INSIDER CHURCH

Insider Church offers a fresh and helpful analysis of an important phenomenon in the missiological world today. By spotlighting the watershed issue of ecclesiology, Antonio brings greater depth and clarity to the implications of the insider movement paradigm. Antonio strives to give the movements under discussion a fair and even-handed treatment. The concluding chapter's evaluation of each of the six key aspects begins with strengths found in the insider paradigm before moving to address weaknesses and offer helpful recommendations. I affirm his well-substantiated summary that "the insider movements paradigm simultaneously supports and undermines the biblical nature of the church." I recommend this book as well-researched, soundly biblical, and thoughtfully written— a valuable contribution to ongoing missiological discussions about God's work in advancing his kingdom in the Muslim world.

DAVE COLES
co-author of *Bhojpuri Breakthrough: A Movement that Keeps Multiplying*
co-editor of *24:14— A Testimony to All Peoples*
lead facilitator of Bridging the Divide Network

Insider Church offers readers a balanced exploration and healthy critique of the major issues surrounding insider movements. It is a must-read for everyone interested in the topic.

GENE DANIELS
author of *Searching for the Indigenous Church*

Making disciples of Jesus in frontier contexts is a venture filled with risk, excitement, and uncertainty. We still have much to discover, especially regarding the types of churches that are yet to be developed. *Insider Church* provides us with a robust, biblical ideal worthy of our goals. This book is a comprehensive ecclesiology that pioneer workers involved in church multiplication will be referencing for years to come.

WARRICK FARAH, DMISS
missiologist, One Collective
co-editor of *Margins of Islam: Ministry in Diverse Muslim Contexts*

Great doctrines require great voices. Some blaze forth God's truths as visionaries, others defend truth as apologists, still others harmonise reconcilable differences as peacemakers. Antonio is the latter. Antonio writes into a known controversy in order to promote better understanding. He follows Paul in giving "honour to whom honour is owed" yet auditing how both parties fall short in their ecclesiology. He uses "strength" and "weakness" equally in the text (30x) as he searches for both good kingdom yeast and unbiblical Islamic yeast. Aware that he cannot "settle the intractable debate and controversy," he resists the temptation to pronouncing whether insider churches are legitimate Biblical churches. He concedes insider "churches" are embryonic in nature but in desperate need of the right DNA based on the whole counsel of God from Scripture. You will be drawn into a fresh chronological treatment of God's household and offering excellent ecclesiology rubrics for the Old and New Testament.

REV. BENJAMIN LEE HEGEMAN, PHD
career missionary with SIM in North Benin, West Africa
co-founder of the Lilias Trotter Center

I have long agreed that ecclesiology is one of the most overlooked issues in current missiological discussion. This is true within the insider movement controversy, certainly, but also within the entire evangelical missiological enterprise. "Church" is one of those words that everyone thinks they understand until one begins to define it! As such, *Insider Church* is a timely and important contribution well beyond the insider movement context. As an advocate of insider movements myself, I also want to add that the author took great pains to reach out to myself and others for input and comment. As such, while we will continue to differ on important topics, the book models a truly crucial approach, much needed in this hour of history: a better way to seek understanding before seeking to be understood.

Kevin Higgins, PhD
general director, Frontier Ventures
president, William Carey International University
long-term worker in South Asia

In this well-crafted and considered book, S. T. Antonio brings his considerable theological acumen and missional experience to bear on the question of how and whether insider movements make not just disciples but the churches that will strengthen and sustain discipleship over the long-haul. Antonio is at once generous and principled, eager to learn from insider advocates and think creatively about the nature of the church, while remaining steadfast in his commitment to a biblical vision of the church, even in sensitive and insecure contexts. I cannot imagine a more timely or effective addition to the current conversation about mission in the Muslim world.

Matt Jenson, PhD
professor of Theology, Torrey Honors College, Biola University
co-author of *The Church: A Guide for the Perplexed*

Antonio has written a penetrating and irenic study of insider ecclesiology that highlights most of the positive, innovative aspects of insider advocates' understanding of church and then systematically, yet graciously, critiques its shortcomings. I believe that *Insider Church* has significant potential to break some of the deadlock between deeply held positions. Antonio clearly examines beliefs about the nature of the church held by many advocates of the insider paradigm (that are sometimes implicit and unexamined), and then offers a gentle but compelling series of biblical and missiological critiques. Whether you are new to this vital conversation, or long enmeshed in it, I strongly encourage you to take the time to read this invaluable contribution.

Don Little
missiologist, Pioneers and director of the Lilias Trotter Center
founding facilitator of the Bridging the Divide Consultations
author of *Effective Discipling in Muslim Communities*

Insider Church provides a wise, biblically and theologically informed, and missiologically sensitive perspective on one of the most controversial missiological issues today. The author is not only thoroughly at home in the relevant academic literature, he is also a seasoned practitioner with significant ministry experience among Muslims. Both sides of the debate will profit from this thoughtful discussion.

Harold Netland, PhD
professor of Philosophy of Religion and Intercultural Studies, Trinity Evangelical Divinity School

INSIDER CHURCH
Ekklesia and the Insider Paradigm

Insider Church: Ekklesia and the Insider Paradigm
© 2020 by S. T. Antonio
All rights reserved.

No part of this book may be reproduced, stored in a retrieval system, or transmitted in any form or by any means—electronic, mechanical, photocopy, recording, or otherwise—without prior written permission of the publisher, except brief quotations used in connection with reviews in magazines or newspapers. For permission, email permissions@wclbooks.com. For corrections, email editor@wclbooks.com

Scripture quotations are from The ESV® Bible (The Holy Bible, English Standard Version®), copyright © 2001 by Crossway, a publishing ministry of Good News Publishers. Used by permission. All rights reserved.

Published by William Carey Publishing
10 W. Dry Creek Cir
Littleton, CO 80120 | www.missionbooks.org

William Carey Publishing is a ministry of Frontier Ventures
Pasadena, CA 91104 | www.frontierventures.org

Cover and interior design: Mike Riester
Copyeditor: Andrew Sloan
Indexer: Rory Clark
Managing editor: Melissa Hicks

ISBNs: 978-1-64508-272-9 (paperback), 978-1-64508-274-3 (mobi), 978-1-64508-275-0 (epub)

Printed Worldwide

24 23 22 21 20   1 2 3 4 5   IN

Library of Congress Control Number: 2020947043

INSIDER CHURCH
Ekklesia and the Insider Paradigm

S. T. Antonio

Available at missionbooks.org

This book is dedicated to my friends and co-laborers serving
Muslims in the Arab world.

CONTENTS

Foreword by Craig Ott	xi
Acknowledgments	xiii
Introduction *Insider Movements and the Church: Setting the Stage*	xv

PART 1 *Toward a Biblical Vision of the Church*

CHAPTER 1 *Church in the Divine Drama:* *Narratives and Themes of the Church's Identity*	3
CHAPTER 2 *Clarifying "Church": Six Dimensions*	29
CHAPTER 3 *Contextualizing "Church"*	71

PART 2 *Toward a Fresh Appraisal of Insider Church*

CHAPTER 4 *Clarifying Insider "Ekklēsia"*	91
CHAPTER 5 *Evaluating Insider "Ekklēsia"*	125
CHAPTER 6 *Implications for the Insider Movements Conversation*	167
Epilogue *Recommendations for Multiplying Biblical Churches among Muslims*	175
Bibliography	184
Subject Index	198
Scripture Index	204

FOREWORD

By Craig Ott

The history of Christian encounter with Muslims is a checkered one, ranging from conquest and coercion to compassion and conversation. The results have generally been disappointing and the world of Islam has consistently proven to be one of the hardest soils for the seed of the gospel to take root. Christians who love Muslims and long to see a breakthrough have been hungry for answers. And then enters the "insider movement" strategy. This bold approach to contextualization of ministry among Muslims emerged nearly three decades ago claiming to point to a radical new way forward and reporting remarkable fruitfulness. Stated in the simplest terms, this approach advocates that Muslims who desire to become followers of Jesus should be encouraged to remain not only within their network of social relationships, but also to continue to participate in many (if not most) Islamic practices and self-identify as Muslims. In this way, so it is claimed, movements can emerge by not extracting believers from their natural social ties and by developing new contextual forms of believing communities without imposing foreign culture or theological categories.

Not surprisingly, this approach released a firestorm of controversy which has not only engulfed discussions among mission strategists and practitioners, but has overflowed into church mission committees and theological faculties. Everyone seems to have an opinion, whether well-informed or not; opinions that generally lack nuance. As a result, there are many cases where the flow of mission funds shifted and where missionaries were asked by supporting churches to sign new policy statements. Denominations drew lines in the sand. Bloggers received fresh red meat to keep readers clicking. From the extreme flanks of the conflict volleys have been exchanged, including explosive missiles such as "heresy," "unbiblical," "syncretism," "ethnocentric," "traditionalist," and "cultural imperialism." After a quarter century of debate there is seemingly not much new left to be said and, for the most part, an uneasy ceasefire has settled in. Meanwhile, to shift metaphors, a host of variations on the insider movement theme have also been composed and performed under new names.

But there is one important, indeed extremely important matter of central missiological and theological concern that has been largely underdeveloped and at times downright overlooked in the debate: *ecclesiology*. What does it mean to be the church? Most of the arguments relating to insider movements pro and con have centered around questions of culture, religious identity, evangelistic effectiveness, discipleship, Bible translation, syncretism, and local Christian expression. But more fundamentally, we need to ask: do insider movements result in communities of Christ followers that bear biblical marks of a church? Nearly everyone agrees that the goal is not mere conversion, but discipleship and the formation of believing communities that the New Testament calls churches. There is also consensus that Scripture allows considerable freedom in local expressions of the church, and that churches everywhere needn't look like traditional Western churches—that is *not* the debate. But what *kind* of churches should be the fruit of mission work? More specifically, to what extent does the insider movement strategy by its very nature contribute to or actually hinder the emergence of biblical communities of faith? That is the subject of this book, and S. T. Antonio is the right person to write it. With biblical faithfulness, academic precision, and practical experience, he digs deep into this fundamental question.

It is my hope that this volume will stimulate fresh discussion—not merely to reignite old debates, but to move the discussion forward in a helpful and biblical manner. After providing a bird's eye view of the larger insider movement conversation, Antonio zeroes in on the ecclesiological crux of the matter. He provides an urgently needed antidote to "knee-jerk response syndrome," and administers a healthy dose of careful theological reflection. Even readers who disagree with Antonio's conclusions cannot ignore them and will be stimulated to examine afresh these most basic questions. These are questions that must be answered by everyone engaged in the endeavor to not only communicate the gospel, but to see transformational communities of disciples emerge that become local expressions of the body of Christ, manifest the kingdom of God, and glorify him in the power of the Spirit.

Craig Ott, PhD
Trinity Evangelical Divinity School

ACKNOWLEDGMENTS

The journey of this book includes assistance from many who helped shape, refine, and elevate the final product beyond my own capabilities. I was first introduced to the topic in Craig Ott's contextualization course at Trinity Evangelical Divinity School, which convinced me that he needed to be my thesis adviser. Dr. Ott helped refine the topic and supervise the research that led to this book, and his feedback and encouragement were instrumental in keeping me on a fruitful track. Harold Netland's sage questions and advice at my defense hearing helped sharpen the content and presentation of various aspects of my argument. Ultimately, it was their suggestion to publish this research that gave me the encouragement to do so.

There are many who, without reading the manuscript, contributed to the formation of the ideas in this book. My discussions with classmates at Trinity Evangelical Divinity School and my Pioneers colleagues helped shape my thinking around these topics in important ways.

There are several who read the manuscript and offered constructive feedback, including Don Little, Kevin Higgins, and Warrick Farah. Dave Coles provided detailed comments on multiple versions of the manuscript, and he dialogued with me about its ideas and implications. His enthusiasm for the project, and his tangible support at various stages, were significant in the journey of this book. The astute and patient editorial help of Andy Sloan, Melissa Hicks, and D.G. Wynn helped to refine and elevate the final product to new levels.

One person has been a part of the process from start to finish. My wife, Jeanne, provided feedback on the manuscript, as well as companionship and encouragement throughout the long, lonely journey of research and writing. She never stopped believing in the project, and she tirelessly pushed and encouraged me to keep going at every stage. Without her support, I would have given up ten times over.

I take full responsibility for what is written in this book, including all deficiencies therein. For anything of value, I give glory to God.

INTRODUCTION

Insider Movements and the Church: Setting the Stage

The hard, rocky soil of the Muslim world is beginning to break. In the past few decades, whole communities of Muslims have turned to Christ in ways unheard of and unprecedented in over a millennium (Garrison 2014, 18). God is on the move in the Muslim world like never before, and it is the privilege of his people to joyfully receive and steward this great harvest.

As we welcome this marvelous ingathering of Muslim-born believers into the family of God, some new disciples stand out as different than the rest. As they learn to pray in the name of Jesus, some may continue to join their Muslim community in Friday prayers in the mosque. As they learn to obey the Bible, some may continue to read and revere the Qur'an. While they confess Jesus as the Word of God and the Savior of the world, some may continue to confess Muhammad as a kind of "prophet." Variations abound, but one way or another these "insiders" continue to positively embrace their Muslim identity in some shape or form as something which is not compromised by their faith in Jesus.

Cross-cultural disciple makers and church planters have welcomed this unlikely marriage with surprise, delight, or horror—or all of the above. What do we make of such combinations of faith and folly, of truth and error, of worship and idolatry? Is it possible to follow Jesus and Muhammad, the Qur'an and the gospel? Or have we misjudged Islam all along?

INSIDER CHURCH

After encountering the faith and fellowship of "insider" believers, some mission workers and scholars have reexamined their assumptions about Islam and its incompatibility with biblical discipleship to Jesus, promoting a new paradigm which affirms and encourages a greater degree of synthesis and integration between biblical faith and Islamic beliefs, practices, and identity. The goal is "insider movements," which are multiplying networks of believers in Jesus from non-Christian religious communities who follow Jesus while remaining in their religious communities and retaining their "socio-religious" identities (Travis 2015a, Loc. 796–876). "Insider" movements are not restricted to Muslim contexts; they can take place in Buddhist, Hindu, or Jewish communities as well. In Muslim contexts, insiders come to faith in Jesus, but instead of seeking to leave their Muslim religious community to join a "Christian" community, they continue to positively embrace a Muslim identity. According to advocates, such a decision is biblically legitimate and enables insiders to remain an integral part of their families and communities as they seek to be salt, light, and yeast within the networks and relationships in which they were born.

But "insider movements" are more than just theory—they have been witnessed and documented over the last few decades by cross-cultural workers and missiologists. Several examples and case studies are described and analyzed in *Understanding Insider Movements* (often abbreviated as *UIM* in this book).[1] Observers and participants in these movements see them as examples of a radical, new way that God is penetrating religious groups previously resistant and untouched by the gospel. Insider advocates see these developments as opportunities to rethink our assumptions and approaches to church planting among people of other religions, providing a legitimate model that may be more effective in reaching parts of the world which have been resistant to traditional methods.

However, a significant number of mission workers, church leaders, and believers from Muslim background do not share this enthusiasm for insider movements. Many have been skeptical of insider ministry, with some in declared opposition to the insider paradigm as dangerous to the work of the gospel. Articles and books have been written responding to the writings of insider advocates, at times reflecting fierce, charged debate throughout the mission community. Still others find themselves somewhere in between "hearty advocate" and "fierce critic," confessing the wisdom of Proverbs 18:17: "The one who states his case first seems right, until the other comes and examines him."[2]

---

1 Part 2 of *Understanding Insider Movements* (chaps. 7–19) is devoted to "Examples, Testimonies, and Analysis," featuring thirteen different chapters giving various examples or case studies of insider movements in mostly Muslim contexts, along with a few examples in Buddhist, Hindu, Sikh, and Jewish communities.

2 Farah and Meeker identify a variety of different positions that cross-cultural workers among Muslims reflect besides complete acceptance or complete rejection of insider-level contextualization. They categorize workers' views of contextualization into four basic categories: (1) Triumph Model (Christianity triumphs over Islam), (2) Replacement Model (Christianity replaces Islam), (3) Transformation Model (biblical faith transforms Muslims), and (4) Completion Model (biblical faith completes Muslims) (2015, 370-71).

How should churches, mission agencies, and church planters respond to the phenomenon of insider movements? Do insider movements represent a legitimate mission goal that can help open the door for the gospel among certain least-reached, highly resistant communities? Does the insider paradigm spread the yeast of the kingdom of God in Muslim communities (Matt 13:33), or does it introduce a yeast that contaminates the "unleavened bread of sincerity and truth" in the church (1 Cor 5:6–8)? Should mission agencies and church planters encourage or support "insider" identity as they cultivate disciples and multiply churches in Muslim contexts? How does the church welcome the great new harvest among Muslims in a way that is both fruitful *and* faithful?

A consensus on insider movements has thus far eluded the mission community. Part of the difficulty is that there is a great deal of confusion about what "insider movements," and its related terms, actually mean. Additionally, the sheer complexity of the insider question complicates simple assessment. As some have pointed out, the insider debate is not about one issue only, but rather involves a variety of interlocking issues and assumptions which are interwoven together and at times impossible to untangle (Bartlotti 2013, 138).

My aim in this book is not to solve this debate, but to zero in and focus on one particular issue that is at the heart of the insider paradigm—the nature and identity of the church. By drilling down on this one key issue we not only gain a fresh perspective of insider movements, but we also gain a fresh and deeper perspective on the biblical nature of the church. As we will see, the insider paradigm raises important questions about the nature and identity of the church, and a careful, considered look at these questions has the potential to transform our view of the church—and our view of insider movements.

Before re-envisioning the church and insider movements, it's important to set the stage, which I will do in three ways. First, I "zoom out" to the big picture of the larger insider debate, how it unfolded, and where it stands today. Next, I "zoom in" on our key theme—the nature of the church—and its importance to the insider question. Finally, I outline the plan for the remainder of the book, which offers a fresh look at the insider paradigm in light of the biblical identity of the church.

I begin with an important story that sets the context for my project—the story of the insider movements debate.

The Insider Debate

Nearly a hundred years ago, a task force was convened to investigate the causes for lack of progress of mission to Muslims. For three decades, numerous missionaries had answered the call of Samuel Zwemer to bring the gospel to Muslim lands, yet without the kind of fruit yielded by other fields. The chief obstacle, according to this task force, was the social rupture that would result from public confession of faith and baptism into the church.

INSIDER CHURCH

In response, this task force made a radical suggestion: form fellowships of believers that declare their faith while remaining within their Muslim social-political community (Riggs 1941, 116, 120–21). The proposal was denounced from multiple directions as soon as it was made public, officially disavowed by the council that commissioned the task force, and thoroughly rebutted by Samuel Zwemer, J. Christy Wilson, and other mission leaders.[3] Such ideas would not receive serious consideration in the mission community for another three decades.

In the 1970s, some missionaries began advocating for experimenting with fresh approaches to reaching Muslims rather than being content with the slow progress of traditional methods. Phil Parshall emerged as a key advocate of contextualized "Muslim culture" churches that helped avoid "extraction" of new believers from their community (1974, 42–43, 50; 1979; 1980a; 1980b). He pioneered such a church in Southeast Asia with encouraging fruit, which propelled his initially controversial proposal toward greater acceptance among missionaries to Muslims.

For some, however, Parshall did not go far enough. Parshall drew the line at participating in Islamic prayer (*salat*), confessing the prophethood of Muhammad (*shehada*), and permanent identification as a Muslim (1985, 194). Others, however, explored whether even these elements could also be appropriated by believers of Muslim background, or "BMBs" (Uddin 1989, 267–72; Woodberry 1989, 287–307). A divide began to emerge among advocates of contextualized ministry to Muslims, one which was eventually brought out into the open in the pages of *Evangelical Missions Quarterly*, through the introduction of the controversial "C-spectrum."

Coined by John Travis (pseudonym), the C1-C6 spectrum categorized various "Christ-centered communities" found in the Muslim world based on contextualization of language, culture, and "socio-religious" identity (1998a, 407). The most contested part of the spectrum was C4-C5. C4 groups, while adopting Islamic cultural forms, refrained from participating in key Islamic rituals (like *salat* prayer) and stopped short of identifying as "Muslims," identifying only as "followers of Jesus." C5 groups, on the other hand, retained insider "socio-religious" identity as "Muslim followers of Jesus," and, as Travis later explained (1998b), potentially continued to participate in key Islamic rituals and identity markers.

Phil Parshall, pioneer of C4 contextualization, sounded the alarm over C5 as potentially syncretistic (1998, 405), while John Travis defended it as legitimate "high

---

3 The task force was convened by the "Near Eastern Christian Council" in 1936. Its controversial proposal, and the aftermath, was discussed thoroughly in the 1941 issue of *The Muslim World* (edited by Zwemer) with articles by Wilson and Zwemer (opposed) and Riggs (in favor). Zwemer strongly advocated for a decisive faith commitment and a break with the religious past of the convert (1941, 112). Wilson affirmed that public profession of faith is not for the missionary to decide, but rather a private matter between Christ and the convert; yet he also affirmed that profession of faith and baptism into the church was crucial for spiritual growth (1941, 133). Riggs (whose article was reprinted in *Understanding Insider Movements*, Loc. 8982–9170) was the lone voice urging that "the results of this inquiry deserve more calm and purposeful consideration than they have thus far received" (1941, 122).

spectrum" contextualization (1998b). The entire 1998 issue of *Evangelical Missions Quarterly* was devoted to the debate between Travis and Parshall, an exchange which would set the terms of the conversation for years.

This launched a fierce debate in the mission community over the legitimacy of C5 ministry. Some advocated strongly for C5 as the next phase in pioneering contextualization among Muslims (Massey 1999, 191), while Parshall continued to caution against the way the C5 label was used as a pretext for an array of radical ministry activities (2003).[4] A new terminology emerged alongside of C5—the phrase "insider movements," defined as "large numbers of Muslims who become followers of Christ without changing either their self-perception or their communal identity as Muslims" (Talman 2004a, 5).

The debate continued in various journals and at mission consultations. Mission leaders and theologians such as David Garrison (2004), Timothy Tennent (2006), and Gary Corwin (2007a) registered critiques of C5/insider ministry as problematic on biblical, theological, or missiological grounds. These critiques, serious as they were, sparked a prolific output of responses from insider advocates—many of which were published in the *International Journal of Frontier Missiology*—that vigorously defended, clarified, and developed the emerging "insider paradigm" from multiple angles.[5]

This debate in mission circles eventually caught the attention of the evangelical public, provoking strong reactions from some pastors and denominational leaders. Blog posts and books were written denouncing the insider paradigm.[6] The Presbyterian Church of America commissioned a multi-year study group to respond to insider movements, which resulted in a robust rejection of the paradigm.[7]

While the conversation heated up in the evangelical church, a parallel development sought to "cool down" the conversation and move beyond the impass. In 2011, missiologists Don Little and L. D. Waterman (a pseudonym) formed Bridging the Divide, which gathered mission practitioners from both sides of the

---

4 Massey's article provoked a wave of "Letters to the editor" in subsequent *EMQ* volumes, including both critical and affirming responses, and a further rejoinder from Parshall (2000b). Parshall later included the major articles discussing C5 contextualization in his larger collection, published in the *Philippines: The Last Great Frontier: Essays on Muslim Evangelism* (2000a).

5 The *IJFM* devoted several issues to insider movements (Mar 2000, Dec 2004, Aug 2006, Mar 2007, and June 2007), mostly giving voice to insider advocates. Critiques were occasionally published (e.g., Corwin, and Tennent), though always with thorough responses from insider advocates.

6 Book-length critiques targeting a broader evangelical audience included, *Chrislam: How Missionaries Are Promoting an Islamized Gospel* (edited by Lingel, Morton, and Nikides 2012), and *Insider Movements: Incredibly Brilliant or Biblically Incredible?* (Morton 2012). John Piper critiqued insider movements in a short video on "The Gospel Coalition" website (Hansen and Piper 2012), and D.A. Carson mentioned insider movements in the context of his book on the "Son of God" translation controversy (2012, 70-72). *Christianity Today* brought the issue to the evangelical public through a series of articles on insider movements from a variety of perspectives (Daniels 2013; Travis 2013a; Tennent 2013; Parshall 2013).

7 PCA Ad Interim Study Committee on Insider Movements, 2013, 2014. A dissenting "minority report," authored by Nabeel Jabbour and Tom Seelinger, was also included.

insider issue for annual face-to-face dialogue about their differences in pursuit of greater unity and understanding. The goal was to change the ethos and tone of the conversation from bitter debate to charitable dialogue seeking truth and clarity.

The annual consultations yielded a number of important breakthroughs in the conversation. Besides lowering the temperature of the discussion and encouraging greater Christian charity and grace on both sides, Bridging the Divide produced key points of progress and clarity, many of which were disseminated through conference summaries and journal articles. Misunderstandings were clarified, common ground was identified, and issues of fundamental disagreement were openly discussed, leading to greater nuance and perspective to the issue from both sides.[8]

Despite the important progress made, important differences remain in the mission community regarding insider movements. Advocates have produced multiple books in favor of the insider paradigm, including the tome *Understanding Insider Movements* (ed. Talman and Travis 2015), a compilation a largely insider-affirming collection of articles in a single volume, amounting to a definitive defense of the insider paradigm.[9] Critics of insider movements have been less prolific, but not absent, as seen in the publication of *Muslim Conversions to Christ: A Critique of Insider Movements in Islamic Contexts* (Ibrahim and Greenham 2018). While many evangelical missionaries are increasingly pursuing "movements" as a missional goal, some include "insider" as part of that vision, while others reject "insider" identity as a preferred element of a healthy church planting movement.

And so "the divide" over insider movements remains—the conversation continues as missionaries, organizations, and churches labor to discern the best ways to faithfully steward the Lord's harvest among Muslims. But the issue of insider movements is no longer a simple binary choice between unqualified acceptance and outright rejection—though those positions still have defenders. A number of mediating positions have been identified, creating space for more nuanced, measured responses to the complex challenges in discipling Muslims into healthy, multiplying churches.[10]

---

8 Some of the papers and discussions from Bridging the Divide filtered out to the broader community through articles in the *IJFM* (Bartlotti 2013; Daniels and Waterman 2013), *EMQ* (Daniels 2014), and a special edition of *Evangelical Review of Theology* (37, no. 4). Bridging the Divide posted summaries and conference documents on their website (www.btdnetwork.org), as well as articles that have been discussed at the consultations.

9 This massive 719-page anthology of sixty-four articles, most previously published, represents some of the best and most important articles advocating for the insider paradigm. The volume includes a mixture of examples and case studies of insider movements, biblical and theological foundations for the insider paradigm, and topics such as religion, contextualization, and identity. The book does not aim to present both sides of the debate, but rather to describe, explain, and defend the insider ministry paradigm. As such, it is the definitive resource for a clear, multifaceted understanding and positive defense of insider movements and the ministry paradigm encouraging such movements.

10 One example is an illuminating discussion between Gene Daniels and L. D. Waterman about the ambiguities and difficulties of the term "socio-religious insider"—widely used by insider advocates but which has proven to be an obstacle to clarity and progress in understanding (2013, 59–66). Missiologist Warrick Farah took this discussion even further

Within this larger landscape, there remain a number of important unresolved threads in the insider conversation, which, if followed, hold promise of opening up yet new realms of understanding and insight in our ministry efforts among Muslims. One such thread is the nature and identity of the church, an oft-neglected theme that has fundamental importance to the issue of insider movements.

Ecclesiology and Insider Movements

The insider movements question is like a tangled knot. It is not a single issue, but rather a whole complex of issues bound up together in a complicated, interlocking web. Our convictions about the nature of Islam, contextualization, the role of the Holy Spirit, the nature of the church, theology of religions, the nature of authority—and other issues—all impact the way that we assess the insider paradigm. This makes it challenging to offer a global, definitive assessment; it is even more challenging to demonstrate such an assessment with others who have differing convictions in one or more areas (cf. Bartlotti 2013, 138).

A fruitful way forward is to focus on one particular issue in the insider debate, and use that issue to shed light on the question as a whole.[11] In this book, I aim to shed new light on the insider question through focusing on ecclesiology.

Ecclesiology is our vision of the nature and purpose of Christ's church. It is the communal dimension of biblical discipleship—how life in Christ is "life together" in the family of God.[12] It is no mere intellectual exercise, but is profoundly practical as we carry out the Great Commission among Muslims. Our beliefs about the nature and mission of the church directly shape the goal that we envision and work towards as we make disciples. Significantly, both insider advocates and critics have utilized presuppositions about "how to be and do 'church'" to defend or debunk the insider paradigm (ibid).

The nature of the church has been tightly intertwined in the fabric of the insider debate from the very beginning. Ecclesiology lurked in the background of "Christ-centered communities" of the C1-C6 spectrum, and people have debated whether an "insider movement" can be a "church planting movement." The Bridging the

---

by highlighting the ambiguity of the term "insider" itself, noting that there are at least five different expressions of "insider-ness": cultural insider, sociocultural insider, "dual belonging" insider, "reinterpreting" insider, and syncretistic insider (Farah 2015).

11 We have seen the kind of progress that can be made when zeroing in on one particular issue or "lens" of the insider-movement discussion—for example, in the fresh application of identity studies to the issue of insider movements by Tim Green (2013a, 2013b, 2013c), Kathryn Kraft (2012), and Jens Barnett (2013, 2015). While the concept of identity has been extensively employed for decades in the insider debate, people like Green, Kraft, and Barnett helped to "clean the lens" and gain a more nuanced view of identity, providing fresh categories that better account for the complexities of insider identity and that have helped move the discussion forward. A fresh appraisal and application of ecclesiology to insider movements can likewise provide increased understanding and progress in the ongoing conversation.

12 "Life together" comes from Dietrich Bonhoeffer (2009), *Life Together: The Classical Exploration of Christianity Community*.

Divide consultations highlighted the centrality of biblical *ekklēsia*[13] in the insider question, as well as the important ecclesiological common ground on both sides of "the divide." Critics have charged insider movements with deficient ecclesiology, while advocates have responded by clarifying, developing, and commending an insider-affirming ecclesiology.

The insider paradigm clearly raises fundamental questions about the nature and identity of the church, particularly as it takes shape in new cultural and religious contexts. Our assumptions on these matters significantly influence how we assess insider movements, which raises an important question. To what extent are our assumptions about the church rooted in Scripture, and to what extent are they extra-biblical imports from our cultural background? This question can only be answered by returning to the Scriptures, submitting our ideas about the church to the Word of God, and realigning our vision with Christ's vision for his church.

This book is an invitation to take a fresh look at the nature of the church, in Scripture and in the insider paradigm. Not only does a robust, biblical and theological account of the church shed important light on the insider paradigm, but the challenge of the insider paradigm yields new insights on the nature of the church.

Such a task is not without its challenges. Evangelicals have not been known for strong, robust ecclesiology, and the global evangelical mission force among Muslims come from a variety of ecclesiological backgrounds. Our diverse experiences of church unavoidably influence our personal hopes, fears, and dreams of "church" taking root in Muslim communities.

Despite these challenges—and perhaps because of them—it is imperative that we give focused, renewed attention to the fundamental questions about the nature of the church, what that means for our mission practice, and how that impacts our assessment of the insider paradigm. If the mission community is to move toward greater unity in our witness, then we must seek out and preserve a common biblical core that can bind us together and undergird a unified witness among Muslims. My aim in this book is to outline a fresh and robust biblical vision for the nature of the church that can illuminate the insider paradigm and ultimately guide our efforts in multiplying churches among Muslims to the glory of God.

In the first three chapters, I propose a framework for a robust, biblical vision of the church. Chapter one argues that the identity of the church is inseparable from the story of the people of God with its manifold themes and transformations. Chapter two fleshes out the many dimensions of the church's identity—such as local-universal, visible-invisible, core essence, and mission in the world. Chapter three tackles the church's relationship to culture and the parameters of authentic, biblical contextualization of the people of God.

---

13 Ekklēsia (pronounced ek-klay-SEE-ya) is the Greek word translated as "church" in the New Testament. In this book, I often use the word ekklēsia as synonymous for "church" or biblical "church-ness."

The final three chapters turn more specifically to insider movements. Chapter four outlines the vision of ekklēsia advanced by the insider paradigm, and chapter five assesses this vision, identifying where it enhances and where it endangers the flourishing of biblical ekklēsia. Implications for the insider debate are discussed in chapter six, and an epilogue offers concluding recommendations for multiplying biblical churches among Muslims which reflect the fullness of Christ's vision for his church.

A few clarifications may prove helpful to my readers. While I occasionally reference the functions, practice, and mission of the church, my primary focus is the first, fundamental question of ecclesiology: *"What is the church?"* I wholeheartedly affirm the full authority and truthfulness of Scripture and the uniqueness of Christ as the only hope for the eternal joy of Muslims. My own church heritage includes a mix of Baptist, free church, and non-denominational influences, but I write for a broad evangelical audience regardless of denominational background. I eagerly desire to see Christ exalted among all nations, especially those least touched by the gospel. My own context is church planting among Muslims in the Middle East, but I write for anyone working with Muslims—knowing that any suggestions should be tested and adapted according to the specifics of each context.

The ultimate aim of this book is to deepen and sharpen our vision of the church as we seek to invite Muslims to join the number of the redeemed. If we want our disciple making efforts to be both fruitful and faithful to the Lord of the harvest, we ought to align our vision with the Lord's own vision for his church. God's vision for his church is found in his revealed Word: not in the form of a theological or sociological definition, but in the form of a story—an unfolding drama about God and the community he is creating for himself. To this grand story we now turn.

PART ONE

*Toward a
Biblical Vision
of the Church*

CHAPTER ONE

The Church and the Divine Drama: Narratives and Themes of the Church's Identity

The church is the light of the world. But in Muslim-majority lands, it can also be a stumbling block. My Muslim friends have complicated and varying views of the church. Many see the church as the Christian counterpart to the mosque—a house of prayer deserving of respect. Some see the church as a source of strange, deviant worship, which intrigues the curious while repelling the devout. With the Eastern and Oriental Orthodox churches being some of the largest and oldest Christian communities in the Middle East, many Muslims associate "church" with icons, incense, and black-robed, bearded priests. For many Muslims—including those living in "unchurched" parts of the Middle East—their views of the church are just as likely to be shaped by stories about the Pope and the Vatican, or the varied portrayals of churches in Hollywood movies.

Some of my friends view the church and Christians fairly positively, as a community of peace in a region too often at war. Yet some still see the church as a potential danger—as an alternative, competing community that can pose a threat to Muslim society if it lures Muslims to abandon their religion, family, and nation.

INSIDER CHURCH

How do we multiply churches among people for whom "church" carries such unwieldy baggage? Is it possible to bypass Muslim suspicions of "the Christian church" altogether by reimagining "church" as *Muslim,* insulated completely from the institutional Christian church? What are the possibilities and dangers presented by such a proposal?

Any answer to the above questions requires answers to a completely different set of questions. What is *church*? What is essential to its biblical identity, and what is secondary? How does the church express itself in diverse cultural and religious contexts? The way we define *church,* and its interaction with cultural context, is foundational for how we see the church taking shape in Muslim contexts. It also determines in large measure how we assess the insider vision of the church.

This chapter and the next tackles the fundamental question of the nature and identity of the church, laying the groundwork for later discussion on the church's relation to culture. The goal is to provide a biblical and theological vision of the church that is sound and robust enough to engage the messy realities of mission to Muslims and the complex problem of the insider paradigm. As will be shown in later chapters, this biblical and theological framework sheds light on both insightful strengths and worrisome weaknesses of the insider vision of the church which must be addressed in a clear-eyed, responsible assessment of the insider paradigm.

To define the identity of the church, there is no better starting point than Holy Scripture. The inspired Word of God discloses the mind of God—who designed and created the church. Furthermore, God's Word illumines, corrects, and relativizes all human ideas and experiences of church. But as we look to Scripture, we see that the church is not presented as an abstract philosophical concept, but as a concrete reality—a living, historical community, enmeshed in the story of God and his people. We cannot understand what it means to "be and do church" apart from the overarching narrative of the people of God which defines the church's identity.

In the remainder of this chapter, I trace the way that Scripture unveils and shapes the identity of the church through the unfolding narrative of the people of God, from Abraham to the New Jerusalem.[1] As we trace this story in its key stages, we will get a glimpse of the rich array of themes, images, and teachings that contribute to the

---

1 This approach is similar to what Klink and Lockett refer to as "History of Redemption" (BT2) in their fivefold taxonomy of approaches to biblical theology in *Understanding Biblical Theology: A Comparison of Theory and Practice* (Grand Rapids: Zondervan), 22–23. This is also the approach represented by the New Studies in Biblical Theology series edited by D. A. Carson. The series preface states that one of the key goals of the series is "the delineation of a biblical theme across all or part of the biblical corpora" (Carson 2006, 9). This approach is employed masterfully by Christopher Wright (2006) in *The Mission of God: Unlocking the Bible's Grand Narrative,* as he argues that a biblical-theological theme that is traced through the canon also serves as a distinctive lens through which to read the biblical story line from creation to Christ to consummation—providing an interpretive framework or "map" to aid understanding Scripture as a whole. It therefore should be judged for its "heuristic fruitfulness," or its ability to either illumine or distort the biblical text as a whole (ibid., 68–69).

fabric of the nature of the church in Scripture.[2] As later chapters show, the insider paradigm emphasizes particular images and biblical themes to support its vision of *ekklēsia* for insiders. In order to accurately assess both the strengths and weaknesses of insider biblical theology, it is crucial to grasp the fullness of the biblical narrative and array of images that define the identity of the church in Scripture.

The story of the people of God will be traced along four key stages and an excursus, each of which reveals and shapes the identity of the church in crucial ways: (1) the Old Testament people of God, (2) the kingdom community of Jesus, (3) the Pentecostal church of the Spirit, (4) the apostolic teaching about the church, and (5) the triumphant church of the Lamb. Each stage provides an important block in our biblical foundation for defining the church, and each deserves careful attention.

"I Will Be Your God, and You Will Be My People": The Old Testament Backdrop

The word *church* does not appear in the Old Testament. Yet we cannot fully understand the nature of the church without grasping its roots in the Old Testament story of God and his people, which forms the essential backdrop for the emergence of the church of Jesus Christ in the New Testament.[3] The significance of the Old Testament to the church can be captured in three identity-defining moments in the story of God and his people: (1) the Covenant with Abraham, (2) the Exodus and Sinai revelation, and (3) the Exile and the Remnant.

The Covenant with Abraham: Origins of the People of God

The story of the people of God has a backstory—the story of God and his creation. God's good purposes for the world were frustrated by the rebellion of Adam and Eve, sparking a downward spiral of violence and evil, from the crime of Cain to the arrogance of Babel. But then a new history begins of God choosing, forming, and redeeming a people for himself. The call of Abraham in Genesis 12:1–3 is a turning point in the biblical story and in the history of the world, "the beginning of God's answer to the evil of human hearts, the strife of nations and the groaning brokenness of his whole creation" (Wright 2006, 199).

---

2 See, for example, Paul Minear's classic, *Images of the Church in the New Testament*, which names ninety-six different images in the New Testament related to the church, organized under four major controlling images: people of God, new creation, fellowship in faith, and body of Christ.

3 My approach in beginning a biblical theology of the church with an Old Testament theology of the "people of God" is an alternative approach to that which would take a systematic theological definition of the church (such as the company of all who are truly saved by Christ) and read this understanding back into the Old Testament, as certain strands of Reformed theology would do in speaking of "the church" in the Old Testament. Instead, I attempt to preserve the distinctive contribution of Old Testament theology to an overall biblical theology of the church by allowing the Old Testament to speak on its own terms before seeing how it is developed and fulfilled in the theology of the New Testament. Edmund Clowney (also Reformed) follows this general approach by examining the nature of the church in the context of redemptive-history as first the people of God, then the disciples of Christ, and then the fellowship of the Spirit (1995, 29). Others who affirm the importance of a biblical theology of the people of God to ecclesiology are Payne 2009, 41; Millar 2000, 685; Tidball 2000, 407; and Wright 2010, 29, 114.

INSIDER CHURCH

The promise to Abraham reveals God's plan of creating a people to bless all peoples, and within this covenantal call, Israel would later find the essence of its own identity as the people of God. As Harrington says, "Gen. 12:1-3 contains in brief compass many features characteristic of Israel's sense of peoplehood: the divine initiative, the communal nature of salvation, the central significance of God's fidelity and the gift of the land, and the place of Israel with reference to other peoples" (1980, 5). The Abrahamic promise introduces language that will reverberate throughout Scripture of God's resolute determination to create a people for himself and to identify as "their God" (Gen 17:7-8).

This foundational covenant with Abraham extends to Abraham's children (e.g., Gen 12:7; 15:1–21; 17:1–8), and in the new covenant, this incredible honor is bestowed upon all who are united to Christ, the Seed of Abraham (Gal 3:29). The essence of the church ultimately finds its origin in God's radical decision to choose one man and fashion him into a nation that would bless the world—the first defining moment in the formation of the people of God.

Exodus and Sinai: God Takes Israel to Be His People

The exodus from Egypt inaugurates a new era in the formation of the people of God, a critical juncture which would forever re-define the identity of God's people. The exodus was a fulfillment of God's promise to Abraham and a new horizon for his people (Ex 2:24; 6:2–5). For the first time, God formally reveals his personal name, *Yahweh* (6:2–3), and refers to Israel as his people, signaling a new level of intimacy and identification between Israel and their God: "I will take you to be my people, and I will be your God, and you shall know that I am the LORD your God, who has brought you out from under the burdens of the Egyptians" (Ex 6:6–7).[4] In language reminiscent of betrothal, God promises to make Israel into a nation that belongs to and his blessed by him, in fulfillment of his promise to Abraham.[5]

The exodus culminated in the "day of assembly" at Mt. Sinai, where Israel's identity is solidified through the ratifying of the covenant and the giving of God's law (Clowney 1995, 30).[6] Nowhere is this identity better captured than in

---

[4] God powerfully asserts ownership of his people to Pharaoh: "Let *my people* go, that they may serve me in the wilderness" (Ex 7:16).

[5] The image of Israel as the bride of God, betrothed at the exodus, is used throughout Scripture, often to mourn Israel's unfaithfulness to the covenant (Hos 1:2–3; 2:1–13; Jer 2:1–3; 3:1–20), sometimes to look forward to a new exodus and restored covenant relationship (Hos 2:14–23; 3:1–5), and eventually as background for the image of the church as the bride of Christ (Eph 5:25–32; 2 Cor 11:1; Rev 19:7–8; 21:1–4; cf. Matt 9:15; Mark 2:19–20). Cf. Minear, who discusses the bride of Christ as one of his "minor" New Testament images of the church (as opposed to his four "major" New Testament images of the church as "people of God," "new creation," "fellowship in faith," and "body of Christ"); however, Minear does not discuss the Old Testament backdrop for the image (2004, 54–56).

[6] The word for "assembly" is the noun *qahal*, which has two different usages, according to Brown-Driver-Briggs (BDB): either (1) an assembly called for a particular purpose, or (2) "congregation, as organized body" (BDB 874). The verb form of *qahal* occurs in the Niphal ("to assemble") and in the Hiphil ("to summon/call an assembly") (BDB 874–75). Both the

Exodus 19:4-6, which is "a seminal definition of the community of God" (Millar 2000, 684). Christopher Wright calls this passage "a key programmatic statement by God ... like a hinge in the book of Exodus, in between the exodus narrative (Ex 1–18) and the giving of the law and covenant (Ex 20–24). It defines the identity of Israel and the role God has for them" (Wright 2006, 330). This statement—which shapes not only the identity of Israel, but also the New Testament church (1 Pet 2:9; Rev 1:6)—deserves careful unpacking.

The people of Israel are defined first and foremost by *God's prior act of redemption*: "You yourselves have seen what I did to the Egyptians, and how I bore you on eagles' wings and brought you to myself." As in the new covenant, it is God's "past grace" which provides the context for understanding the identity of the people of God (Wright 2006, 116–17). The deliverance from Egypt is the definitive sign that God has graciously elected Israel—the basis of Israel's privileged status and mission (Harrington 1980, 9–10; cf. Deut 7:6–9).

The people of Israel are also defined by virtue of *a covenant relationship with the God who redeemed them:* "Now therefore, if you will indeed obey my voice and keep my covenant ..." (19:5). Israel is given both promises and obligations, and in order to become all that God intends them to be as his people, they must remain faithful to the stipulations of the covenant as revealed in God's law.

What follows is a threefold statement that defines who the people of God are in relation to God and to the surrounding nations. (1) *God's special possession* (19:5, cf. Deut 7:6). The Hebrew word used here (*segulah*) indicates the personal royal property of a king, the idea being that King *Yahweh*, who owns the whole earth, has claimed Israel for his personal, kingly possession (Wright 2006, 256). Israel's cherished status would also be highlighted through being God's "firstborn son" (Ex 4:22) and the "apple of [his] eye" (Deut 32:10; Clowney 1995, 33).

(2) *A kingdom of priests* (19:6a). Chris Wright explains this difficult Hebrew phrase as:

> a term implying a representative mediatorial role. Israel would bring knowledge of YHWH to the nations (just as the priests taught the law of YHWH to the people) and would ultimately bring the nations into covenant fellowship with YHWH (just as the priests enabled sinners to find atonement and restored fellowship through the sacrifices). Israel's very existence in the earth was for the sake of the nations, and it had been since God's promise to Abraham. (2006, 260)

---

noun and verb refer to a variety of purposes for the gathering/assembly, including for war, an evil council, a group of returning exiles, for judgment, for political decisions, or for religious purposes (to hear God's words at Sinai, to celebrate a feast/festival, etc.) (ibid.). A related word is *edahee*, which refers to "a company assembled together by appointment, or acting concertedly," referring variously to a group of angels, people, the righteous, evildoers, animals, (e.g., a swarm of bees), or Israelites (BDB 417). There is a clear overlap in meaning/usage between the two terms, though a slight difference in nuance, in that *qahal* highlights the actual gathering/assembling more than *edahee*. The LXX normally translates *qahal* as *ekklēsia* (73x), and sometimes as *sunagoge* (35x). The word *edahee*, on the other hand, is always translated as *sunagoge* (147x), and never as *ekklesia* (Giles 1995, 231, 233).

The "kingdom of priests" statement encapsulates a "missional identity and role" of Israel containing both centripetal (nations coming to God) and centrifugal (God's law/justice going out to the nations) dimensions (Wright 2006, 331–32).[7]

(3) *A holy nation* (19:6b). Abraham became a "great nation," and Israel was to become a "holy nation": a people set apart from the surrounding nations, reflecting the holiness of their God. This was both a divine work and a human calling: God sanctified and set apart Israel to be his people (Lev 20:24–26, 22:31–33), and Israel was called to "be holy" as God was holy, following God's law and remaining "set-apart" from the surrounding nations (Lev 18:3–4; Wright 2010, 123).

At the center of the "holiness" of the nation is the presence of the "Holy One" in her midst, the physical dwelling of God with Israel in the tabernacle and later the temple (Clowney 1995, 33; Wright 2006, 334–35). In the words of Moses, "Is it not in your going with us, so that we are distinct, I and your people, from every other people on the face of the earth?" (Ex 33:16). It is the personal presence of *Yahweh* God in the midst of his people that ultimately set Israel apart and became a key defining feature of the identity of the people of God.

God's past redemption, a special covenantal relationship, and a privileged status and role with respect to the surrounding world—these elements capture the essence of what it meant for Israel—and later, the church—to be the people of God. Declared and solidified at the "the day of assembly" at Mt. Sinai (cf. Deut 9:10), such truths would be remembered for generations as future assemblies and festivals of Israel—and the church—would look back and commemorate this original identity-defining gathering (Heb 12:18–24; Clowney 1995, 30).

The Exile and the Remnant: The Death and Rebirth of the People of God

If the exodus is the high point of the story of the Old Testament people of God, the exile is the low point. Israel had failed to live up to its calling as a kingdom of priests and holy nation, falling into a downward spiral of rebellion that fractured their relationship with God and threatened to unravel their identity as God's covenant people (Hos 1:9). In a reversal of the exodus, Israel was expelled from the land of promise and sent into exile

But God, in his grace and love, did not fully reject Israel. After judging his people, God promised he would again return to them in mercy and salvation, regathering them from exile and restoring them as his people (Hos 2:23, cf. 3:16–22; 1:10–11), and along with them he would also gather Gentiles, seen in splendid images of people from all nations streaming to Israel to worship God in fulfillment of God's promise to Abraham (Isa 2:2–4; 25:6–8; 66:20–21; Jer 3:17; cf. Clowney 1995, 36).

---

[7] This theologically and missionally significant title would later be ascribed (with slight variation) to the church three times in the New Testament, once by Peter (1 Pet 2:9a, *basileion hierateuma*, "a royal priesthood," following the LXX translation of Ex 19:6), and twice by John (Rev 1:6, *basileian hiereis*, "a kingdom, priests"; and 5:10, *basileian kai hiereis*, "a kingdom and priests").

In the context of exile, the prophets introduced an important new transformation in the identity of the people of God which paved the way for the new covenant church—the concept of *the remnant*, which means "what is left."[8] In Ancient Near Eastern cultures, "remnant" was often used to refer to "what is left of a community after it undergoes a catastrophe" (Meyer 1995, 669; cf. Elliott 2000, 723). In the Old Testament, *remnant* highlights God's action in saving or preserving a group of people, as in the case of Jacob's family, whom God preserved from famine through Joseph (Gen 45:7). God's action is also highlighted in 1 Kings 19:18, which uses an active verb to describe those that God "left/caused to remain" in Israel who had not bowed the knee to Ba'al in the time of Elijah—later picked up by Paul in Rom 11:4–5 to describe the remnant of Jews who believe in Christ (Elliott 2000, 724; Millar 2000, 685).[9]

In the prophetic literature, the theme of the remnant is elevated to express a new stage of the people of God, a complex theology which intertwines the themes of judgment and mercy (Elliott 2000, 724; Millar 2000, 685). On the one hand, the theme of remnant can highlight the judgment of God: "The catastrophe undergone by the community is so great that only an insignificant remnant survives, or none at all" (Meyer 1995, 670; e.g., 2 Kings 21:13–15, Isa 17:4–6; Jer 8:3). Though God made Israel "numerous as the sand of the sea"—the promise of Abraham—only a remnant would survive God's judgment in exile and be restored (Isa 10:22).

The remnant theme can also highlight the mercy and salvation of God (Meyer 1995, 670; cf. Isa 1:25–26; Obad 17; Mic 2:12; Zeph 3:1–13). This goes beyond mere preservation and survival to restoration and renewal—God's covenant love to Israel would be renewed, and Israel's status as God's people would be restored (cf. Mic 7:18). The prophets unpack the remnant theme in terms of God's undeserved grace to his people, all of whom deserve judgment (Ezra 9:8, 13–15; Jer 5:10, 18; Mic 7:18–20), as well as a purifying purpose in judgment—purging the people of their sin and leaving behind a righteous, faithful people (Ezra 9:13–14; Isa 1:25–26; 4:2–4; 10:20; Jer 50:20; cf. Meyer 1995, 670; Elliott 2000, 723).

Thus, the remnant represents a critical development in the story and identity of the people of God. In the wake of covenant unfaithfulness and divine judgment, the future of God's people was restored through prophetic promises of a new covenant enjoyed by the remnant (Jer 31:31–34). The true people of God are not simply the physical descendants of the twelve tribes of Israel; they are the preserved and purified remnant who survive the judgment of the exile and who faithfully

---

8 I credit my former teacher, Dr. Timothy M. Stafford, for first alerting me to the idea of "remnant theology."

9 While the noun *remnant* does not appear in 1 Kings 19:18, the related verb for "remain" is used in the Hiphil form, meaning "I cause to remain" (i.e., "I leave" or "I have left"). This passage is picked up by Paul in Rom 11:4–5 in his theology of the remnant and put to use in addressing the reality of prevalent Jewish unbelief in the Messiah.

await the promises of God's redemption. The remnant would experience new and greater acts of salvation: a "new exodus," and life under a greater David (Isa 11:10–16; 28:5–6; Jer 23:3; 31:7–9; Mic 2:12–13; Zeph 2:7–9; cf. Meyer 1995, 670). The covenant formula, undone in exile, is reaffirmed as a prophetic hope for the remnant of Israel, as well as for many Gentiles who would join the remnant in the worship of God (Isa 2:1–5; 66:18–19; Zech 8:20–23; cf. Thielman 2005, 708).

The covenant with Abraham, the exodus and assembly at Sinai, the exile and emergence of the remnant—these are three key turning points in the history of the people of God, a story which forms the essential backdrop to the emergence of the new covenant people of God, the church.

"I Will Build My Church": Jesus' Kingdom Community

The climax of the story of God's people is the life, death, and resurrection of Jesus Christ, which we find narrated in the four Gospels. The fulcrum of the Bible, the Gospels, play an indispensable role in unpacking the way the life and work of Christ inaugurated a new era in the story of the people of God.

The Gospels begin where the Old Testament ends: with the remnant in expectation of redemption. John the Baptist arrives to prepare a faithful remnant for the promised kingdom. Not all ethnic Israelites would enjoy God's kingdom, but only those who exhibited true repentance (Matt 3:2–10, esp. v. 9; Luke 1:17; cf. 7:26–28). In his baptism by John, Jesus endorses John's message and identifies with the faithful remnant (Lunde 2006), even as he prepares to transform that remnant into the new covenant church.

It is fashionable to claim that Jesus was preoccupied with the kingdom of God and gave little thought to "the church." The word "church" (*ekklēsia*) occurs only three times in the Gospels (all in Matthew), compared to "kingdom" (*basileia*) occurring some 126 times across the Gospels.[10] Surely we must at least prioritize the "kingdom" ahead of the church, the argument goes.

However, as will become clear below, this line of thinking risks a superficial reading of the Gospels that focuses on word count at the expense of a robust understanding of the full range of ways that Jesus talked about and inaugurated his new covenant people. A more accurate picture emerges when we take a closer look at the ministry of Jesus and its place in the story of the people of God.

To understand Jesus' vision of the church, it is crucial to understand the two main activities of Jesus' ministry: (1) announcing and demonstrating the presence

---

10 *Ekklēsia* occurs once in Matthew 16:18 and twice in Matthew 18:17. The predominant theme of Jesus' teaching is clearly the kingdom of God (*basileia tou theou*), or "kingdom of heaven" (*basileia ton ouranon*), as often in Matthew. The kingdom of God/heaven is said in various places to be the central theme of Jesus' proclamation (e.g., Matt 4:17, Mark 1:15, Luke 4:43). Marshall notes that critical scholars have even claimed that Jesus was not interested in founding the church because he expected (incorrectly) the immediate advent of the kingdom (Marshall 1992, 122; Ladd 1993, 104).

of the kingdom, and (2) forming a community of disciples.[11] These two activities, and their dynamic relationship, reveal the critical role of the church in the ministry of Jesus. I begin with the second before unpacking the first.

Jesus' Community of Disciples
From the beginning of his ministry, Jesus calls people to follow him (Matt 4:19; 8:22; 11:28–29; Mark 1:16–20; Luke 5:27–28). But such a call, while personal, was never private. The call to discipleship has always been a call to follow Jesus together in community.

This can be seen in the communal images Jesus uses to describe his disciples. His disciples are a "little flock" (Luke 12:32), a "city on a hill" (Matt 5:14), and a planted field (Matt 13:24; 15:13; cf. Marshall 1992, 123). It can be seen in the second-person plural "you all" verbs in the Sermon on the Mount, "because it is the corporate impact of the disciple community, as an alternative society, which is in view here" (France 2007, 171; cf. Hagner 2008, 176).

Three important themes help illumine Jesus' vision for his emerging (and future) community of disciples. They are: (1) the "Jesus family," (2) renewed and restored Israel, and (3) the "ekklēsia" of Jesus.

THE "JESUS FAMILY"
One of the most pervasive, and yet neglected, images that Jesus uses to describe his disciples is that of "family" (Marshall 1992, 123; Minear 2004, 171; Hellerman 2009). Joe Hellerman's sociocultural study of the Gospels shows how Jesus operated within a Mediterranean strong-group model of the family that prioritized sibling relationships and patrilineal loyalty—not unlike that in many Muslim contexts. In this framework, Jesus depicts his community as a surrogate family which trumps natural family ties (2009, 64, 71).[12] R. T. France fleshes out the implicit theology at work:

> Those who follow Jesus have committed themselves to "do the will of my Father who is in heaven," and so have entered into a new relationship with God as also their "heavenly Father." ... And those who are children of the same heavenly Father are thus members of the same family, and are to regard one another as brothers and sisters. ([Matthew] 5:22–24, 7:3–5, 18:15, 18:21, 18:35, 23:8) ... And this extended family under the one heavenly Father (23:8–9) includes Jesus himself, who acknowledges the same Father in heaven, so that he can refer to his disciples as "my brothers" (cf. 25:40; 28:10). (France 2007, 496; cf. also Rapinchuk 2012, 37).

---

11 The launching of Jesus' ministry begins with the proclamation of the kingdom of God (Mark 1:14–15/Matt 4:17), and this is followed immediately by the account of the calling of Simon and Andrew to be his disciples (Mark 1:16–20/Matt 4:18–22).

12 Hellerman helpfully contrasts this with modern Western culture, which prioritizes the individual over the communal and prioritizes the husband-wife relationship rather than the sibling relationship, as in Mediterranean culture (2009, 64). In summary, "Jesus wanted His followers to interact with one another like members of a strong-group, surrogate family characterized by collectivist solidarity and commitment on every front. Such was Jesus' vision for authentic Christian community" (ibid., 75).

Jesus himself stands at the center of this new family. He claims the disciples as his true family—at times over against his birth family (Matt 12:49–50/ Mark 3:31–35), and he expects the same of his disciples. They must be willing, if necessary, to leave behind their natural family to follow Jesus (Matt 8:21–22; Luke 9:59–62), to "hate" their family members for the sake of Christ (Luke 14:25–27),[13] and to endure possible divisions within households (Luke 12:51–53).[14] Yet those who leave behind their natural families are promised to "receive a hundredfold" in their new spiritual family (Matt 19:25; cf. France 2007, 496).

The image of disciples as "family" plays a critical role in Jesus' vision of the nature of his community of followers, as well as the vision of the rest of the New Testament. But there are yet two additional significant themes in Jesus' teaching about his group of disciples.

THE RESTORED REMNANT OF ISRAEL

In addition to a "family," Jesus also pictured his disciples as the restored remnant foreshadowed by the prophets. Jesus' choice of *twelve* apostles signified a reconfiguration of the true people of God, organized not around the twelve tribes but around Jesus and his apostles, the core of the eschatological remnant (Matt 16:19; cf. Ladd 1993, 107; Wright 2010, 212; France 2007, 367–77).[15] All who believed in Jesus and joined his community of disciples became a part of the restored, righteous remnant of Israel and therefore heirs of the eschatological promises in the prophets.

The leaders of Israel, however, rejected the Messiah, which led them (and their followers) to forfeit their place in the restored people of God. The result was that Israel, as a nation, found itself outside the kingdom, which was taken away from them and given to "a people producing its fruits"—the new "Jesus community" of believing Jews and Gentiles (Matt 21:43; cf. Mark 12:9; Blomberg 1992, 325; cf.

---

13 This would have been an affront in the first-century cultural context, highlighting a reality that following Jesus would at times result in alienating one's family (Bock 1994–96, 1285). This teaching of Jesus shows his "stark refusal to allow filial duty to take priority over discipleship," which "underlines the radical newness and overriding importance of the message of the kingdom of heaven; even the most basic family ties must not be allowed to stand in its way.... The kingdom of heaven apparently involves a degree of fanaticism which is willing to disrupt the normal rhythms of social life. Jesus can hardly have been surprised that true discipleship remained a minority movement, and that popular enthusiasm for his teaching and healing generally stopped short of full discipleship. Many are invited, but few are chosen ([Matt] 20:16, 22:14; cf. 7:14)" (France 2007, 330–31).

14 Jesus taught his disciples to expect to be delivered over to persecution and hated by their own family (Luke 21:16–17). As Bock says, "To confess Christ might mean being hated by one's own kin. One must be ready to face the family's hostile reaction, not by maliciously separating from them, but by preparing for their hostile reaction to one's confession of Christ" (1994–96, 1672). Such things are quite relevant to ministering in Muslim contexts.

15 The selection of the Twelve was the "nucleus of a reconstituted and remnant community of Israel" (Keener 2012, 752), indicating that "a new era had come and that the old Israel was not responding to God in a proper manner and needed restructuring under the direction and ministry of Jesus, whom God had sent" (Bock 2007, 77). This may be analogous to the Qumran community, which also had a leadership council of twelve members (plus three priests) and portrayed themselves as "miniature Israel" and the righteous remnant (Keener 2012, 752; Thielman 2005, 708; France 2007, 744; cf. 1QS ["The Community Rule" Qumran Scroll] 8:1–4).

France 2007, 816–17).[16] R. T. France unpacks it this way: "Israel, [the religious leaders] have assumed, is where God rules, but they have rejected his will and so find themselves outside his domain, while he will rule over a reconstituted 'Israel' which acknowledges his sovereignty" (France 2007, 817).[17]

The new "Jesus family," then, is not a deviation from the story of Israel, but rather its resolution. The community of disciples were the restored remnant of Israel, the true heirs of the promises to Abraham and to the prophets of Israel, a community which would later welcome in the Gentile nations—a community that would become *the church*.

THE EKKLĒSIA OF JESUS

Jesus refers to his disciples not only as his family and the restored Israel, but as "*my church.*" While the word *ekklēsia* only occurs three times in the Gospels, one of them is in a moment of prime significance and revelation—Peter's confession of Jesus' messianic identity (Matt 16:13–20). After acknowledging the divine revelation behind this confession, Jesus states: "And I tell you that you are Peter (*Petros*), and on this rock (*petra*) I will build my church (*mou tein ekklēsian*), and the gates of Hades will not overcome it" (Matt 16:18 NIV).[18] Jesus does not expound on the precise form of his church, but this passage (as well as Matthew 18) provides a definitive contribution to Jesus' overall vision for his church.

Jesus combines several metaphors in describing his ekklēsia. First, Jesus' church is an "assembly" of people—the basic meaning of the word *ekklēsia*. But this is no ordinary assembly—it the assembly *of Jesus*,[19] which potentially echoes the

---

16 Dative form of *ethnos*.

17 The theology of Jesus' community as "the new Israel," while containing some element of truth, needs to be refined and further nuanced to do full justice to the nature of the church, the nature of Israel, and the relationship between the two. France preserves a distinction between the church and Israel by referring to the Jesus community as an "alternative 'Israel'" (France 2007, 367–77), which is a "new entity" composed of Jews and Gentiles "characterized not by ethnic origin but by faith in Jesus" (France 2007, 816–17); Bock talks of the Jesus community functioning "parallel to" the nation of Israel (Bock 1994–96, 541). Goldman notes that Luke–Acts portrays what is taking place in Jesus and the church as a fulfillment, and not a dashing, of Israel's hopes, as seen in devout believing Jews (Goldman 2012, 42–43; cf. Luke 3:4–6; 4:17–21; Acts 2:16–21; 15:15–18).

18 Marshall notes that the ekklēsia of Jesus has as its "antecedent" the remnant and the "saints of the Most High" in Daniel 7 (Marshall 1992, 124). Thus, the ekklēsia of Jesus fits into the broader sweep of the history of the people of God as laid out in Jesus does not provide many details as to the organization or form of his messianic congregation. However, in Matthew 18:15–20, where we find the other two occurrences of ekklēsia, Jesus envisions his messianic community gathering as taking the form of smaller, local communities bearing the authority and presence of Jesus to make important decisions such as dealing with unrepentant sinners in the community (cf. especially v. 17).

19 The personal pronoun is fronted in Greek (*Mou*, in *mou tein ekklēsian*, rather than the more common *tein ekklēsian mou*) emphasizing that this assembly is "the congregation of *me*, the Messiah" (Marshall 1992, 124; emphasis added), who builds the messianic community around himself (France 2007, 623; Ladd 1993, 108). There is no basis for an apostolic succession, but one should not ignore the clear wordplay and say that it simply refers to Peter's *confession* of faith (Blomberg 1992, 252; Marshall 1992, 124; Morris 1992, 423; France 2007, 622). Rather, the foundation on which the church is built is "Peter as the man who has received revelation" (Morris 1992, 423), or Peter as a representative of the twelve confessing Jesus as Messiah. The rock is "Peter the confessor," who later becomes "the rock of stumbling" when he opposes

"assembly of Yahweh" in the Old Testament. Second, Jesus' assembly is *something Jesus builds*—and that on a solid foundation. "Building" a people is a common Old Testament concept (Ladd 1993, 107; cf. Ruth 4:11; Ps 28:5; 118:22; Jer 1:10; 24:6; 31:4; 33:7; Amos 9:11), which led to a Jewish expectation that the Messiah would build a congregation within Israel (e.g., the Qumran community; cf. Blomberg 1992, 252–53; Marshall 1992, 124). Third, Jesus' assembly is *victorious over death* (i.e., "the gates of Hades"; cf. France 2007, 623-24).[20]

In addition, two further points should be made regarding Jesus' use of the word *ekklēsia*. First, it is likely Jesus is referring to the post-ascension community of the church (cf. the future tense in Matthew 16:18, and the mode of Jesus' presence in Matthew 18:20). Second, Jesus seems to envision the church as both a singular community ("my church" in Matt 16:18) as well as local, gathered communities bearing the authority and presence of Jesus to make important decisions such as dealing with unrepentant sinners in the community (cf. Matt 18:17).

The occurrences of *ekklēsia* are few, but they provide an important window into Jesus' vision for his church—his messianic assembly, built on the rock, strong in the face of death, bearing his authority in gathered fellowship. These truths factor into the larger fabric of themes that together express a robust vision of the church in the teaching and ministry of Jesus.

Jesus' formation of a community of disciples was a critical aspect of his ministry. Another central part of his ministry was proclaiming and demonstrating the kingdom of God. Understanding the nature of this kingdom, and its relationship to the ekklēsia of Jesus, is crucial for a sound biblical vision of the church.

The Kingdom of God in the Ministry of Jesus

The term "kingdom of God" is a rich, dynamic idea shaped by a variety of factors.

Jesus' plan to go to the cross (Ladd 1993, 108–9). This imagery of Jesus building his *ekklēsia* on the rock of Peter and the apostles bears similarities with other passages in a broader New Testament theology of the church. In 1 Corinthians 3:10–11, Christ is pictured as the foundation and the apostles' work is the "superstructure" (France 2007, 622). In 1 Pet 2:4–8, the Christian community is pictured as a spiritual temple of "living stones" built on the cornerstone of Jesus Christ. In Eph 2:20–22, the foundation is expanded to include the "apostles and prophets," with again Christ as cornerstone. In Rev 21:14, the New Jerusalem has the names of the twelve apostles in the twelve foundations (France 2007, 622).

20 The word *ekklēsia* in Greek can mean one of three things: (1) an assembly, (2) a group of people who are assembled, or (3) a community/congregation of people (BDB, 303). Its original usage in Greek was "the popular assembly of the full citizens of the Greek city state" who made judicial and political decisions (O'Brien 1987, 90; cf. Giles 1995, 24; BDB, 303). However, it also came to refer to any spontaneous or casual gathering of people (cf. Acts 19:32), or to a community or group of people (BDB, 303). In the Septuagint (LXX), ekklēsia was used to translate Hebrew qahal, which refers to a group assembled for some purpose (Blomberg 1992, 252). The normal usage of the word in both the LXX and in Greek literature for an assembled people shows that the word ekklēsia does not carry an inherent theological or cultic meaning (Banks 1980, 35; cf. Giles 1995, 25). However, it is possible that Jesus (as well as Paul) are invoking a theologically pregnant notion of Israel as God's covenant community, the "assembly of Yahweh" (Clowney 1995, 30; Harrison and Dvorak 2012, 11; Ladd 1993, 107; France 2007, 623). Ekklēsia translates qahal in the LXX in the phrase "the day of assembly," the day Israel received the law at Sinai (e.g., Deut 4:10; 9:10; 18:16), as well as "the assembly of Yahweh," which referred to Israel gathered to worship the Lord (cf. Deut 23:1–9).

As Ladd explains, the term

> cannot be reduced to a single concept but is a complex concept with several facets. Its root meaning is the reign or rule of God. It can designate the eschatological act of God when God acts in kingly power to destroy his enemies and save his people. It can also designate the future realm of salvation into which God's people will be gathered to enjoy the blessings of his reign. As such, it is interchangeable with the Age to Come. (Ladd 1993, 68)

The Old Testament background is the kingship and sovereignty of God over all of his creation (e.g., 1 Sam 8:7; Ps 103:19; 145:11–13), combined with the anticipation of God acting to demonstrate and manifest his sovereignty in history (Dan 2:44–45; 7:26–27). In a word, "God is now the King, but he also must *become* King" (Ladd 1993, 61; emphasis in original).

The Jews largely expected the kingdom to coincide with the ultimate defeat of Israel's enemies and the restoration of the nation of Israel in the promised land under God's rule alone (ibid., 60), and after the exile, this expectation of the coming kingdom was associated with the restoration of the Davidic monarchy (cf. Isa 9:6–7; Ezek 37:24–28; Dan 7:13–14, 27; Mic 5:2–5).

This background illumines Jesus' teaching on the kingdom, which drew on the Old Testament but countered the Jewish expectations for the kingdom in surprising ways. The kingdom would not come all at once (Mark 3:30–32; Luke 19:11–27); it would exclude certain Israelites while including Gentiles (Matt 21:43–44; Luke 13:24–30); and it would not be implemented through the sword but through the cross (Mark 8:31–35; 10:32–45; cf. Clowney 1995, 39).

The kingdom involved both a present (Luke 11:20; 17:20–21) and a future dimension (Matt 25:1–13; Luke 19:11–27). God's promised reign had "come near" in Jesus' ministry, "a present inbreaking in history in his own person and mission … a new realm of redemptive blessing into which people enter by receiving Jesus' message about the kingdom of God" (Ladd 1993, 68; cf. Matt 12:28, Mark 4:26; 10:14–15; Luke 7:28; 10:9–11). And yet, the kingdom will not be fully consummated until the end of the age when the Son of Man returns in final judgment and salvation (cf. Matt 7:21; 8:11–12; 13:43; Luke 13:29; 19:11–27). The present and future dimensions of the kingdom provide an "already/not-yet" dynamic tension, held together by the fact that the kingdom primarily refers to the *reign/rule* of God, dynamically manifested in Jesus' ministry as a sign and foretaste of its full realization at the end of the age (Cullmann 1964, 84–86; cf. Bruce 1958, 103).

Relationship between the Kingdom and the Church in Jesus' Ministry

The kingdom and the church are not competing values in Jesus' vision—they are inseparable and integrally related. Understood properly, the "concept of the kingdom of God implies a community … a group of people who own him as king and the establishment of a realm of people within which his gracious power is manifested" (Marshall 1992, 123). The kingdom and the church are necessary to one another:

> There can be no Kingdom without a church—those who have acknowledged God's rule—and there can be no church without God's kingdom; but they remain two distinguishable concepts: the rule of God and the fellowship of men and women. (Ladd 1993, 117)

The church and kingdom are distinct realities which are dynamically related to one another in various ways (Ladd 1993):

- The kingdom creates the church—the presence of the kingdom results in people entering the kingdom and becoming "the new people of God, the children of the Kingdom, the true Israel, the incipient church" (p. 111).
- The church witnesses to the kingdom—Jesus sends the church to announce the kingdom, while the church itself has "a dual character, belonging to two ages. It is the people of the Age to Come, but it still lives in this age" (p. 112).
- The church is an instrument of the kingdom—the church demonstrates the reality of God's reign in various ways (p. 114; cf. Matt 10:8; Luke 10:17).
- The church is the custodian of the kingdom—previously stewarded by the nation of Israel, the kingdom is now entrusted to the Jesus community (p. 115).
- The church is a "sign, instrument and foretaste" of the kingdom (Newbigin 1988, 138).

Bringing these strands together, the church-kingdom relationship can be summed up as follows:

> The church is the community of those who believe in Jesus and his preaching of the kingdom. It preserves and repeats Jesus' preaching and tries to be faithful to it. It lives its life against the background or horizon of the kingdom. As the community of Jesus Christ it is the sign and symbol of hope … that the kingdom of God has been inaugurated in the person of Jesus and will come to completion whenever God wishes. (Harrington 1980, 26–27)

Therefore, we should recognize that the proclamation of the kingdom goes hand-in-hand with the creation of the church in the ministry of Jesus. As Marshall says,

> All this material shows that Jesus proclaimed the rule of God and urged people to return to God in repentance and obedience, that he called them to be his own disciples and constitute the *ekklesia* of the Messiah, that he saw them as children of God called to be brothers and sisters. It may surely be affirmed that here we have the essence of the church. (Marshall 1992, 124)

It is clear by now that the kingdom of God should not be construed as eclipsing, or marginalizing, the church in Jesus' vision. Rather, the kingdom of God is an important theme in the whole network of themes that fills out the fuller picture of the church in the ministry and teaching of Jesus.[21]

---

[21] The teaching on the kingdom is not featured in the Gospel of John, though it is not absent (cf. John 3:3). The Gospel of John features different terminology to refer to the church,

Proclaiming the kingdom and forming his emerging ekklēsia were all a prelude to the climax and central purpose of Jesus' coming—his crucifixion, resurrection, and ascension. Contrary to all expectations, Jesus inaugurated the kingdom, not through the sword but through the cross. Receiving universal authority, King Jesus commissioned his church to implement his universal reign through discipleship of the nations, which involved baptizing them into the growing community of the triune God (Matt 28:19–20). And after Pentecost, that's exactly what his disciples did:

> The origins of the church lie in the entire action of God in Jesus Christ, but the decisive moment was the resurrection when *the proclaimer of the kingdom became the one proclaimed.* God's action of raising up the crucified one and pouring out the Spirit *turned the group of disciples into the church.* (Harrington 1980, 27; emphasis added)

This paves the way for the next key moment in the unfolding story of the people of God—Pentecost—when "The people of God, claimed by Christ in the blood of the New Covenant, are made the fellowship of the Spirit as they await their returning Lord" (Clowney 1995, 50).

Pentecost: The Coming of the Spirit and Emergence of the Church

One could say that Jesus "founded" his church the moment he poured out the Spirit on his community of disciples. The decisive moment was dramatically marked with the unique, powerful sign of tongues, signaling the last days and the inauguration of the eschatological people of God from all nations and languages.

The book of Acts narrates the emergence and expansion of the church in Jerusalem and beyond. Beginning at Pentecost, Luke describes believers as being both saved and immediately "added" (*protisthemi*) to the church by the Lord (2:47; 5:14; 11:24), a word used in Jewish proselyte literature for Gentiles who are joined to the people of Israel.[22] Whether added "to the Lord" (e.g., 5:14; 11:24) or "to their number" (2:47), the meaning is the same—believers are naturally joined to the growing Jesus community—the church.[23] This pattern continues in Paul's ministry, in which he intentionally gathers believers into churches, led by local elders (Acts 14:23; cf. Banks 1980, 33). From beginning to end, the book of Acts tells a story in which the advance of the word to the ends of the earth brings the expansion of the church (6:7; 9:31; 12:41; 16:5; cf. Carson 2008).

---

such as "children of God" (John 1:12; 11:52), the flock of God and his Son (10:12, 16), and "branches" of Jesus the vine (15:5–6). Cf. Olbricht 2012, 62. In the high priestly prayer of John 17, Jesus looks forward to the future church as a "growing community governed by love" (ibid., 79). The church, in John, is defined by the mission of the Son, "a community that has its being in the sending of Jesus" (Ferreira 1998, 200).

22 For example, LXX Esther 9:27 ("The Jews firmly obligated themselves and their offspring and *all who joined them* that without fail they would keep these two days according to what was written and at the time appointed every year") and LXX Isaiah 14:1 ("For the Lord will have compassion on Jacob and will again choose Israel, and will set them in their own land, and sojourners *will join them and will attach themselves* to the house of Jacob"). Ott and Wilson 2011, Loc. 570, citing Reinhardt 1995, 99–100.

23 "Their number," *epi to auto*, is a phrase which acquired semi-technical meaning in the early church to refer to the gathered community of believers, as in Acts 1:15; 2:1; 1 Cor 11:20; 14:23 (Metzger 1971, 305; cited in Ott and Wilson 2011, Loc. 9569, n. 7).

INSIDER CHURCH

The inclusion of the Gentiles in the church is a major theme in the book of Acts. Forecasted by Jesus (Acts 1:8) and the sign of tongues (Acts 2:1–10)(Acts 2:1-10), the inclusion of the Gentiles is realized as the gospel moves beyond Jerusalem to Samaria (8:48), to Gentile God-fearers (chapter 10), and to others throughout the Roman Empire (11:19–26; chapters 13–14). This surprising inclusion of non-Jews in the people of God is divinely validated by subsequent "Pentecosts," additional dramatic outpourings of the Spirit as the gospel crosses new barriers (8:14–17; 10:44–49).

No passage is more important to this theme than the Jerusalem Council in Acts 15. The council concludes with the apostles recognizing that they are witnessing the promised ingathering of the Gentiles, itself a sign of the promised restoration of the people of God in the last days (Bock 2007, 502–3, cf. Acts 15:17, quoting Amos 9:11–12). It is now clear that Jesus is saving and including uncircumcised Gentiles as his people through faith in him, and that a new era has dawned which no longer requires circumcision and Mosaic law-observance to be full members of God's covenant people (15:10–11, 19). This watershed moment propels the apostle Paul to continue his mission throughout the Gentile world, even reaching Caesar's doorstep.

In the book of Acts, a distinctive community identity emerges around the church, seen first in the vivid descriptions of its unique community life—learning from the apostles, sharing possessions, worshipping in public and in homes, and breaking bread in ways that echo the Lord's Supper (2:42–47; 4:32–37). A variety of terms are used to "name" this community, the most common being "brothers" (30x), "disciples" (28x), and the "church" (23x), and less common being "believers" (10x), "the Way" (6x), and "Christians" (2x) (Giles 1997, 197).

The word *ekklēsia* has a variety of usages in Acts. It can refer to: (1) a secular assembly (e.g., 19:32–40); (2) a local community of disciples in a particular city (cf. 11:22, 13:1, 18:22, 20:17); (3) the community of believers in a larger region (e.g., *the church* throughout all Judea, Samaria, and Galilee, 9:31); and (4) *multiple* communities of believers throughout a region (e.g., 14:23; 15:45; 16:5). The predominant usage is a local congregation of believers, against the background of a clear interconnectedness with local communities in other places, bound together by a common identity of faith in Jesus and recognition of the authority of the apostles (Bock 2007, 227; Ladd 1993, 389).

The Jewish community had an ambivalent relationship with the early church. On the one hand, the first believers did not actively seek to break from the Jewish community, evidenced by their continued participation in Jewish worship in the temple and in the synagogue (Acts 2:46; 3:1; 13:14–15). Ladd notes,

> Jesus and his disciples did not form a separate synagogue, nor start a separate movement, nor in spite of constant conflict with the Jewish leaders break with either the temple or synagogue in any outward way. His disciples formed an open fellowship in Israel whose only external distinguishing mark was their discipleship to Jesus. (1993, 380; cf. Marshall 1992, 124)

The believers insisted they were not contradicting the Mosaic law and that the gospel was the fulfillment of the Hebrew Scriptures (e.g., Acts 2:14–36; 3:18–26). Thus, the early church in Acts "considered themselves a movement within Judaism and were considered such by others" (Harrington 1980, 30; cf. Acts 2:46; 3:1; 13:14–15).

On the other hand, the "followers of the Way" distinguished themselves with a unique, distinctive community identity—one which repelled many Jews and attracted many Gentiles. The use of ekklēsia and other terms signify the development of an "identifiable religious community" in the form of local gatherings of disciples with a sense of solidarity and unity with other congregations throughout the empire (Bock 2007, 227, 372). This distinction was brought into fuller relief through the full acceptance of uncircumcised Gentiles into fellowship, further distinguishing themselves from their non-believing Jewish countrymen.

The church in Acts is the continuation of what Jesus "began" in his earthly ministry. After creating a community of disciples, Jesus builds them into the church, empowered by the Spirit, sent as witnesses to Jesus among the nations. A multi-ethnic movement of Jews and Gentiles, local communities of "the Way" multiply throughout the empire and develop a solidarity together with the growing Jesus-community around the world. This portrait of the church is a continuation of the Jesus-community in the Gospels:

> The most important aspects of the ecclesiology of Acts can be traced back to Luke's Gospel. Like Jesus, the church follows the leading of the Spirit, includes outcasts, helps the poor, and practices table fellowship. That is the best description of Luke's vision of what the church should be. … Luke describes the church as a community of believers in Jesus who continue what Jesus "began" to do and to teach. (Goldman 2012, 57)

The ecclesiology of Acts—and the rest of the New Testament—is nothing less than an outgrowth of the ecclesiology of Jesus.

It is this stage in the biblical story where we should see ourselves—in between the first and second comings of Jesus, in the age of gospel proclamation and expansion of the church to the ends of the earth. And like the early church, we can sit "at the apostles feet" receiving their teaching—if not in person, then in their Spirit-inspired epistles—which further unpack the richness of the identity and nature of the church.

Excursus: Apostolic Teaching about the Church in the Epistles

The apostles were commissioned by Christ as cofounders of his church (cf. Matt 16:18; Eph 2:20), and they authoritatively instruct the church—in person and in writing—not just what to do, but *who we are*. If Acts reveals the nature of the church as it emerged and spread after Pentecost, the Epistles further unfold the identity of the church in personal apostolic communication specifically addressed *to local churches*. The Epistles therefore must not be neglected in a biblical vision of the church, for they provide a rich set of teachings and images of the church which complement the narrative perspective of the people of God. Below I highlight important contributions in the letters of Paul, 1 Peter, and the letter to the Hebrews.

The Church in Paul's Letters

The church is everywhere in the epistles of Paul. Out of the 114 occurrences of *ekklēsia* in the New Testament, 62 are found in Paul's letters (O'Brien 1987, 91; Giles 1995, 23). Nine of his thirteen[24] letters are specifically addressed to local church communities,[25] one to an individual with a church community as a secondary audience (Philemon; see vv. 1–2), and three to individuals regarding how to lead/administer the church (1 and 2 Timothy, Titus). Through a variety of themes, images, and metaphors, Paul's letters offer a dynamic vision of the church of Jesus Christ.

EKKLĒSIA IN PAUL

As in Acts, Paul's usage of *ekklēsia* is flexible and without a fixed, technical meaning (Giles 1995, 23). The majority usage refers to a local congregation or community of believers, either "as assembled" (1 Cor 11:18; 14:19, 28, 34, 35) or without reference to an actual gathering (Giles 1995, 114, 127–28).

At times no location is specified,[26] but the church is often identified by the city,[27] region,[28] or house in which it meets.[29] In a minority of cases (especially in Ephesians and Colossians), *ekklēsia* refers to the whole body of believers in Christ.[30]

This range of usage of *ekklēsia* highlights the centrality of the local congregation for Paul, as well as a larger dimension of the church that transcends the local congregation to include the larger believing community.

Whether viewed locally or globally, the church is no ordinary community to Paul, but an extraordinary society of divine significance. Paul sometimes speaks of *ekklēsia theou*, "the church of God" (1 Cor 1:2; 10:32; 11:22; 15:9; 2 Cor 1:1; Gal 1:13), yet another possible echo of the ancient "assembly of Yahweh."[31]

---

24 I assume in this book the traditional authorship of the so-called "disputed" Pauline letters. Carson and Moo (2005) provide compelling and in-depth scholarly defenses of traditional authorship of all of the Pauline letters.

25 Five of these nine epistles specifically mention *ekklēsia* (either singular or plural) to describe the recipients being addressed, five describe the recipients as "saints" (*hagioi*), and two describe them as "faithful/believing ones" or "faithful/believers in Christ."

26 For example, 1 Cor 6:4; 10:32; 11:22; 14:4; 14:5; 14:12; 14:23; 1 Tim 3:15; 5:16. See also references to "all the churches" or "in every church" in Rom 16:16; 1 Cor 4:17; 7:17; 11:16; 14:33; 2 Cor 8:18, 19, 23, 24; 11:8; 11:28, 12:13; 2 Thess 1:4.

27 For example, at Cenchrae (Rom 16:1), in Corinth (1 Cor 1:2; 2 Cor 1:1), in Philippi (Phil 4:15), of the Laodiceans (Col 4:16), of the Thessalonians (1 Thess 1:1; 2 Thess 1:1).

28 For example, the churches of Galatia (1 Cor 16:1; Gal 1:2), of Asia (1 Cor 16:19); of Macedonia (2 Cor 8:1); of Judea (Gal 1:22; 1 Thess 2:14).

29 For example, in Prisca and Aquila's house (Rom 16:3–5; 1 Cor 16:19), in the house of Nympha (Col 4:15), in Philemon's house (Phlm 2), in Gaius' house (assumed in Rom 16:23).

30 For example, Ephesians 1:22; 3:10, 21; 5:23–32; Col 1:18, 24. Possibly also 1 Cor 12:28; 15:9; Gal 1:13; Phil 3:6.

31 The LXX phrase is *ekklēsia kuriou* ("assembly of the Lord"), which likely translates the Hebrew *qahal Yahweh* (O'Brien 1987, 90; Dunn 2011, 166; Thielman 2005, 708).

Paul uses a variety of pregnant terms to describe the church, including "holy/sanctified ones" (*hagioi*, cf. Rom 1:7), the "brothers" (*adelphois*, cf. Col 1:2), the "called ones" (*kleitois*, cf. 1 Cor 1:2), "beloved ones" (*agapetois*, cf. Rom 1:7), and the "faithful/believing ones" (*pistois*, cf. Eph 1:1). Such terms point to a deeper reality that gives the church significance in Paul's vision—the mystery of the gospel.

THE GOSPEL AS BASIS OF THE CHURCH

The gospel—God's act of redemption through Christ and the Spirit—is central to Paul's vision of the church. Faith in Christ not only justifies—it incorporates believers into God's people as sons of Abraham (cf. Gal 3:6–29; Rom 4). Salvation in Paul is a "community-creating event":

> getting saved and becoming a member of the people of God are inseparable, simultaneous events: "For we were all baptized into one body—whether Jews or Greeks, whether slaves or free—and we were all made to drink of one Spirit" (1 Cor 12:13).... In Eph 2:14–18, we see that in the cross, God not only created reconciliation with God, but reconciliation between Jew and Gentile "to create in himself one new man" (i.e., the new humanity, the church). (Hellerman 2009, 123, 130–31)

As in the exodus, so in the cross, God's redemption creates a community, that God might dwell with his people. The core of the church's identity, according to Paul, is the good news of God's wondrous redemption.

The gospel also provides the key to understanding the significance of the church in the story of the people of God. Paul views the church in a key moment in redemptive history, when a long-hidden "mystery" is revealed to humans and spiritual beings (Eph 3:10–11)—the surprising way the cross of Christ opens the floodgates of the people of God to all nations. Previously alienated, Jews and Gentiles, slaves and free, high and low class, male and female—all are reconciled as one in Christ, brothers and sisters in God's family and coheirs of the promises to Abraham, Moses, and the faithful remnant of Israel (Rom 4:12; 10:24–27; Gal 3:27–29; Eph 2:12; 3:5–6).

Foretold by the prophets, the unique and unprecedented community represents the climax of world history; and the church is God's trophy, displaying his wisdom and glory in heaven and earth. Such is the privileged identity of the church in light of God's great redemption in Christ. It is no surprise that such a wondrous reality inspires a variety of metaphors and images to express the church's identity in Paul's teachings.

IMAGES OF THE CHURCH IN PAUL'S LETTERS

Paul gives us some of the most developed and important biblical metaphors of the church, providing a wealth of insight into the church's identity. One metaphor is the church as *building*: not the physical meeting structure, but the community itself, which "builds itself up" as a body—a project in which all members participate (Banks 1980, 52–53; cf. Minear 2004, 49–50).[32] The metaphor is flexible, referring

---

32 For the church as a building which is built by the apostles and evangelists, see Galatians 2:18; 1 Corinthians 3:10–14; 2 Corinthians 10:8; 12:19; 13:10; Rom 15:20; Ephesians 2:20;

to the local congregation on the foundation of Christ (e.g., 1 Cor 3:10–14) and to the global church on the foundation of the apostles and prophets, with Christ as cornerstone (cf. Eph 2:21–22).

A related metaphor is the church as *temple* (Banks 1980, 52; cf. Minear 2004, 96–97), showing the church as no ordinary "building," but the very structure in which the Spirit of God dwells—a fulfillment of God's ancient promise to dwell among his people, as well as the basis for the church's holiness (1 Cor 3:16–17; 2 Cor 6:16–18 [quoting Lev 26:12 and Isa 52:11]; Eph 2:21–22). The temple metaphor is likewise ascribed both to the local congregation (1 Cor 3:16) and to the global community of faith (cf. Eph 2:21–22).

The church is also pictured as a *field* (1 Cor 3:9) and a *plant/tree* (Rom 11:17–24; Col 2:7; Eph 3:17)—an inspiration for the modern metaphor of "church planting." These metaphors resonate with Old Testament teaching on Israel as God's vineyard (cf. Isa 5:17), which the apostle John finds fulfilled in Jesus (John 15:1–6). Paul also depicts the church as *unleavened bread*, a metaphor which invokes the Passover and connects in important ways to the Lord's Supper (1 Cor 5:6–7; 10:14-17; Gal 5:9). Other important images are the church as a *new humanity* (rooted in Christ, "the Second Adam") and a *new creation,* metaphors which situate the church in God's plan to renew his creation (Eph 2:10, 15–16; Rom 5:12–21; 1 Cor 15:20–23; 2 Cor 5:17) (Banks 1980, 53; cf. Minear 2004, 35–36, 48–49).

One of Paul's more pervasive metaphors continues a theme from the Gospels—the church as *family* (cf. Minear 2004, 165–72). Sibling/kinship terms are found in nearly every chapter in Paul's epistles (Hellerman 2009, 211), and his favorite term for describing his audiences is familial: *adelphoi* ("brothers" or "brothers and sisters") (Banks 1980, 55). These terms are full of theological significance, rooted in the church's relationship with God (i.e., adopted sons of the Father in Jesus the Son, cf. Rom 8:12–17; Gal 4:4–7) and bearing profound, costly implications for relationships (e.g., Rom 12:10, 1 Cor 8:13). Connected to this is Paul's depiction of the church as household (*oikos*), such as in Galatians 6:10 and Ephesians 2:19, both of which refer to the global community of faith.

Another important Pauline metaphor for the church is the *body of Christ*. Rich and multifaceted, this metaphor has different functions and nuances in different passages (Minear 2004, 173).[33] In some cases, it refers to the *physical body of Jesus* crucified on the cross, through which believers die to the law (Rom 7:4) and in which they are reconciled to God—Jew and Gentile alike (Eph 2:16). In another usage, it signifies the one unified community into which believers are baptized, with a diversity of functions in building up the community, like in a human body (Rom 12:4–6; 1 Cor 12:12–27; Eph 4:4, 11–16). The basis of this "unity in diversity" is the church's spiritual union with Christ (1 Cor 12:12–13).

4:12. For the church as a body which "builds" itself up in love, see 1 Corinthians 14:5, 12, 26; Rom 14:19; Colossians 2:7; Ephesians 4:16 (Banks 1980, 52).

33 See Minear's extensive treatment of the metaphor in chap. 6 of *Images of the Church in the New Testament*, 173–220.

It should be noted that, as with other images, Paul views both the local congregation (1 Cor 12:27; cf. Banks 1980, 63) and the universal community of faith (1 Cor 12:13; Rom 12:5) as the "body of Christ." The universal dimension, while hinted at in Paul's earlier letters, is brought to full flower in later letters (Banks 1980, 66), developed in terms of the intimate union of Christ with the church (like a husband and wife, cf. Eph 5:22–33), the authority of the exalted Christ over the church (Eph 1:22; Col 1:18), and Christ as the source and goal of the church's growth (Eph 4:16).

The body of Christ is just one of many metaphors that make up the array of images that depict the multifaceted glory of the identity of the church in the vision of Paul—along with the family/household of God, building/temple, God's field/plant, unleavened bread, and new humanity/creation. In the context of personal, passionate teaching to the early church, Paul takes us deeper into the mystery and wonder of the church of Jesus Christ and its multifaceted, glorious heritage. Another important apostolic contribution to the church is found in 1 Peter—without a single mention of the word *church*.

THE CHURCH IN 1 PETER

The apostle Peter, the alleged "rock" of the church, provides significant teaching on the church in a variety of terms. Throughout his first letter, Peter refers to scattered Christian communities using terms classically used for the people of God—God's "elect" (1:1; cf. 2:9), the "called" (1:15; 2:9, 21; 3:9; 5:10), and God's "flock"/"sheep" (2:25; 5:2–4; cf. Black 2012, 231). In a rich crescendo, Peter strings together several pregnant Old Testament phrases (from Ex 19:6 and Isa 43:20–21) and applies them to the identity of believers in Jesus—"a chosen race, a royal priesthood, a holy nation, a people for his own possession" (1 Pet 2:9).[34] It is the clearest identification of the church as the people of God in the New Testament (Harrington 1980, 81). Peter also addresses the believers as "sojourners and exiles" (2:11; cf. 1:1, 17), an image which draws upon Israel's exile and scattering among the nations.

Peter calls the church to "be holy" as God is holy (1:15; cf. 2:11-12), a calling which shapes the church's relationship to the world (ibid., 229–30, 235). The church is a living, growing temple, with Christ as the cornerstone, and with believers being both "living stones" and priests in the temple (2:4–8; Black 2012, 231; Clowney 1995, 46). And like Paul and Jesus, Peter also describes the church as a family (1:22; 2:17; 3:8; 5:9; Black 2012, 231).

Both complementing and confirming the Pauline vision, Peter's teaching on the church offers a significant contribution to several aspects of the biblical vision of the church—as does the letter to the Hebrews.

---

34 "What allows the application of Israel's titles to the Christian community is faith in Christ the living stone (see Ps 118:22) and incorporation into Christ in baptism" (ibid., 83).

The Church in Hebrews
There are two significant ways Hebrews fills out a biblical vision of the church. First, Hebrews shows how the church possesses a new and better covenant (8:6), a greater High Priest (4:14–5:10; 7:26–28), a superior sacrifice (9:11–13), and greater access into God's presence (9:24; 10:22). These central themes of Hebrews are foundational to the identity of the church, providing an impetus for believers to maintain the regular habit of assembling together to encourage and sharpen each other in anticipation of Christ's return (10:25).

Second, Hebrews provides a heavenly picture of the church as "the assembly of the firstborn" gathered on Mt. Zion, with all the angels and saints, in the presence of God and Christ in the heavenly Jerusalem (12:18–24). This image hearkens back to the assembly at Sinai, surpassing it in both terror and glory (12:18–21, 25–29) while looking forward to the final assembly in the heavenly Jerusalem (12:22). Yet the author of Hebrews vividly depicts this gathering as a present reality—the church is in some sense already gathered in this heavenly assembly (12:22; O'Brien 1987, 97), echoing Paul's depiction of the church as already seated with Christ at God's right hand (Nicuum 2012, 132, 138; cf. Eph 2:6; 3:10; Col 3:1–4). This picture of the church remains in tension with the "this-worldly" picture of the church in the rest of the New Testament: small groups gathering in homes, scattered throughout the world as aliens and strangers, enduring persecution, patiently awaiting the Lord's return. However, such is the tension of the kingdom of God—already manifest, still awaiting full realization.

The teaching of the apostles on the church—as seen in the Pauline letters, 1 Peter, and Hebrews—is an invaluable part of the biblical vision of the church, helping us find our place in the biblical story. Addressed directly to the church, the Epistles help us grasp and embrace our glorious identity as the church, an apostolic vision that anticipates the final vision given to John, the culmination of the story of the people of God. If the Epistles unpack the identity of the church now, Revelation gives a glimpse of the identity of the church as it will be.

The Completion of the Church in the Book of Revelation

Addressed to the "seven churches of Asia"—representative of the worldwide church—Revelation gives a suggestive, mysterious glimpse of the church's final destiny. But this glorious vision of the future of the church is addressed to the imperfect church of the present: a church called to repent, witness, and persevere in faithfulness (cf. Peters 2012, 263).

One image of the church in John's vision is the lampstand. Seven times in Revelation the image is used, picturing the worldwide church as seven lampstands, with Christ standing at the center. The imagery comes from both the tabernacle (Ex 25:31–40) and the promise of the rebuilt temple (Zech 4:2–10), picturing the church as the place where Christ rules and dwells (Osborne 2002, 86–87; cf. Peters 2012, 245–46).

Perhaps Revelation's greatest contribution to our understanding of the nature of the church is the window it gives into the church's final form. One such glimpse is the picture of the uncountable, white-robed, worshipping assembly from every nation and tribe, bought by the blood of the Lamb (Rev 7:9–10; cf. 5:9–10). The Abrahamic blessing to all families of the earth, the prophetic hope of the ingathering of the nations, and the mission of the church to the nations inaugurated at Pentecost—these purposes are finally complete in this final vision of the people of God.

The final form of the church emerges again at the end of Revelation. Chapters 20–21 present the church with combined imagery: as both Bride of the Lamb and the Heavenly City of Jerusalem descending from heaven in the new creation (Peters 2012, 261–62). Reflecting and fulfilling the Old Testament theme of Israel as the bride of Yahweh (cf. Hosea 1–3; Jer 2:1–3), the wedding imagery signals a happy ending to the love story between God and his people, a story with moments of betrayal and estrangement, but one which concludes with full restoration and intimacy. The Bride and the New Jerusalem are identified together in the text (Rev 21:9-10), setting it in contrast to Babylon, the prostitute-city (ch. 17). The New Jerusalem is thus both a "people" and a "place"—an image of both the people of God and the final home of the people in the new creation (cf. Osborne, 733).

The heavenly Jerusalem signals the final realization of God's plan from the beginning of creation—God's perfect, unadulterated, permeating presence with his people (Rev 21:3), underscored by the absence of temple, sun, or moon in the new creation. The consummation of the church in the new heavens and new earth is a restoration of Eden, signaled by the tree of life, the healing of the nations, and the removal of the curse (22:1–5).

Such glorious images are intended to help the present church see its identity in light of what will be at the consummation. At present scattered, persecuted, racked with sin and strife, and a marginalized minority—it will one day be holy, vindicated, unified, and eternally honored in God's presence. The identity and nature of the church is not merely something to be observed in the present, but a reality in which to hope with anticipation; and thus Revelation—and the biblical story—fittingly concludes with the church and the Spirit eagerly beckoning the return of the King (Rev 22:17, 20).

The Defining Narrative of the Church

The identity of the church is not revealed all at once. It is progressively unfolded in the great drama of God and his people, from Abraham to the New Jerusalem—a story still unfolding. To define the church biblically, we must attend to this story, along with the cornucopia of images and sub-themes which express the multi-faceted nature of the church. We have traced the story of God's people in five stages, summarized as follows:

(1) The Old Testament people of God,
(2) are transformed into the kingdom family of Jesus,

(3) who become the Spirit-endowed church of Pentecost,
(4) who grow and mature through the apostolic teaching on the church,
(5) anticipating their future glory as the Bride of Christ in the New Jerusalem.

The unfolding narrative of God's people, along with the manifold imagery expressing the nature of this community, is summarized in the table below.

Table 1. Themes and Images of the People of God in the Biblical Narrative

Stages in the Story	Form	Themes and Images of the People of God
Abrahamic Covenant	Family of Abraham	Children of Abraham
Exodus and Sinai	Redeemed Nation	Kingdom of Priests, Holy Nation
Judgment and Promise	Remnant in Exile	Scattered Exiles, Believing Remnant
Messiah and the New Covenant	Kingdom Community of Jesus	Community of Disciples, the Jesus Family, the Church of Jesus, Restored Israel, Salt of the Earth, City on a Hill, Jesus' Flock, God's Vine
Death, Resurrection, and Ascension of Christ **Outpouring of the Spirit at Pentecost**		
The "Last Days"	The Apostolic Church of the Spirit	The Church of Spirit-filled Witnesses from Jerusalem to the Nations
	(Apostolic Teaching on the Church)	Household of God, Body of Christ, Temple of the Holy Spirit, New Humanity, New Creation, Unleavened Bread, Chosen People, Holy Nation, Royal Priesthood, Strangers and Sojourners, Heavenly Assembly of the Firstborn, Planting of God
The Consummation in the New Creation	Perfected Bride of Christ in the New Jerusalem	Lampstand; the Persecuted, Victorious Faithful; Redeemed Multitude from Every People, Bride of the Lamb; New Jerusalem

The biblical narrative, and its array of images and teachings, provide a wealth of resources to guide and shape our vision for what it means to see the biblical church multiplied among Muslims—and the value of the insider paradigm in particular. The insider paradigm emphasizes particular themes and particular parts of the biblical storyline to support its vision of ekklēsia, and its biblical foundation must be evaluated in light of the full scope of the biblical teaching on the church.

But reinvigorating our vision of the biblical story of the people of God, in all of its glory, is only the first step to defining the nature of the church. The biblical teaching on the church raises certain critical questions that, if answered, help to reliably guide a sound, constructive assessment of the insider paradigm as we seek to multiply churches among Muslims. The next chapter dives deeper into several crucial issues related to the nature of the church.

CHAPTER TWO

Clarifying "Church": Six Dimensions

Driving through the desert, the national pastor and his American visitors arrived in a small, far-flung village. The pastor told about how he and his church members had been visiting this village for a few years, and how several individuals and families believed in Christ. "We have several house churches in this village," the pastor said. This impressed not only these short-term guests, but also some long-term missionaries eager to partner with nationals to reach "the unreached."

But after several months of getting involved, the missionaries learned more about the house churches. Although there were a number of people and families professing Christ, they did not interact with other believers in the community. Believing families did not have any regular habit of prayer, worship, and Bible study as a family; they would only do so when the pastor or another church member visited from the city and led a "house church meeting," which happened on a very sporadic basis. While these missionaries praised God for the openness to the gospel and the new believers in this village, they realized that this national pastor had a low bar for calling a group a "church."

Back in the city, other national pastors had a much higher bar for defining a church. To start a church, a building or a rented apartment for church activities would be essential, as well as a charismatic, strong-willed pastor—normally paid a full-time salary, and often seminary-trained—who would be responsible for the bulk of the ministry. There should be at least three church meetings per week: the Sunday worship service, a midweek prayer meeting, and a youth meeting. The worship service would be a hybrid between local and Western cultural elements, involving worship songs in the local language and musical style accompanied by keyboard and guitar, followed by a thirty- to forty-minute sermon in a format similar to evangelical churches in the West. If someone wanted to start a church, they would seek these things. If any of them were missing, it simply would not feel like *church*.

These two real-life scenarios assume two different definitions of the church, both of which are inadequate. If we have too high of a bar for defining the church, we risk burdening the church with unessential foreign cultural elements, making churches less reproducible and less accessible to many Muslims. On the other hand, if we have too low of a bar for defining the church, we risk fooling ourselves (and others) into thinking we have planted a church, when in reality, we have only just begun.

The insider paradigm brings with it an implicit understanding of ekklēsia, and later chapters make clear where it falls on the spectrum of defining the church. A sound assessment of the idea of "insider church" requires a sound definition of the church which avoids both minimalist and maximalist errors, capturing the fullness of the biblical nature of the church while excluding non-essential, cultural elements from the church definition. In the previous chapter, I argued that such a definition should begin with the biblical narrative of the people of God which provides the foundational story and network of themes which define and shape the church's identity. But this is only a start, as there are a number of key issues regarding the nature of the church which remain in need of clarification, especially for those seeking to multiply the church among the least-reached. In this chapter, I tackle several critical issues that are essential to clarify in order to realize a full, robust, biblical vision of the church among Muslims. As later chapters show, the insider vision of ekklēsia offers a unique set of answers on each of these critical issues, ideas which in, the end, both facilitate and hinder the biblical nature of the church in different ways.

Each of the following topics represents a window into a different aspect of the nature of the church, and each has ramifications for how we assess church planting strategies among Muslims—including the insider paradigm. The key issues are: (1) the "core essence" of the church, (2) the church *local* and *universal*, (3) the church *visible* and *invisible*, (4) *marks* of the church, (5) *salvation* and the church, and (6) the church in the *world*.

The Core Essence of the Church

When you strip away everything else, what makes the church *the church?* In all of its forms, local and universal, what is the essential identity, the "core essence," that distinguishes the church from every other social or religious community? Is it claiming the name "Christian" or "church"? A specific culture or set of rituals? Adherence to certain beliefs or practices?

Our answer to this question has important implications for how we conceive of a "church" for Muslims and how such a church identifies itself in relation to the Muslim society around it. The insider vision for ekklēsia is to see communities of Jesus-followers that continue to embrace some level of Muslim social identity. This raises the question: What distinguishes these communities, if anything, from the non-Jesus-following community around them? If the goal is that Muslim-born believers will eventually express "church" in their context, what is the essential core that marks off this community from other groups, and how does this core ecclesial identity shape and interact with their social identity and other community memberships?

Some define the essence of the church in terms of ascription to specific theological doctrines, as found in certain creedal statements. Others define it in terms of certain practices, perhaps the practices of the early in church in Acts. Both biblical orthodoxy and orthopraxy have their place in defining the biblical nature of the church, as subsequent discussion will show. However, the core identity of the church is not fully encapsulated by either consent to specific propositional truths nor the practice of a particular set of activities.

The essential identity of the church—what sets it apart from every other community—is ultimately found in its *unique relationship to the living God*. The church, as we have seen previously, is *the people of God*, and it is this identity which ultimately sets apart *this* people from every other people. As Lesslie Newbigin said, "Here we are dealing with the Church or congregation of God. It derives its character not from its membership but from its Head, not from those who join it but from Him who calls it into being. It is God's gathering" (Newbigin 1954, 21; emphasis added). The distinguishing feature of the church is not found within itself, but outside itself—in the God to whom it belongs and who gave it birth.

But what exactly is the unique relationship God has with his church? God is creator of all peoples and nations, and all people in some sense are "offspring" of God (cf. Acts 17:28–29). The *people of God*, however, are set apart from creation by virtue of a *redemptive relationship* with God—they are adopted "sons and daughters" in reconciled relationship to their Father (cf. Gal 4:4–7). A redemptive relationship has always defined the people of God, beginning with Israel, whose covenant relationship was based on God's prior redemption of Israel, particularly in the exodus redemption. In the New Testament, the church is defined by the greater redemption in Christ by the Spirit, transforming and elevating the identity of the church through a deeper revelation of God as the Father who redeemed us by sending his Son and his Spirit.[35] This new revelation about God revealed to us in the gospel gives us a new, triune dimension to the covenant refrain, "I will be your God and you will be my people" (Lev 26:12; cf. 2 Cor 6:16; Clowney 1987, 14).[36] The essential character of the church is defined by its saving relationship with the the triune God.

First-century Jews, like Muslims, had great difficulty understanding and accepting the Trinity. Nonetheless, the New Testament clearly reveals the redemption of Christ as a triune act that shapes the church's relationship with God in distinctive ways.

(1) The church is the *family of God, chosen and adopted by the Father*. We are a spiritual family who have been rebirthed by God (1 Pet 1:3) and given a spiritual inheritance in his kingdom (Rom 8:17)—the basis for the biblical theme of the church as family (cf. France 2007, 496).

(2) The church is the *body of Christ and fellow heirs with the Son*. We enter God's family through faith and discipleship to Jesus Christ (John 3:16; 8:31; Eph 2:8–9), which is ultimately accomplished through union with Christ in his death, burial, resurrection, and ascension (Gal 2:20; Rom 6:1–11; Eph 2:6; Col 2:11–13; 3:1–3). This saving, transforming union with Christ is at the core of our identity as the redeemed church (1 Cor 12:12–13, 27).

(3) The church is the *temple of the Holy Spirit*. At Pentecost, the Spirit was sent to indwell, empower, and teach the church, spearheading its witness to the ends of the earth (John 14:15–17; Acts 1:8, 2:1–4, 38–39). In the old covenant, God dwelt with Israel in the tabernacle and temple; in the new covenant, the Spirit of God indwells the church, a downpayment of the full presence of God in the new creation (1 Cor 3:16; 2 Cor 6:16; Eph 1:14, 2:21–22).[37]

The redemptive work of the Father, Son, and Spirit defines the very essence of the church's identity as the saved people of God. What distinguishes the church from all other social and religious communities—what makes the church *the church*—is not a specific building, cultural forms, a certain creed, practices, or any human or government recognition. What makes the church *the church* is that *this* community is God's precious possession, bought by the blood of the Lamb and sealed by the Holy Spirit.

---

35 As Fred Sanders (2010) argues in *The Deep Things of God: How the Trinity Changes Everything*, salvation in the New Testament has an undeniable Trinitarian shape: it is a Trinitarian act that reveals the Trinitarian character of God. That is, the one God of Israel revealed his triunity when the Father sent the Son and the Spirit for our salvation.

36 Del Colle says, "The church exists within the missions of the Son and the Spirit, the divine economy of the incarnation of the Son and the outpouring of the Holy Spirit" (2007, 255; cf. also Jenson and Wilhite 2010, 191).

37 Many theologians of the church acknowledge the Trinitarian shape of the church in one fashion or another (e.g., Clowney 1995, 29; O'Brien 1987, 116; Erickson 1998; Dunn 2011; Ott and Wilson 2011, chap. 1, "What Is a Church?").

This understanding has important implications for how we define the biblical church, and what it looks like for a group of believers to mature into a biblical church which relates properly to other communities. As we will see later, such considerations impact the way that we assess insider ekklēsia, and the limits of "retaining socio-religious identity" in Muslim societies.

The church, in all of its forms, is set apart by its identity as the ransomed people of the triune God. This reality impacts all aspects of our biblical vision of the church, including the local and universal church.

The Church Local and Universal

The expressions "local church" and "universal church" do not occur in Scripture. However, from the beginning of Jesus' vision of his ekklēsia, and throughout Acts and the Epistles, it is clear the church takes the shape *both* of local congregations *and* a universal fellowship. We have already detailed the ways that the word *ekklēsia*, as well as many key images of the church, are used to refer to localized communities as well as the larger family of believers. This raises important questions: What are the defining features of the local church, and how do the local and universal church relate?

The Local Church

It is important to recognize that the church began as a local church—the Jerusalem church at Pentecost. As the church expanded beyond Jerusalem it took the form of local congregations springing up throughout the empire. When Paul conducted his mission journeys, he intentionally left behind local churches under the leadership of appointed elders (cf. Acts 14:23), congregations to which he would periodically return for encouragement and edification (cf. 15:41). It is not surprising that the majority of usages of *ekklēsia* in Paul's letters refer to the local church (Gehring 2004, 164).

The local church has profound significance in the eyes of God. It is called the church of God (1 Cor 1:2), God's household (1 Tim 3:15), God's field and building (1 Cor 3:8), God's temple (1 Cor 3:16), and the body of Christ (1 Cor 12:27). The local church is not described as a *part* of the body of Christ, or as one "pillar" in the temple of God, etc.; such titles are predicated directly and fully of the local church—warts and all—a fact that speaks volumes regarding its inherent theological identity (Banks 1980, 63; Ladd 1993, 391).[38]

But what is the nature of these local communities to which the New Testament ascribes such significance, and what are its essential elements? Is a group of believing friends who meet regularly for prayer and accountability a "church"? What about a Christian denomination? A seminary community? A weekly Bible study for seekers and believers?

---

38 Banks notes this with regard to the predication of "body of Christ" to the church at Corinth: "This suggests that wherever Christians are in relationship there is the body of Christ in its entirety, for Christ is truly and wholly present through his Spirit (v. 13). This is a momentous truth. We find here further confirmation of the high estimate Paul had of the local Christian community" (1980, 63).

INSIDER CHURCH

Clarifying the essential elements of the local church is of critical importance in church planting among Muslims. First, it shows what elements need to be in place for a church to be considered established or "planted"—crucial for knowing whether a disciple making (or insider) movement is a *church* planting movement. Second, clarifying the elements of the local church is important in order to distinguish them from *secondary cultural elements* in traditional church forms, freeing us up to be hospitable to new church forms more appropriate to new cultural contexts.

Our definition of the local church largely depends upon our choice of biblical passages to define the church. Those who lean heavily on Matthew 18:20 produce a "two-or-three-gathered ecclesiology" (cf. Bartlotti 2013, 139), while those who look primarily to Acts 2:42-47 will provide a largely functional, activity-based definition of the church.

Whatever the case, a robust defintion of the local church should avoid making any single passage bear the full weight of defining the church. Both of the above verses have their place in a definition of the church, but neither was intended to provide a full and comprehensive definition of the local church.[39] Over-reliance on one or two passages risks an incomplete, or even distorted, understanding of the local church. A better way forward is to allow the whole scope of the New Testament teaching to shape our understanding of the local church.

I propose that five essential elements can be discerned in the local communities that the biblical authors refer to as churches in the New Testament. The first two are related to the "core essence" of the church; the final three involve the activity and organization of the church. They are: (1) shared experience of salvation, professed in baptism, (2) solidarity and identity as "ekklēsia," (3) regular gathering as "ekklēsia," (4) biblical patterns of community, and (5) appointed elders.

A community that reflects only two or three of these elements may resemble a church, but it does not yet reflect the communities that are called "churches" in the New Testament. These different components can take a variety of forms in different cultural contexts, but local churches will reflect the following elements in some form or fashion.

---

39 The context of Matthew 18:20 is primarily about the spiritual authority of the church to confront sin in the church and the proper steps to do so, and verse 20 itself does not claim to define the local church, but rather assures the presence and authority of Christ when two or three gather in Jesus' name. While a gathering of believers in the name of Christ is a crucial aspect of the local church (see point 4 below), the full New Testament witness adds more important information we should also include in our biblical definition. Acts 2:42-47 is a narrative, and in applying narrative it is important to discern what is descriptive and what is prescriptive in narrative descriptions. One way to see if something is prescriptive is to see whether it is repeated in the narrative (a way that an author puts forward something as an example to emulated); another way is to see if it is explicitly taught elsewhere in Scripture. Acts 2:42-47 provides much that is repeated elsewhere in the book of Acts and is taught elsewhere in Scripture; therefore, we are justified in seeing it as largely prescriptive, or better, an exemplary model that Luke is presenting to us, an original ideal that Luke is calling us to emulate. This passage plays an important role in our definition of the church, but it must be taken together with the rest of the New Testament. Defining the church based on Acts 2:42-47 results in a strong focus on specific church practices, which are important (see point 4 below), but it misses other important elements which are implicit and which other New Testament teaching brings out more fully and directly.

(1) Shared Experience of Salvation, Professed in Baptism
Without a group of redeemed people, there can be no church. The core essence of the church is its redemptive relationship with the triune God, and a group is not a church unless they enjoy that relationship. A church may have a building, an educated pastor, an orthodox doctrinal statement, and practice communion and baptism, but if there are no spiritually reborn people, then it is not a church. A group of seekers studying the Bible together on a journey towards faith in Christ is a wonderful, encouraging sign of spiritual progress, but they are not yet a church until there is a commitment to Christ and experience of salvation.

The New Testament clearly attests to the fact that salvation in Christ—symbolized in baptism—is the basis for the creation of, and incorporation into, the gathered local church. On and after Pentecost, those who are added to the church are added *as they are saved* through faith, which is professed in baptism (Acts 2:41, 47). It is through receiving the Spirit by faith that a local congregation is "baptized" into the body of Christ and constituted as the church (1 Cor 12:12–13, 27). The imperative of Christian unity in the local church is based on shared salvation in Christ: "There is one body and one Spirit—just as you were called to the one hope that belongs to your call—one Lord, one faith, one baptism, one God and Father of all" (Eph 4:4–6). The basis of the church's fellowship is none other than their common salvation in Christ, symbolized in their common baptism.

It is not enough for believers to be united in Christ—they must be *aware* of this union, and *they must say so to one another*. In the country where I live, we have encountered a number of secret believers who came to faith online, but they do not know of other believers. These secret believers are united together spiritually in the universal church, but they do not yet constitute a local church. An essential step towards a group becoming a local church is to declare their faith to one another—which raises the question of baptism.

Baptism in Muslim contexts is a notoriously challenging issue, as it can tend to galvanize familial or communal backlash against new disciples. In the New Testament, however, baptism plays an important role in expressing, and acknowledging, the redemption that creates the church and unites it in one body. In the act of baptism, the baptized, the baptizer, and any other witnesses together bear witness to at least two things: (1) the repentance and faith of the baptized (Acts 2:38), and (2) the work of the Spirit in spiritually uniting the believer to Christ (1 Cor 12:13). As Paul makes clear, this union with Christ is the basis of our unity with one another in the church (1 Cor 12:13). Thus, despite the contextual challenges, baptism plays an important instrumental role in facilitating the formation of the local church.

A local church is first and foremost a community of people who have been united in the body of Christ by the Holy Spirit, and who know this to be the case. They not only have a common experience of salvation, but they also acknowledge this to one another, including in baptism.

(2) Solidarity and Identity as "Ekklēsia"

A local church not only recognizes common salvation, but takes the next step of committing to one another and *claiming together their identity as the ekklēsia of Jesus*. The radical, transformative reality of Christ's redemption creates solidarity and fosters commitment to group identity as a biblical church/ekklēsia. A local church will internalize and embrace an "ekklēsia identity"; that is, a corporate identity reflecting the core essence of the church—a community redeemed by the God of the gospel (Waterman 2011, "Concluding Thoughts").

Solidarity and identity as the "church" is an integral part of the New Testament vision. The early Jerusalem church naturally and beautifully developed a special solidarity and community identity immediately following the outpouring of the Spirit; they were a distinct and recognizable community in Jerusalem, with unique practices and claims, bearing a distinct community name—"the Way" (Acts 2:42–47; 4:32–37). As the Jerusalem church multiplied, local congregations sprang up in various places, each carrying a particular community identity—the "church in Antioch," the "church in Corinth," the "church in Prisca and Aquila's home," etc. The apostles taught local churches about the reality of their communal solidarity in Jesus and the richness of their identity as the body of Christ, the temple of the Spirit, brothers and sisters in the family of God, etc. (cf. 1 Cor 12:12–31, Eph 4:4–6, 1 Cor 12:12–31).

In the New Testament, the word *ekklēsia* is one of the most common identifying terms for local churches; however, as we have seen, there are also many other terms used to express the identity of the local church, such as believers, the brothers, the Way, the body of Christ, household of God, family of Jesus, etc. Each context is free to consider the linguistic options for conceptualizing and naming biblical ekklēsia, and each community has the freedom to choose what to "name" themselves. Whatever label is chosen, the *content* of their communal identity as a church/ekklēsia should remain constant and be increasingly shaped by all the Scriptures say about the church.

In movements around the world, groups of seekers and believers who study and obey God's Word are multiplying. For such groups to develop into biblical churches, they must discover, and claim together, their inheritance as the people of God. As they read the story of the people of God, they must eventually realize that this is *their* story. As they read about local churches in the New Testament, they must eventually say to one another, "Hey, that's us! Let's be one of those." As they encounter the images of the church in Scripture, they must recognize and receive the voice of God, applying and internalizing this identity as a group: "*This is who you are.* You are my royal priesthood ... the body of my Son ... the temple of my Spirit ... my treasured possession."

The first two elements of the local church are applications of the core essence of the church—a community redeemed by the triune God. First, a local church recognizes and professes its common redemption by God in Christ through the Spirit. Second, a local church commits to one another and identifies together as the people of God, the ekklēsia of Jesus, the temple of the Spirit. However, these first two elements are more than a matter of concepts and labels; they take shape in visible, tangible community, which leads us to the remaining three elements that focus on the form of the local church.

(3) Practice of Regular Gathering as "Ekklēsia"

In the New Testament, the form of the people of God changes from a centralized, largely mono-ethnic nation in a defined land to a multi-ethnic fellowship of scattered communities living as sojourners and strangers throughout the world. Unlike the Old Testament, which prescribed in rigorous detail the specific form of community for God's people and their worship (as in traditional Islam), the New Testament leaves undefined or undescribed the precise organization or form of the church. Instead, the New Testament provides key elements and principles, in the context of Spirit-led freedom from the law, and individual churches in different contexts and times have opted for an array of different expressions of "church." The New Testament is not completely silent on the form of the local church, as some key elements can be discerned as present (or assumed present) in New Testament churches. In each of these elements, it is important to distinguish precisely what is essential in biblical churches, and precisely where the New Testament is silent and leaves freedom for contextual variation.

One of these key elements is the regular practice of gathering. For a group to be a local church, it must not only identify together as a church—it must express this solidarity in Christ through the *ongoing practice of intentionally gathering together as church*. Regular gathering has been part of the church from the beginning (Acts 2:42–47), and the Epistles assume a church that meets regularly (1 Thess 5:27), often giving these gatherings specific instruction, direction, or rebuke (1 Cor 5:4; 14:26; Eph 5:18–20; Col 3:16). Meeting regularly is specifically commanded of believers as essential for catalyzing godly character in anticipation of Christ's return (Heb 10:24–25); and the "one-another" instructions assume and require ongoing gathering (e.g., Col 3:8, 12–17; Eph 4:25–5:1; Rom 12:3–13).

The centrality of gathering to the local church is found in the word *ekklēsia* itself—which originally meant "assembly." The identification is so close that sometimes ekklēsia refers to the church gathering itself—the event of assembly (1 Cor 11:18; 14:19, 28, 34–35; Col 4:16), analogous to the secular usage of *ekklēsia* for a spontaneous gathering (cf. Acts 19:39, 41). At times, the church *is* the gathering. The word *ekklēsia* is expanded, of course, to refer also to the *community of people* who regularly gather (Acts 8:1; 12:1; 13:1; 1 Cor 6:4; 10:32; 11:22; 12:28;

1 Tim 3:5; 1 Thess 1:1; 2 Thess 1:1; 1 Cor 1:2; Rom 16:1).⁴⁰ *Ekklēsia* is not the only word used for the church in the New Testament, but it is the most common word used, which shows how essential "gathering" is to being a local church.⁴¹

Without regular gathering, a group of believers is not yet a local church. Any understanding that believers may have about their identity as the ekklēsia of Jesus remains abstract and ethereal without regular gathering in tangible community. Imagine a city where there are several believers from Muslim background. They come to know one another, declare their faith to each other, and welcome one another as fellow brothers in Jesus—an incredible breakthrough! However, due to fear of family pressure, or for desire to keep their faith secret, they meet only occasionally and sporadically, and thus they are not yet a local church.

Imagine another city, where several believers from Muslim background study the Scriptures together, and they come to discover and embrace their identity as the ekklēsia of Jesus—and commit to do so together. It will be impossible for them to do so without regularly meeting together; not only is regular meeting a clear feature of the New Testament church, but it is also necessary for them to fulfill all of the functions of the New Testament ekklēsia—such as those described in the next section.

While regular gathering is essential to the local church, the New Testament does not prescribe a specific day/time, a required frequency, nor a required location. The first church gathered daily in Jerusalem (Acts 2:46), and two other passages describe or imply a Christian gathering on the "first day of the week" (Acts 20:7, implied in 1 Cor 16:2). However, there is no clear prescription for how and when the local church should gather, beyond the fact that it is a regular occurrence (Banks 1980, 40–41).⁴²

The place of gathering in the early church was often in believers' homes, which seems quite suitable to the high-persecution context in the New Testament which

---

40 As Volf says, "The life of the church is not exhausted in the act of assembly. Even if a church is not assembled, it does live on as a church in the mutual service its members render to one another and in its common mission to the world. The church is not simply an act of assembling; rather, it assembles at a specific place (see 1 Cor. 14:23). It is the *people* who in a specific way assemble at a specific place" (1998, 137). To this I would add that many of the other metaphors and titles which are ascribed to the church (e.g., family, body of Christ) imply a *community* which continues to subsist in between gatherings.

41 Therefore, I would agree with Banks' overall point that the "chief importance [in Paul's usage of ekklēsia] lies in the way it stresses the centrality of meeting for community life" (1980, 51). However, I disagree that "Paul's predominant usage of ekklēsia … refer(s) to the actual gatherings of Christians, and *nothing more*" (Banks 1980, 51; emphasis added). While the actual gathering seems to be clearly in view in some of the usages, there are many cases—both in Paul and outside of Paul—where the gathering of the church is not clearly part of the context, as noted above (cf. Tidball 2000, 408; Giles 1995, 113–21; cf. also Stegemann and Stegemann 1999, 264). It is not necessary to restrict the meaning of ekklēsia to a Christian gathering in order to acknowledge that regular gathering is essential for the local church.

42 Banks notes that it is not clear from the passages which mention gathering on the first day of the week that this is a regular (or only) day in which the church gathers together (1980, 40), and thus there is no clear biblical mandate that the gathering of the church must be weekly and on Sunday.

demanded a low profile and flexibility. Scripture nowhere prescribes homes as a place of community gathering; the specifics of the "where" and the "when" of the gathering are flexible and nonessential to the nature of the church, and thus believers are free to respond to pragmatic needs and concerns in this area.

For a group of believers to be a local church, there must be some ongoing pattern of gathering together as a church, though the time, frequency, and location of such gatherings can vary from context to context. Gathering together is not so much a requirement to be enforced, as it is a gift to be cherished. At times, extenuating circumstances make it difficult, if not impossible, to gather. A season of persecution may temporarily scatter the church. Believers might be isolated from other believers, physically or socially. A pandemic may lead churches to close their doors for a time to prevent infection. Such circumstances underscore the privilege it is to gather together and how essential it is to allowing a group to function and flower as a local church.

The "gift of gathering" is essential to the local church. A temporary pause does not make a group cease to be a local church, but a permanent stop would. Despite the challenges, the church of Jesus Christ is resilient, even in the face of death. When persecution comes, the church gathers in catacombs. When pandemics arise, the church tends to the sick, meets online "in spirit," and endures until able again to meet "in body." The church is much more than a gathering, but it is not less. However, it is not just *any* kind of gathering that makes a group of believers into a local church, but rather a peculiar kind of gathering with certain key activities.

(4) Patterns of Biblical Community

The local church not only gathers regularly, it also establishes a set of patterns that reflect the biblical functions of the church. The New Testament does not prescribe a fixed liturgy for the church, but rather provides models and basic guidelines for its gathered community. I propose that the essential functions of the local church include the following basic elements: (1) true worship, (2) Christ-centered testimony/teaching, (3) authentic fellowship, and (4) Spirit-empowered edification.[43] Integrally related to one another, they are also overarching categories that include a variety of biblical practices.

First, church gatherings are characterized by *worship of the God revealed in Jesus*. It does so together as a community, responding corporately in gratitude and praise

---

43 These four correspond to Bate's five "gospel values" of the church's praxis in the world: *martyria* (witness), *koinonia* (relatedness), *diakonia* (service), *kerygma* (message), and *leitourgia* (worship or sacrifice) (Bate 1994, 102). We have subsumed *kerygma* under *martyria*, since the proclamation of the message is part and parcel of the church's mission as witnesses of the risen Christ (Acts 1:8). Ott and Wilson list a variety of "biblical purposes" for which the church gathers, including "prayer, worship, evangelism, instruction, edification, service, celebration of the ordinances of baptism and the Lord's Supper, exercise of church discipline, and the sending of missionaries" and "embody[ing] the values of the kingdom of God" (2011, chap. 1, "What Is a Church?").

to God for who he is and what he has done.[44] In both the descriptions of the church and the instructions of Paul, it is clear that praise and "spiritual songs" have always characterized the church (Acts 2:47; Eph 5:19–20; Col 3:16). In the Old Testament, the Levitical priests facilitated sacrificial worship, but in the New Testament, all believers are a "royal priesthood" offering spiritual sacrifices of praise to God through Christ, our High Priest (Heb 10:19–25, 13:15; 1 Pet 2:4, 9). The praise and glory of God is the ultimate end for which God redeemed his church (Eph 1:6, 12, 14; 1 Pet 2:9); it should pervade every aspect of life (Col 3:17; cf. Rom 12:1–2), including the gatherings of the local church. "All-of-life" worship and gathered, corporate worship are part of the same whole, feeding into and stimulating one another: the church gathers in order to spur one another on toward lives of obedience offered in worship to God.

Second, church gatherings involve *testimony to and immersion in the truth of Christ*. The church has always been characterized by "devotion to the apostles' teaching," an expression of the identity of the church as a "pillar and foundation of the truth" (1 Tim 3:15), as well as a community of disciple-students learning at the feet of Master Jesus. The apostles played a key role in defining and transmitting the authentic teaching of Christ to the church once and for all—which we have in the New Testament—and other leaders (pastors, teachers, prophets, elder-overseers) are commissioned to preserve the apostolic teaching about Christ in a world full of counterfeits. The New Testament envisions not only the leaders, but all members of the church "speaking the truth [about Christ] in love" to one another for the growth of the body (Eph 4:11–16). All are called to "contend for the faith once for all entrusted to the saints" (Jude 3) and to "let the word…dwell in you [all] richly" (Col 3:16)—which includes not only clarifying and commending the truth, but also embodying and living it out.

Testifying to the truth is not for the benefit of believers alone. As the church proclaims and lives out the truth, it does so before a watching world. Church gatherings are not closed communities, but open ones where "not-yet-believers" can encounter the truth of Christ (1 Cor 14:24). The church gathers to be filled up, and prepared to be sent out as bold, Spirit-filled witnesses into the world (Acts 4:23–31); it also prayerfully sets apart and sends missionaries to further the Great Commission (Acts 13:3; cf. Ott and Wilson 2011, Loc. 264). Both to believers and to the world, the local church gathers for the sake of testifying to and living out the truth of Christ.

---

44 Banks says that in Pauline theology, "worship" is not the purpose of gathering, but rather mutual edification, since "worship" is a broader term which encompasses the entire response of believers to the mercies of God in salvation, while mutual upbuilding of the local body is the image which uniquely describes what is distinctive in the gathering of the local church (i.e., Rom 12:1–2; cf. Banks 1980, 92–93). However, as Carson argues, Christians gather *both* for mutual edification *and* for worship—for worship should be offered both individually *and* corporately, in daily living as well as within the context of the local church gathering (2002, 26, 45, 49).

Third, church gatherings are characterized by *authentic fellowship in the Spirit*. Fellowship means sharing in a common life together—spiritually and physically. The Greek word for fellowship (*koinōnia*) refers to participation or sharing in something (Witherington 1998, 160), often physical resources. The fellowship of the church begins spiritually in shared fellowship with God—an expression of the core essence of the church (Acts 2:42; 2 Cor 13:14; 1 John 1:3; Phil 1:5; 2:1). This spiritual fellowship also finds expression in physical fellowship. Sharing of resources was exemplified by the early Jerusalem church (Acts 2:42, 45; 5:34–37) and the church at Philippi (Phil 1:5–7; 4:14–16); it is also an ongoing expectation for all churches (1 Cor 11:17–34; James 2:14–17; 1 John 3:16–17). The spiritual "koinonia" of the church also finds tangible expression in practices such as baptism, the Lord's Supper, fellowship meals, laying on of hands, etc. (Banks 1980, 80–90). The fellowship of the church/ekklēsia reflects the important theme of the church as family.

Fourth, the local church gathers for *Spirit-empowered edification* (Rom 12:3–8, 1 Cor 12–14,[45] Eph 4:7–16, 1 Pet 4:8–11; cf. Banks 1980, 92–93). All members of the church are assigned ministry roles by the Spirit in which they are to serve and build up the body, so that it matures through the diverse ministries of its members—including teaching, mercy, administration, and many others (Berding 2006). This function reflects the church's identity as the body of Christ (diverse members/roles, one body), royal priesthood (everyone is a "priest" and ministers to the body), and community of disciples (a community of learners growing towards maturity).

These four key functions of the local church characterize the central purposes and orientation of the local church according to the New Testament. Each of these purposes are fleshed out in the New Testament with a variety of activities, such as baptism, the Lord's Supper, prayer, discipline, singing, giving, etc. These four functions are not separate from one another, but interrelated, with several of them often present in the same practice. For example, the Lord's Supper is an act of worship, fellowship, edification, and testifying to the truth, all at once.

For a group to be a local church, its gatherings and community life must have a specific intentionality and purpose—that of worship, teaching/witness, fellowship, and service. If they lack these, such groups are not yet a local church. For example, a group of believers who regularly gathers to play games, or to discuss Christian books, is not a local church.

While the New Testament provides a significant amount of teaching on these purposes that the local church fulfills, it does not prescribe a fixed, detailed liturgy for the church, nor does it dictate any specific linguistic or cultural forms that must be practiced by all churches. The heart and fundamental orientation and character of the

---

45 Paul explicitly states mutual edification as the overarching goal of the variety of ministries that take place in the gathering of the church. As Paul states in 1 Corinthians 14:26, "Let all things [in the assembly] be done for building up [one another]," a key theme which recurs throughout 1 Corinthians 14 (cf. vv. 4–5, 12, 19).

church gatherings are defined, but there is a great deal of space for the freedom of the local church in developing its own liturgy and specific practices in the way it worships, practices fellowship, testifies to the truth, and edifies the body in its gatherings.

In the Middle East, traditional Orthodox, Catholic, Oriental, and Assyrian churches use liturgies that have been passed down historically for generations. Evangelical Arab churches have adopted forms learned from missionaries and their evangelical churches in the West, adapted into a hybrid of Arab and Western evangelical culture. New church movements among believers of Muslim background (BMBs) in places where there is no existing Arab church, or where they choose not to join an existing church, are also free to adopt new, biblical ways of worshiping God, engaging in fellowship, testifying to the truth, and edifying one another in the Spirit.

In Muslim communities around the world, groups of believers have emerged who meet together regularly to discover and respond to God's truth in the Scriptures. In many cases, these groups multiply, spawning other discovery groups which themselves start new groups, sometimes leading to exponential multiplication. For these believing groups to become local churches, they should begin to live out the biblical teaching on corporate worship, Christ-centered testimony/teaching, spiritual and physical fellowship, and mutual ministry/edification. Until they do so, these believing groups are still "on the way" to becoming local churches.

Another concrete example is what happens when a whole household comes to faith in Christ together, as in the book of Acts. This is an ideal situation and strategic goal to pray for and work towards, as it provides significant social support to new believers from the beginning of their faith journey. For these believing households to become local churches, they would need to not only identify themselves as a local church/ekklēsia, but also develop some kind of pattern of regular meeting as a church/ekklēsia which involves all the biblical functions of the local church.

A local New Testament church is characterized by biblical patterns of worship, truth, fellowship, and edification. A final essential element addresses the question of leadership.

(5) Biblical Leadership

New Testament churches are led by biblical elder-overseers who provide spiritual oversight for the congregation. A variety of words are used in the New Testament for these church leaders—elders (*presbuteroi*), overseers (*episkopoi*), leaders (*egoumoi*), and "shepherds" and teachers (*poimenas kai didaskalous*), all of which seem to be used interchangably to refer to the same designated role of biblical elders.[46]

---

46 This is clear not only from the way these terms are used, but the ways all of these terms appear to describe the same role. In Titus 1:5-7 Paul uses both elder (*presbyteros*) and overseer (*episkopos*) interchangably. Both Peter (1 Pet 5:1-5) and Paul (Acts 20:28) describe the role of elders (*presbyteros*) in terms of "shepherding" (imperative *poimanate*) God's flock. It is possible that the term "leaders" in Hebrews 13:17 is broader and includes deacons (*diakonos*) as well, but it is more likely that this also refers specifically to the office of elder-overseers, since their role is described as watching over the souls of the church as those who will give an account, which clearly fits with the way the office of elders-overseers is described.

Paul's clear practice was to make sure elders were appointed in the congregations he started (Acts 14:23; Titus 1:5). While such congregations were still referred to as "churches" before the elders were appointed (Acts 14:23), the New Testament picture of the church indicates that eventual appointment of elders was expected, and not optional, for New Testament churches.

Appointment of elders is not something to be rushed. Paul warned Timothy against appointing recent converts (1 Tim 3:6; cf. 5:22), which may explain why he did not always appoint elders immediately, but sometimes did so on a subsequent trip (Acts 14:21).[47] However, it is a critical final step of "committing [the church] to the Lord" (Acts 14:23) that should not be postponed indefinitely (Titus 1:5).[48]

The appointing of elders is superintended by the Spirit, for "the Holy Spirit has made you overseers, to care for the church of God, which he obtained with his own blood" (Acts 20:28). However, human selection also plays a role, and Paul gives criteria for selecting elders, centered mostly on character and reputation, as well as ability to teach (1 Tim 3:1–7; Titus 1:5–9).[49]

Elder-overseers have the role of spiritual oversight of a congregation—undershepherds who care for Christ's flock, accountable for the people under their care (1 Pet 5:1–5; cf. Heb 13:17). The church must honor and submit to elders, while elders must lead the flock willingly and in gentle humility (1 Pet 5:1–5).

The establishment of a church, then, appears to be "finalized" once biblical elders are appointed. From Paul's perspective, the appointment of elders would seem to mark the completion of the apostolic work of "planting" the church, handing over the ongoing spiritual responsibility to elders who continue "watering" the church as it grows to maturity.[50] While Paul continued to participate in ongoing "watering"

It is possible that Eph 4:11 is referring to "shepherd-teachers" (or "pastor-teachers"), however, it is more likely that it is referring to a group of leaders consisting of elders and non-elder teachers, grouped together because of the overlap of their responsibilities. Paul expects that all elder-overseers are "able to teach" (1 Tim 3:2). However, 1 Tim 3:11 clearly implies that some, and not all, elder-overseers "labor in preaching and teaching." Elders clearly have the responsibility of preserving the apostolic truth and protecting the flock from false teaching, but this does not restrict *all* teaching to elder-overseers.

47 Paul did not appoint elders on his first trip to Pisidian Antioch, Lystra, and Iconium (Acts 13:14; 14:1, 8), but rather appointed them later when he made a return trip to those cities (14:21).

48 As Waterman says, "The appointment of elders was an early and foundational priority. Apparently, a pattern of Paul's apostolic ministry was that elders were not necessarily immediately appointed on the formation of a new church, but that once a church had been formed, the appointment of elders was considered important unfinished business, to be accomplished as soon as possible and appropriate." (Waterman 2011, "Church in the Context of Scripture")

49 Interestingly, having a high education or formal theological training is not included as criteria for biblical elders. This does not imply that education and formal training have no value, only that they are not biblical qualifications for elders.

50 The distinction between "planting" ministry and "watering" ministry comes from 1 Corinthians 3:6, where Paul refers to his pioneering work in starting the church in Corinth as "planting," while referring to Apollos' building on Paul's foundation through teaching and instruction as "watering." As Ott and Wilson say, "Whereas the ministry of planting involves primarily evangelism, discipleship, and congregating, the ministry of watering involves further teaching and strengthening churches that have already been gathered" (2011, Loc. 292). Of course, Paul also did some "watering" as well, but his primary focus was "planting" the church where

of established churches through periodic visits, written correspondence, and prayer, the appointed elder-overseers clearly carry the main, ongoing responsibility for the spiritual care and growth of the flock (Heb 13:17).

The clear New Testament pattern is that local churches are elder-led. A group of believers who regularly gather together for worship, prayer, and Bible study, but never appoint biblical elders, have not yet developed into a full local church. Scripture does not specify a specific organization or form of leadership, leaving a great amount of freedom for the way leadership can be expressed (Ladd 1993, 579). The precise number of elders is not mandated; in most cases, there seems to have been a plurality of elders (Acts 14:23; 1 Thess 5:12–13; cf. Longenecker 2002, 84).[51] The particular title used for these leaders is not essential (pastors, elders, overseers, etc.), nor is their organization (overseeing a house church, or a church network, cf. Titus 1:5). At the same time, Scripture has much guidance on the responsibilities of biblical elders, the criteria for their selection, as well as kingdom leadership values. Each context has great leeway, however, in discerning how to structure the leadership of their church in light of the teachings and values of Scripture.

When God redeems people in Christ, he redeems them into a community. Reconciled to God in Christ, believers enter into a "new humanity," a community of disciple-apprentices, a new Jesus-family. But this new community is not merely an idea that exists in people's minds—it takes shape in the world, and in all of its contextual diversity, it expresses certain key defining elements. To synthesize the above, I propose the following definition of the local church: *a group of baptized believers in Jesus who commit to one another and identify together as a church, meeting together regularly and practicing patterns of biblical community characterized by worship, truth, fellowship, and edification under the oversight of biblical elders.*[52] Such a community reflects the churches in the New Testament, and such a community can be expressed in a variety of forms and organizational structures, varying levels of formality, and in multiple types of locales. It can take the form a mega-church with an impressive building and organization, or a decentralized house-church network. However, any such organization—no matter how impressive or sturdy—which lacks the essential features listed above is not a local church in the biblical sense.

Christ had not yet been named, handing over to local elders the responsibility of "watering" the churches he planted (Ott and Wilson 2011, Loc. 279–292).

51 In at least one case, it is ambiguous whether it was a plurality or a single elder-overseer for each church/city (Titus 1:5).

52 See a similar definition by Ott and Wilson, who define the local church as "a fellowship of believers in Jesus Christ committed to gathering regularly for biblical purposes under a recognized spiritual leadership." Four of my five essential components generally correspond to Ott and Wilson's four elements of *believers, gathering, purpose,* and *leadership* (Ott and Wilson 2011, Loc. 262). Cf. also Waterman's definition, with which I essentially agree: "A biblical church is a significant group of Jesus' followers having an identity as a church (*ekklesia*) who gather together regularly on an ongoing basis, with recognized leadership under the headship of Christ, to worship God and encourage one another in obeying all his commands (including, but not limited to baptism and the Lord's Supper)" (Waterman 2011, "Concluding Thoughts").

In planting and growing local churches, it is important to remember that all five elements may not appear simultaneously. As it takes time for a baby to grow into a boy and then a man, it takes time for people to begin professing faith, to commit to one another in solidarity as the church, to develop rhythms and practices of biblical gatherings, and to produce biblical elders. However, such things do not happen automatically, but require intentionality in learning about and adopting the essential elements of the biblical church.

The local church is certainly central to the biblical vision of the church. But the church is not just a local fellowship, but also a global family, which raises additional important issues for planting churches among least-reached Muslims.

The Universal Church

It can be argued that the universal church is simultaneously the greatest obstacle and the greatest treasure for Muslims coming to faith. The universal Christian community stands as a competing *umma,* and Muslims believe that to become a "Christian" means to leave their *umma* and join another—branding them an apostate, outcast, and even target for execution. This well-known obstacle has led some to discourage BMBs from calling themselves "Christians" or joining the established Christian church. At the same time, Muslims who come to faith are people who highly value community and eagerly desire to belong and be honored in a worldwide fellowship. Many have forfeited, to some degree, aspects of their status, honor, and place in their family or community, and they deeply long for acceptance and belonging of the universal family of God to replace what they lost in the Muslim *umma*. For disciple-makers, navigating these complex dynamics of the relationship between BMBs and the global body of Christ can be quite challenging, one which requires a clear, robust understanding of the universal church.

The global or universal church refers to the entire community of believers in Christ throughout the world. As discussed previously, such a claim is firmly rooted in the biblical pattern of applying ecclesial metaphors and themes to both local congregations and the larger community of believers (e.g., Matt 16:18; Acts 9:31; Eph 1:22; 3:10, 21; 5:23–32; Col 1:18, 24; 1 Pet 2:9–10). The universal church is the fruit of the universalizing nature of the gospel, which goes from Jerusalem to the ends of the earth, summoning the nations to join Christ's ever-growing community of disciples (Col 1:6; Matt 28:19–20; Acts 1:8).

The identity of the universal church is illumined by images of the church as "family" and "body of Christ." As adopted children of God, believers—regardless of whether they are in fellowship in the same church—are brothers and sisters in the family of God (cf. Eph 3:15; 4:6). The same spiritual unity that binds believers together in the local church also connects them to believers in the universal church (Banks 1980, 55). This also applies to the "body of Christ" metaphor, which defines relationships both inside and outside the local church. All believers, wherever they exist, are united by virtue of being baptized by one Spirit into one body.[53] The Spirit's work of uniting believers with the crucified and ascended Christ is the basis for their corporate identity as the body of Christ, not only within their local congregation but also with believers throughout the world (cf. Rom 12:5; 1 Cor 12:13; Eph 2:13–22).[54]

But the universal church is also eschatological, a foretaste of the coming kingdom. It is a sign of the last days, the firstfruits of the eschatological ingathering of the nations foretold by the prophets (cf. Isa 2:1–5; 66:18–19; Joel 2:29–29; Zech 8:20–23). As Christ builds his church through his Spirit, the church grows more universal, encompassing more ethnic groups, until the universal church is completed at the end of the age, when men and women from every tribe and nation will assemble as one to praise and serve God in the New Jerusalem (Rev 7:9–17).

This glorious future is also, in some sense, a present reality. The church is now spiritually united with the ascended Christ in heaven (Eph 1:20–23, 2:6–7; Col 3:1–4), participants with the angelic hosts and "spirits of the righteous made perfect" in the heavenly assembly (Heb 12:22–24; cf. Gal 4:26). Presently hidden to the world (Col 3:3), this is the church's true identity (Col 3:1) that should shape the church's life in the world (Col 3:5–25)—a reality with important implications for how the church interfaces with ethnic, national, and social identities in its context. As Steve Kang says, the eschatological vision of God's global, multiethnic people means that

> the prior socio-cultural multiplicity of all God's people—infinite variations of the confluence of sociocultural constructs, such as race, ethnicity, class, gender, and others that construct various people groups in the world—is not obliterated, but redeemed and transformed by the sovereign and gracious work of the Holy Spirit.... . The church is not merely a voluntary gathering of like-minded people with similar interests, as in a homogeneous unit. The church is the earthly embodiment of the risen Christ, the community of all God's people in Jesus Christ in time and space that draws near to the Triune God. (2007, 236)

If the church is a sign and foretaste of the coming kingdom, and the universal church on the last day is a global, multiethnic community from every tribe and tongue, then the church today must find ways to make room for people of other ethnicities and social classes. Social and cultural identities are relativized and redeemed in light of the larger identity and narrative of the global church—a company in which divisions and hostilities that divide peoples are obliterated at the cross, reconciling them into one new humanity. A biblical vision of the universal church calls the church to be a foretaste of its final form in the New Jerusalem.

---

53 What is stated about "all" believers is later applied to the "you" (plural) of the local Corinthian church for the purpose of encouraging them toward living out their spiritual unity in diversity (1 Cor 12:27).

54 Banks says that it is not the ekklēsia that is described as the body of Christ, and that *soma* and ekklēsia terminology "do not completely overlap, since the former has a wider reference than the latter" (1980, 63). However, such a judgment ignores the interchangeable usage of both terms in 1 Corinthians 12:27–28 ("Now you are the *body of Christ* and individually members of it. And God has appointed in *the church* first apostles, second prophets ..."), not to mention the clear identification of ekklēsia with Christ's soma in Ephesians 1:22–23 and 5:23 and Colossians 1:18.

The universal church is not merely a theological doctrine; it is a glorious reality. For Muslim-born believers in Jesus, it means that they are not alone; although outnumbered in their communities, they are a part of a worldwide family that cannot be counted, a great cloud of witnesses across time and space, the international *umma* of Christ. Though marginalized or stigmatized by their own families and communities, they are recompensed "a hundredfold" with new brothers, sisters, and mothers in the family of God (Mark 10:29–30). The universal church has a major responsibility to find wise ways of welcoming these new believers and emerging churches into the global family of God in ways which encourage and empower them to grow and multiply. Such a transition will not leave social and cultural identities unchanged, but relativized and transformed by a new belonging to the global body of Christ.

Having defined the local and universal church, it remains to clarify their relationship to one another. Are they two different churches, or is one part of the other? Can someone be in one but not the other?

Relationship between the Local and Universal Church

The local church and the universal church are not two different churches—they are two aspects of the one church of Jesus Christ. The church is local, for it takes shape in local congregations of believers who gather regularly for worship, truth, fellowship, and edification. The church is also universal, for the body of Christ is a worldwide community of brothers and sisters, united in the Spirit. Both perspectives are complementary to one another in order to provide a complete picture of the nature of the church in Scripture.

It is proper, therefore, to distinguish between the local and universal church, but not to separate them. When individuals are saved and baptized into Christ, they are adopted into the worldwide family of God, becoming brothers and sisters with all others throughout the world who are redeemed in Christ. In the age to come, we will be united as one community living in the presence of God, but in this age our identity in the body of Christ is to be lived out and realized in tangible community in the context of local churches scattered throughout the world. The New Testament teaches that those who become a part of God's family (Eph 2:19) are to live in familial and brotherly relationship with believers in a local congregation (1 Cor 8:11–12); those who have been incorporated into Christ's body (1 Cor 12:13) are to live out this reality through a local body whose members mutually edify each other (1 Cor 12:14–30).

Believers who are unable or unwilling to participate in a local congregation are unable to fully develop and express their identity as members of the body of Christ. Their identity as part of God's family remains dormant; if such a state continues, their growth in Christ will be stunted, since the body of Christ is the sphere in which growth in discipleship takes place (Eph 4:15–16). In biblical thinking, the worldwide church is "tangibly evident … *kat' oikous* [from house to house], that is, in the gatherings of the individual local churches" (Gehring 2004, 165).

At the same time, members of a local church should recognize they are part of the larger, worldwide family, comprised of all believers in Christ from every tribe and nation. The bond which unites them locally unites them with all in Christ, and they should welcome as brothers and sisters any who confess Jesus as Lord (Rom 15:7; 3 John 10). Aside from church discipline, refusing fellowship with believers outside (or inside) our local congregation denies the reality of unity in the global body of Christ which transcends culture, gender, social status, or any other human barrier (Eph 2:13–22; Gal 3:27–29). Muslim-background churches and established Christian churches must therefore learn to accept one another as full members in the family of God.

The church is both local and universal in nature, and a biblical vision of the church will neglect neither. Biblical churches will reflect the essential components of a local church as well as its participation in the larger, universal community in Christ. This is a key point which qualifies any particular cultural expression of the church; every church should make room in its "church concept" for other cultural expressions of church besides its own. Cultural specificity must never deteriorate into cultural exclusivity, since Christ has reconciled people of all cultures into one new humanity.

The local-universal distinction highlights two important dimensions of the church's identity. Next, we look at another significant distinction: the so-called "visible" and "invisible" church.

The Church Visible and Invisible

Is there such a thing as an invisible church? Historically, theologians have distinguished between the "visible" church—all who profess to be Christians in the "established" church—and the "invisible" church—all true believers in Christ throughout all time. But how valid is this distinction, and does it create any space for an "invisible" church that has no connection to the visible church? Such questions require taking a fresh look at the visible-invisible distinction in light of Scripture.

History of the Visible/Invisible Distinction

The notion of a "visible" vs. "invisible" church can be traced back to Augustine. A group called the Donatists, believing in a "pure church," separated from the Catholic church due to the moral failure of church leaders (Chadwick 1993, Loc. 3307). Contra the Donatists, Augustine argued that the church in this age is a "mixed assembly" of true and false believers, a mixture of "wheat" and "tares" not to be separated until the end of the age (cf. Kelly 1958, 415). For Augustine, history is a tale of two cities, and "these two cities are entangled together in this world, and intermixed until the last judgment effects their separation" (City of God, Chapter 35, Loc. 3062–74). On the one hand, "the city of God has in her communion … some who shall not eternally dwell in the lot of the saints," while on the other hand, "among her enemies lie hid those who are destined to be fellow-citizens" (ibid.).

The Reformers revived this theme and expressed it in terms of a "visible" and "invisible" church. Calvin argued that *church* can refer to two different communities:

(1) "that which is actually in God's presence into which no persons are received but those who are children of God by grace of adoption, and true members of Christ by sanctification of the Holy Spirit … all the elect from the beginning of the world"; and (2) "the whole multitude of men spread over the earth who profess to worship one God and Christ" (1959, 1022).[55] Like Augustine before him, Calvin taught the necessity of fellowship with the visible church: "Just as we must believe, therefore, that the former church, invisible to us, is visible to the eyes of God alone, so we are commanded to revere and keep communion with the latter, which is called 'church' with respect to men" (ibid). For Calvin, the words "visible" and "invisible" indicate human ignorance of the final makeup of God's true people.[56]

Luther added a different angle to the visible/invisible church. He affirmed that the true church is the "hidden" church with a spiritual nature whose source is the word and grace of Christ. Without this "hidden" spiritual nature, a group is a false church, not a true one. However, the true church is not fully invisible, but reveals itself to true believers through the marks of the true church: "The church must appear in the world. But it can only appear in a covering (larva), a veil, a shell, or some kind of clothes which a man can grasp, otherwise it can never be found" (Luther in *Briefwechzel* as quoted in Noll 1974, 83; cf. Kerr 1943, 125–26). Whereas Calvin emphasized the membership of the church, Luther emphasized the spiritual nature and source of the true church; both affirm—with Augustine—the imperative of participation in the "visible" church.

The visible-invisible church distinction continued to be debated by later theologians, and some warned against a tendency to exalt the "invisible church" as the true church and the "visible church" as inferior and secondary. One example is that of missionary-theologian Lesslie Newbigin, who eloquently defended the priority of the visible church:

> The church itself is the visible company of those who have been called by Him into the fellowship of His Son. The great Pauline words about the Church as the Body of Christ, the Bride of Christ, the Temple of God, are addressed to the actual visible and sinful congregations in Corinth and in Asia Minor, and indeed are spoken precisely in connection with the urgent need to correct the manifold sins and disorders which the apostle found in them. (1954, 22)

Newbigin highlights the way the images of the church in Paul are not merely reserved for an ideal, invisible community of true believers, but are ascribed to specific, imperfect, visible churches. The biblical church is a visible community.

In a similar vein, Dietrich Bonhoeffer emphasizes the necessity of visibility to our church vision:

---

55 The reader should note that both Calvin's statements here refer to the universal church, not the local church.

56 In referring to the "visible" church, Calvin appears to be referring to what should be considered true churches in which the Word is truly preached and the sacraments are administered according to Christ's teaching (cf. Calvin 1959, Book IV, Chapter 1, Section 9, 1023).

> The body of Christ takes up space on earth.... Anything which claims space is visible. Hence the Body of Christ can only be a visible Body, or else it is not a Body at all.... This is why he called his disciples into a literal bodily following, and thus made his fellowship with them a visible reality. (Bonhoeffer 1995, 248)

Combining the "body of Christ" metaphor and the physical nature of discipleship, Bonhoeffer presents a picture of the church, not as an invisible, ethereal communion, but of a visible, tangible community that follows and represents Jesus in the world.

Theologian John Webster complements these insights with a rich description of the relationship between the visible and invisible church, worth citing at length. The biblical church, according to Webster, is

> the "phenomenal" church—the church which has form, shape and endurance as a human undertaking, and which is present in the history of the world as a social project ... visible in the sense that, as a genuinely creaturely event and assembly, it does not occur in "no-space" and is not a purely eschatological polity or culture.... it engages in human activities (speech, washing, eating and drinking); it has customs, texts, orders, procedures and possessions, like any other visible social entity. (2005, 101)

For Webster, the church is visible in the sense that it is a human society that exists in time and space, with observable activities, habits, and gatherings, as in other social groups. But the church's "visibility" is special, different than all other visible social communities:

> But how does it have these things? It does and has these things, and so it is what it is, by virtue of the work of the Holy Spirit. Only through the Holy Spirit's empowerment is the church a human assembly; and therefore only through the same Spirit is the church visible.... The church, therefore, is natural history only because it is spiritual history, history by the Spirit's grace. And so also for the church's visibility: it is through the Spirit's work alone that the church becomes visible, and its visibility is therefore a special or "spiritual visibility," created by the Spirit and revealed by the Spirit. (ibid., 101–2)

According to Webster, empircal or sociological explanations of the church's visibility are not sufficient to explain the church's visibility. It is ultimately the Spirit who makes the church visible, which means that the visibility of the church is a sacred sign of God's presence, integrally connected to the spiritual, "invisible" nature of the church.

The concepts of the "visible" and "invisible" church have been significant in discussions of the nature of the church from Augustine to the present day. But how viable are these concepts, and what applicability do they have as we conceive of planting biblical churches among Muslims?

A Healthy View of the "Visible-Invisible" Church

Distinguishing between the "visible" and "invisible" church has its dangers, but if done judiciously, it highlights important aspects of the nature of the biblical church with key implications for those multiplying churches among Muslims. It is important to keep the visible-invisible church rooted in its biblical foundation, which is a synthesis of three strands of biblical theology.

(1) *The biblical church is visible.* In biblical perspective, the church's identity cannot be extracted from the tangible fellowship of local congregations. Visible, life-on-life community is essential, and not secondary, to discipleship and the nature of the biblical church. Any concept of the church that diminishes the importance of visible fellowship has gone astray from the biblical picture of the church.

(2) *The biblical church is an imperfect community.* The parables of the weeds, the fish in the net, and the sheep and the goats all indicate the church in this age is indeed a "mixed assembly." The New Testament's frequent warnings to persevere in Christ imply that the church contains some who may not persevere to the end (e.g., Mark 13:13; John 15:5–6; Col 1:23; Heb 3:12; 1 John 2:19). Only God knows his true children and who will be finally welcomed into the New Jerusalem (2 Tim 2:19; cf. Erickson 1998, 1057–58; Horton 2011, 852).

(3) *The full glory of the church is presently hidden to the world.* The church is visible, but its true identity cannot be reduced to its observable social community. The visible church has a hidden, spiritual identity and origin, known now "by faith," but one day "by sight." The church owes its existence to the invisible work of the Holy Spirit in the heavenly places, who unites believers to the risen and ascended Christ, thereby joining them in the one body of Christ, the church (1 Cor 12:12–13; Eph 2:14–16, 4:4–5); and one day, the full glory of the triumphant church, known only to God, will be fully unveiled to all creation in all of its splendor.

While acknowledging this biblical foundation, it is also important to allow Scripture to define what the "visibility" of the church can look like—especially in high-persecution contexts. While some of us come from contexts where the church has the freedom to pursue a higher level of visibility, the New Testament church is a better model of what "visible community" looks like in a high-persecution context, in terms of both the local and universal church.

The visibility of the local church in the New Testament was not expressed in terms of official legal recognition, public membership rolls, or having a clearly-marked building with a church sign. Rather, visibility is evident primarily in the local church's gatherings "house-to-house," where the church would break bread, sing praise, share possessions, and testify to the truth and power of Jesus Christ. The remarkable community life of the first church was clearly visible to their surrounding neighbors, giving them "favor with all the people," which presumably contributed to the attraction of new disciples that were added daily to their number (Acts 2:47). The visibility of the local church could not avoid persecution, but this did not prevent the church from continuing to find ways to gather as a visible, tangible community (Acts 12:12; cf. Heb 10:24–25).

The New Testament not only provides a model for visibility in the local church, but also visibility in the universal church. However, visibility of the universal church in the New Testament is not expressed in terms of a single worldwide organization or a unified institution, but rather in other ways, such as the following.

(1) *Communication.* The global body of Christ is visible through correspondence, sharing news, and exchanging of greetings among churches that encourage others and promote open fellowship and mutual acceptance within the wider family of God (e.g., 1 Thess 1:6–9; 1 Cor 16:19).

(2) *Hospitality.* The universal church is visible through sending and receiving visitors between and among congregations (2 Cor 8:16–24, Eph 6:21–22; Col 4:7–8; Rom 16:1–2). By extending and receiving hospitality, the bonds of the universal church are made visible.

(3) *Partnership.* The universal church is visible as different churches participate together in the mission of the gospel, whether financially (Phil 1:3–11; 2:25–30; 4:14–20) or through sending/supporting laborers to "plant" and "water" churches (Acts 11:22–25; 12:25; 13:1–3; 14:24–28).

(4) *Meeting Needs.* As in the local church, the universal church also shared resources to meet physical needs. A clear example is Paul's collection among the Gentile churches for the needy church in Jerusalem (Rom 15:25–29; 1 Cor 16:1; 2 Cor 8:1–9:15), which Paul saw as a visible expression of the spiritual unity and fellowship of the Jews and Gentiles in one body (Rom 15:27).

(5) *Consultation and Consensus.* The universal church is also visible when believers consult together to discern the Lord's will and seek Spirit-led consensus (Gal 2:1–10; Acts 15). When people from different sectors of the church come together and forge agreement, the "unity of the faith" in the universal church is made "visible."

These New Testament patterns represent ways of visibly expressing the universal church. It is not so much an *organizational* visibility, as in a global corporation—it is more of a *familial* visibility, like a large extended family scattered geographically. Organizational unity is one way that local churches can express their familial unity in the universal church, but it is not the only way, nor is it biblically mandated. For high-persecution contexts where official affiliation with existing Christian denominations may create problems, the model of the New Testament may provide alternative, fully legitimate ways to visibly express the universal church. Scripture provides important guidance on what visibility of the church can look like at both the local and global level.

It is also important, however, to complement an emphasis on visibility with a recognition of the invisible, spiritual nature of the church. In addition to affirming and pursuing appropriate visibility, we must also recognize that the true church is more than the visible church. God alone is the owner, creator, and gatekeeper of his church, which is grander and more glorious than our feeble attempts at visible community, a crucial reminder for those living and working in difficult contexts where persecution and sinful immaturity can sometimes hinder the full expression of the visible church.

It is an encouragement to know that the true church includes all who are (and will be) united to Christ, whether or not they are presently known to us or active in the visible church. Our understanding of the church and its membership is limited; God alone has the complete perspective of the full membership of all who are in Christ. Additionally, true membership in the body is not dependent upon acceptance by the visible church, but solely upon God, who knows his own and unites them to the body of his Son. Like Elijah, we are often unaware of the hidden remnant of God's true people who have "not bowed the knee to Baal" (1 Kings 19:14–18). Our perspective on the church, and our feeble, imperfect attempts at visible community, are only a small sliver of the full reality of all God is doing and will do to build his church and gather his Bride from every tribe and tongue.

Ultimately, the visible and invisible church—like the local and universal church—do not represent two churches, but two aspects of the one church, integrally related to one another in at least two ways. The visible and invisible church are related as *body and soul*. First, the core essence or "soul" of the church is the invisible reality of its spiritual identity, and yet this reality takes visible shape in the world in observable, "bodily," local gatherings of disciples, united in familial global ties. The "body" without the "soul" is not a church, but neither is the "soul" without the "body."

Second, the visible and invisible church are related as *already* and *not yet*. The "mixed assembly" of the visible church (presently known to us) looks forward to the full, final company of God's people (known to God, not yet revealed). In this sense, the "invisible" church is "the final form of the visible church on the last day that is known only to God and will be revealed on the last day" (Horton 2011, 717). The relationship is therefore between the church "as it is" and the church "as it will be" at the consummation (Vanhoozer 2004, 47).

Therefore, the visibility of the church is, in one sense, a partial visibility; the fullness of the church's true identity and nature have yet to be revealed to the world. The full and complete membership, perfect unity, and final glory of the church are at present hidden and will remain so until the return of the Bridegroom (Matt 13:24–30; Col 3:3–4; Eph 5:27; Rev 21:2–4). Until then, we are a mixed assembly; a universal church that is yet scattered and divided in the world, a holy nation often obscured by sin and brokenness in our communities.

Yet in our imperfect visible communities, our future glory is not completely hidden. Our feeble attempts at human community offer glimpses and signs of that future fullness that is our true identity as the church, providing a foretaste of the coming kingdom of God. As the people of God gather in visible communities of faith, they do well to remember in faith and hope that the nature and identity of the church is more glorious and grand than what they see in their humble gatherings, mixed communities, and imperfect relationships. By the power of the Spirit, the imperfect, visible community of the present church provides a partial glimpse and sign of its eschatological identity in the New Jerusalem. A biblical vision of the church affirms the essential visibility of the church, while also rightly understanding this visibility as partial, incomplete, and anticipatory of the final eschatological people of God—not an "invisible" community, but one that is already being revealed and anticipated in the visible church.

Ultimately, the church is both visible and invisible. If we emphasize one at the expense of the other, we risk a partial, distorted view of the church. Emphasizing the visible church at the expense of the invisible church risks thinking too highly of our human efforts at visible community and forgetting that God alone is the owner and creator of his church, and that God's church is more glorious than our limited human perspective. Emphasizing the invisible church at the expense of the visible church risks missing out on the Spirit-produced miracle of life-on-life, flesh-and-blood community in the body of Christ.

A biblical, robust vision of the "visible-invisible" church highlights both strengths and weaknesses in the insider paradigm, as later chapters show. A sound assessment of ekklēsia is also helped by attention to a related question in ecclesiology: if the invisible church makes itself visible in the world, are there any particular attributes or marks by which we can identify the true church?

Attributes and Marks of the Church

The world is full of groups claiming the name of "church," but not all are true churches. This raises the question: how do we distinguish the true church from a false one? One of the ways is to define the essential elements of the local church, as I attempted above. Another time-honored way is to clarify certain key qualities or identifying marks by which we can recognize true churches in the world.

Throughout church history, different sets of attributes or marks have been proposed at different times, two of which have been particularly influential in clarifying the nature of the church: the four "classical" attributes (one, holy, catholic, and apostolic) and the Protestant marks of the church (Word and sacraments). If understood and applied with biblical and cultural sensitivity, both sets of marks have an important contribution to our efforts to foster biblical churches among Muslims.

The Four Classical Attributes of the Church

"*I believe in one, holy, catholic, and apostolic church.*" So reads the Constantinopolitan Creed, circa. AD 381.[57] These four ancient attributes have proven influential through the ages among a broad spectrum of the worldwide church. It is important to remember that they arose in a particular context and reflect the concerns and issues of the time (Duerkson and Dyrness 2019, 34). Furthermore, the church has understood and applied the attributes differently in different ages and denominations,

---

[57] Popularly called the "Nicene Creed." Leith 1982, 33. The statement on the church was preceded by earlier creeds that confessed faith in "the holy church," such as *Epistula Apostolorum* (AD 150), *Interrogatory Creed of Hippolytus* (AD 215), and the *Creed of Marcellus* (AD 340) (cf. ibid., 17, 23). The Constantinopolitan Creed was most likely penned at the second ecumenical council at Constantinople (AD 381), which reaffirmed and supplemented the theology of the Council of Nicea (AD 325) (ibid., 31).

whether as the exclusive property of a specific institution (e.g., the Roman Catholic Church), or as identifying the essence of the church existing in various shapes and institutions (Vanhoozer 2004, 78).

Despite their cultural specificity and diverse reception, the classical attributes (or "*notae ecclesiae*") deserve careful consideration. Their widespread acceptance by a significant consensus of a broad swath of the church across time, place, and denominations indicates a value that transcends their original context. A biblical assessment of these attributes shows that each of them are rooted in Scripture, and each are best understood, not as criteria for being a church, but as indicative-imperatives for the church, "gifts" and "tasks" (Jenson and Wilhite 2010, 65) which simultaneously affirm the spiritual identity of the invisible church while calling the church to live out this identity in its visible fellowship.

One Body, Called to Unity

The unity of the church is an accomplished reality before it is an ethical imperative. At the cross, Jesus reconciled the church to God and to one another in one body (Eph 2:13–14). The church *is* one by virtue of its one salvation, baptism, Spirit, and Lord, a present reality in the heavenly places (Eph 4:4–6; cf. 1 Cor 12:12–13;). But unity is also a goal to be realized. Jesus not only makes the church one; he also prays that we would be one (John 17:22). Because we are already one, the church is called to labor "to maintain the unity of the Spirit in the bond of peace" (Eph 4:3). The church does not always do so (1 Cor 1:11–13), which results in recurring apostolic exhortation or rebuke (1 Cor 1:10; Rom 12:16).

As tragic as it is, disunity in the church does not disqualify a group from being a church. The Corinthians, racked with division, are still called "the church of God" (1 Cor 1:2, 12–13). Disunity does represent, though, a serious contradiction with the identity of the church, expressed in Paul's retort, "Is Christ divided?" (1 Cor 1:13).

As we strive to express our unity in the body of Christ, perfect unity is an eschatological hope, already true in Christ, but not fully realized until the consummation, when the redeemed are gathered at the throne, worshipping as one in perfect unison (Rev 7:10).

Like the other three attributes, the oneness of the church is not a "visible demarcation" of the church, but a "theological confession … made by faith, not by sight." It is both a present reality and a calling of the church to "be who you are in Christ."

Made Holy, Called to Be Holy

Holiness, like oneness, is both accomplished fact and ongoing imperative for the church. Believers have been made holy through Christ by the Spirit (1 Cor 6:11; 1 Pet 1:2; Heb 9:13–14)—we are called "saints" or "holy ones" (Acts 9:13; Eph 1:1; 1 Cor 1:2). The presence of the Holy Spirit in the church makes the church God's holy temple (1 Cor 3:16–17).

The holiness of the church also involves a calling to be holy—to live in a manner consistent with its identity as God's holy temple (2 Cor 6:16–18;

1 Pet 1:14–15). Old Testament Israel, likewise, was set apart as holy by God (Deut 7:6; 14:2) before they were called to "be holy, as I am holy" (Lev 11:44–45, 19:2). Whether in Israel or the church, holiness has always been central to the identity of the people of God, both as an ascribed status and as a clarion call to live up to that identity in its life in the world.

Once again, however, holiness is not a qualification for being a church. The church at Corinth is again instructive, as their serious holiness issues (cf. 1 Corinthians 5; 6:15–20; 10:14–22) did not keep Paul from addressing them as sanctified saints (1:2) and God's holy temple (3:16–17). A persistent lack of holiness does, however, indicate a disturbing contradiction with the church's identity as God's holy people.

It is important to remember that the church's holiness will not be fully manifested until the second coming (1 John 3:2–3), when the church will be presented to the Lamb as a pure and spotless bride (Rev 19:7–8; cf. Eph 5:27). However, this eschatological reality is not fully future, but finds present manifestation through ongoing sanctification. The church is an assembly of sinner-saints, ever aspiring to live in a manner worthy of the exalted status, bestowed by grace, of the holy people of God.

The Gift and Task of Catholicity

For many today, the word *catholic* is inseparable from the Roman Catholic Church. The original meaning, however, as used by the church fathers, is "universal" or "general."[58] According to Van Gelder, the "catholicity" of the church has two elements. The first is the expansiveness of the church throughout the world, while the second is the unity/commonality of the church among its varied contexts (Van Gelder 2000, 119). The opposite of "provincial" or separatist, catholicity highlights that wherever the church is found, the church is *the church*. As Karl Barth says, the church is

> one and the same in essence in all places, in all ages, within all societies, and in relation to all its members... . It can be the Christian community only in this identity, and therefore ... it is its task to maintain itself in this identity, and therefore in this identity to will to be, and continually to become and to remain, the Christian community, and nothing else, and therefore the true Church in all these dimensions. (Barth 1956, 708)

Catholicity, then, affirms the essential sameness or identity of the true church throughout space and time. This balances out the diversity and cultural particularity of the global church—which has important implications for contextualization of the church. While cultural form may vary by context, the core essence of the church remains the same. Biblical catholicity does not reside in institutional unity,

---

58 Jenson and Wilhite note that this is the meaning of the term as used by Augustine against the Donatists (2010, 70); the early church fathers used the term to mean "universal" or "general," as used by Justin when speaking of "the catholic resurrection" (Kelly 1958, 190; Van Engen 1991, 61).

organizational unity, nor in a uniform culture or liturgy for the church. Rather, catholicity describes churches which, in all their cultural particularity, participate in and reflect the core biblical essence, identity, and functions of the church shared by all true churches across time and around the world.

Catholicity is not only related to the universal church; it can also be an attribute of a local church.[59] A local church is "catholic" if it is connected to and identifies with the universal church throughout the world and across the ages. Like the previous two attributes, this is both a spiritual reality and an imperative/goal. Every local church, whether it acknowledges it or not, is a part of the worldwide family of God that will one day be gathered together as one on the last day (cf. Rev 7:9–17; Jenson and Wilhite 2010, 75). The local church ought therefore to seek to anticipate that gathering by acknowledging its place in the worldwide community of faith, as well as find ways to visibly express solidarity and unity with the church universal (Volf 1998, 267, 275; Jenson and Wilhite 2010, 75).

Apostolic Foundation, Apostolic Calling
The church is apostolic by design—Jesus built his church on the foundation of his apostles (Matt 16:18–19; Eph 2:20), who had an authoritative role as Christ's appointed vehicles for the revelation of the gospel (Eph 3:5). Churches are apostolic if they are faithful to the gospel that was handed down by the apostles (Gal 1:8; 2 Tim 1:12–13; 1 Cor 15:3): "Apostolicity means in the discipleship, in the school, under the normative authority, instruction, and direction of the apostles, in agreement with them, because listening to them and accepting their message" (Barth 1956, 714).[60]

Like the other three attributes, there remains both an indicative and an imperative aspect of apostolicity. The true church simply is apostolic in that it is built upon the apostolic gospel in continuity with the one church founded by the apostles. But the true church is also *called* to apostolic faithfulness, to be diligent to "guard the good deposit" of the apostolic gospel (2 Tim 1:14).

These four biblical attributes arose in a particular context and have been variously interpreted. However, a biblical appraisal of the classical *notae ecclesiae* highlights important insights for any biblical vision of the nature of the church. Rather than qualifications for being a true church, or the sole possession of a single institution, the classical marks reflect the church's invisible, spiritual identity which it is called to live out in the visible church. Each represents a "gift" and a "task," simultaneously accomplished by God and commanded by him to "become what you are in Christ" as the church journeys toward the New Jerusalem (Vanhoozer 2004, 78–79; cf. Van Engen 1991, 26–27).

---

59 Jenson and Wilhite note that there are some early usages of the word *catholic* (Greek *katholike*) to refer to local churches. They note that Polycarp is referred to as the "bishop of the catholic church which is in Smyrna" in *Martyrdom of Polycarp* (written around AD 156), and Tertullian also spoke of "catholic churches" in the plural (2010, 71).

60 Some have sought to expand the attribute of apostolicity to include apostolic mission in addition to apostolic teaching (Van Gelder 2000, 123; Jenson and Wilhite 2010, 79).

INSIDER CHURCH

A robust vision of biblical churches among Muslims is enhanced by a biblical understanding of the *notae ecclesiae,* envisioning churches which increasingly understand and live in the biblical tension between their identity and their calling as the church, giving the world a sign and foretaste of the coming kingdom in its present visible community. This means churches which understand that Christ has made them *one*—and they vigorously preserve that unity. It means churches which know that they are God's *holy* people—and they prioritize pursuing holiness. It means churches which know that they participate in the body of Christ *around the world and throughout time*—and they find concrete ways to identify with and participate in "such a great cloud of witnesses." It means churches which know their foundation in *the apostolic witness to Christ*—and they are zealous to both preserve it and proclaim it to the ends of the earth.

The four classical marks give important insight into a biblical vision of the church, yet they are not criteria for identifying the "true church." The Protestant Reformers, however, in their attempts to reform the Catholic Church, and later establish their own Reformed churches, felt the need for additional marks to distinguish the authentic church from the inauthentic. The result was a new set of marks which would become a hallmark of Protestant ecclesiology up to the present day.

The Protestant Marks of the Church

In various ways and times, churches in the Protestant tradition have sought to give practical guidance for clear tests of the authenticity of the true church and its faithfulness to Christ (Van Engen 1991, 61–62).[61] Calvin and Luther emphasized two particular marks of the true church which have enjoyed widespread influence to this day: the true preaching of the Word and the right observance of the "sacraments" (baptism and communion). The Protestant marks find classic expression in Calvin's *Institutes*, which describe them as ways by which the invisible church is made visible:

> From this the face of the church comes forth and becomes visible to our eyes. Wherever we see the Word of God purely preached and heard, and the sacraments administered according to Christ's institution, there, it is not to be doubted, a church of God exists [cf. Eph. 2:20]. (1959, 1023)

"Purely preached" does not mean perfectly preached, but rather accurate with regard to what is essential for salvation (Calvin 1959, 1026). However,

> As soon as falsehood breaks into the citadel of religion and the sum of necessary doctrine is overturned and the use of the sacraments is destroyed, surely the death of the church follows—just as man's life is ended when his throat is pierced or his heart mortally wounded. (Calvin 1959, 1041–42)

---

[61] "Thus for the Reformers the three marks of the Church were ways by which members of a local body could ascertain their proximity to Jesus Christ, the one and only true Center of the Church's deep essence ... tests by which the entire Church could be measured as to its faithfulness to its Lord. The presence of the Lord of the Church in its midst would test all the Church's activities, dogmas, and postures of discipline. The Reformers wanted to point to something behind and beyond the four attributes to the Center, to Jesus Christ, to whom the Church owed its life and nature" (Van Engen 1991, 63).

These two practices in particular are marks of the true church, Calvin says, because they always bear fruit by God's grace, and the community that regularly practices and receives them shows their effectiveness in them, therefore showing them to be the true church (Calvin 1959, 1024).

The Word and sacraments as marks of the true church have remained influential among various streams of the Reformation to the present day.[62] But how relevant are these marks to emerging churches among least-reached Muslims? To many, the Protestant marks are inseparable from particular forms of preaching, baptism, and communion, potentially jeopardizing the development of indigenous, reproducible churches.

A healthy perspective on these Protestant marks should clarify and distinguish the "biblically essential" and the "culturally secondary." If handled with care, the Protestant marks make an important contribution to our biblical vision of the church among Muslims.

The Word Proclaimed, Taught, and Obeyed

The proclamation and teaching of the Word of God has strong biblical support and a strong connection to the nature and identity of the church. Proclamation and teaching was a central activity of both Jesus and the apostles, and it had a central role in the birth and growth of the early church in Acts (e.g., Acts 2:42; 4:19–20, 31). Proclamation and teaching of the Word are essential for the church to come into being, as well as for the church to continue to grow. There can be no church without saving faith, and there can be no faith without the Word proclaimed and taught (Rom 10:14–17; Eph 1:13–14; Col 1:4–5).

Teaching and proclaiming of the Word are necessary not only to initiate faith, but also to sustain and mature the church's faith. While certain individuals are appointed by the Spirit to lead and teach the church, the entire body participates in speaking and teaching the Word, as the church builds itself up in love (Eph 4:11–16; Col 3:16). But proclamation and teaching by itself are not sufficient. They must be joined with ongoing, obedient response to the Word (Matt 7:21–23; James 1:22–25 cf. Duerskon and Dyrness 2019, 155). Regular proclamation, teaching, and obedient response to the Word are key indicators that a group of professing Christians are true believers who believe and affirm the truth about Christ. However, two important clarifications are in order.

First, this mark is not a requirement for theological perfection or precision, but rather a growing understanding of, and obedience to, God's truth. At a bare minimum, there should be at least sufficient true content to convey the real Christ and the true gospel and not a counterfeit (Volf 1998, 146; cf. Gal 1:6–9, 1 John 4:1–6), with the goal over time of a deepening of understanding and practice of the whole counsel of Scripture (Col 1:10).

---

[62] The two marks of the Word and sacrament are affirmed by the (Lutheran) Augsburg Confession (Leith 1982, 70), the (Anglican) Thirty-nine Articles (ibid., 273), and implied in the (Reformed) Westminster Confession (ibid., 222).

Second, proclaiming/teaching the Word can take many different forms; it need not conform to any particular cultural form of preaching. Historically, this mark has often been associated with a formal pulpit ministry, with weekly worship services revolving around a professional minister expounding Scripture in a lecture-style format (or sometimes a motivational-speech format). However, we must distinguish the biblical core of "proclaiming/teaching the Word" from the particular cultural form(s) which developed in churches in the Reformed/evangelical tradition. "Proclamation" and "teaching" are biblical terms, but what exactly does Scripture mean by "proclamation" and "teaching" of the Word? *Proclamation* refers to the authoritative announcement or telling of a message—specifically, the message of the gospel declared in the Scriptures; *teaching* refers to helping people understand and obey the message. These two activities went hand in hand in the ministry of Jesus and his apostles, but they took a variety of forms, including parable (Matt 13:1–35), synagogue homily (Luke 4:43–44; Acts 13:15-47), intimate house teaching session (Matt 13:36–43), extended sermon (Matt 5–7; Matt 24–25), disputation/dialogue (Matt 16:13–20; John 14–16; Acts 9:29) public lecture (Acts 17:22–31), long-term, ongoing instruction (Acts 19:9–10), extended talk in a home (Acts 20:7–12), and epistle-writing. The various forms of proclaiming and teaching indicate that Scripture does not circumscribe a specific way that the Word should be taught and preached in biblical churches.

Rightly understood, the preaching/teaching of the Word is an important mark to which the church should aspire as it seeks to visibly express its identity as the church.[63] If the truth of Christ is not declared and taught in some form, it is questionable whether a true church is present. Whether expository sermon, interactive lesson, or inductive Bible study, the truth of the Word should be consistently communicated, taught, and obeyed in biblical churches.

In addition to the Word, the "sacraments"—or "ordinances"—of baptism and communion play an important role in the formation of biblical churches.

Baptism and Lord's Supper

The practices of baptism and the Lord's Supper have strong biblical basis as essential practices for the church. Both are explicitly commanded by the Lord (Matt 28:19; Matt 26:26–29; cf. 1 Cor 11:23–26) and are present from the beginning of the church (Acts 2:38, 41, 46). Paul's epistles assume that all true believers are baptized (Rom 6:3–4; 1 Cor 12:13) and that the Lord's Supper is regularly practiced (1 Cor 11:17–22).

But more can be said about these practices besides the fact that they are commands to be obeyed. Christ commands many things of his followers besides

---

63 Volf states, "This public confession of faith in Christ through the pluriform speaking of the word [i.e., celebration of sacraments, sermons, prayer, hymns, witnessing, and daily life] is *the central constitutive mark of the church*. It is through this that the church lives as the church and manifests itself externally as church" (1998, 150; emphasis in original). See also Webster, who says the church's true spiritual identity is made visible through the church's visible witness/attestation to the presence and work of the triune God in its midst, which he says is primarily through word and sacrament (2005, 107–9).

baptism and communion. These two practices, however, bear unique emphasis for the church, for they are tangible, communal signs by which the church corporately affirms and visualizes its essential identity as the church.

Baptism is a sign of the believer's immersion into Christ's death, burial, and resurrection, by which a person dies to self and is raised a new creation in Christ. No mere individualistic practice, baptism is a corporate act with communal implications. It requires a baptizer, who—along with any witnesses— acknowledges and welcomes the baptized into the body of Christ (Acts 10:47–48; 1 Cor 12:13; Ott and Wilson 2010, Loc. 549).[64] Baptism is therefore a clear marker which denotes a person has identified with Christ and has been incorporated into the body of Christ. By practicing and recognizing baptism, the church declares together its identity as the body of Christ in a visible, tangible way.

Similarly, the Lord's Supper is also a communal act by which the church declares together its spiritual identity as the church. The eating of the bread and drinking of the cup is a community meal by which the church corporately commemorates the body and blood of the Lord that sealed the new covenant, as well as signifies their ongoing participation together in the body of Christ (1 Cor 10:16–17; 11:27). Like baptism, the Lord's Supper is a communal act of corporate profession of a common faith and salvation in Christ, which ties these acts directly to the nature of the church.

There are many important questions as to what form baptism and communion should take in Muslim contexts, questions beyond the scope of this book which should be answered in light of contextual considerations and biblical guidance.[65] The church has observed baptism and the Lord's Supper in a variety of ways throughout history,[66] and Scripture provides precious little detail on their precise form, leaving a degree of contextual freedom for churches to develop forms that fit their cultural context, while retaining their essential biblical identity. But each church should do so as both a local church *and* as part of the universal church, recognizing that these practices are a common inheritance for the whole body of Christ. Contextual meaningfulness should be balanced with some level of continuity with the worldwide church.

---

64 Ott and Wilson note that baptism is more than just an individualistic event: "Indeed it is a public confession of personal repentance and faith, but beyond this it indicates reception into the body of Christ, the new kingdom community.... Similar to proselyte baptism among the Jews, early Christian baptism indicated identification with a community—a meaning we have largely lost today. In other words, to baptize is to enfold into a Christian community, the church" (2011, Loc. 549).

65 One question is the timing of baptism, whether to baptize believers immediately upon profession of faith, or whether to delay baptism until a group can be baptized together, or at least until one can be baptized by another BMB (as opposed to being baptized by a foreigner). Another question relates to the form of communion, how and when it is practiced, and what elements are used.

66 See, for example, Duerkson and Dyrness's discussion of the transformation of communion from an agape meal to a Eucharist service in the early church (2019, 30-33).

Appropriating the Protestant Marks

Baptism and the Lord's Supper are more than just two among Jesus' many teachings we should obey. They are important rituals that Christ has bequeathed to the church by which she corporately declares her identity as the body of Christ. Understood biblically, they are uniquely formative for and sustaining to biblical churches, being explicitly commanded by Christ and integrally related to the nature of the church. When practiced, they visualize and express the church's identity as a believing community, the body of Christ, and the holy temple of God. But these marks are also formative in nature; when practiced, they inherently shape the church's identity, crystallizing a congregation's self-understanding as a spiritual community.

However, we must also recognize the role of cultural context in understanding and applying the marks of the church, which plays out in at least two ways. First, we must distinguish the biblical core (Word, baptism, communion) from the particular institutional forms that developed historically around these practices in the Protestant tradition. Established churches should not insist upon conformity to the historical expressions of these practices, and local congregations should be free to contextualize new forms that faithfully express the biblical core in ways particular to that setting.

Second, while the the Reformers had good biblical reasons for highlighting these particular practices, even a cursory reading of Scripture reveals that these are not the only practices which are indicators of the presence (or absence) of the Spirit in a community of believers. Some Reformers have added church discipline as a third mark.[67] Luther added three additional marks: (1) the consecration of ministers to administer the first three marks, (2) public worship, and (3) bearing the cross/tribulation (Jenson and Wilhite 2010, 90). Menno Simons added holy living, brotherly love, unreserved testimony, and suffering (Duerkson and Dyrness 2019, 148), while the later free-church tradition emphasized personal regeneration and genuine piety (Ott and Wilson 2011, Loc. 226).[68]

---

67 Luther included church discipline ("the office of the keys") in his marks of the church. Calvin also emphasized church discipline, and his later followers explicitly included it as a mark of the church (Jenson and Wilhite 2010, 93). The Belgic confession states: "The true church can be recognized if it has the following marks: The church engages in the pure preaching of the gospel; it makes use of the pure administration of the sacraments as Christ instituted them; it practices church discipline for correcting faults" (Christian Reformed Church n.d., Belgic Confession, Article 29: "The Marks of the True Church").

Church discipline is also commanded by Jesus in one of the few occurrences of the word *ekklēsia* in the Gospels (Matt 18:15–20), as well as by Paul (1 Cor 5:1–13; 2 Cor 2:5–11). In a sense, church discipline can be seen as an extension of the classical mark of the "holiness" of the church. However, we must recognize the biblical balance of holiness with grace and restoration in both passages regarding church discipline. The church should not turn a blind eye toward unrepentant sin, but neither should it approach discipline in a harsh, grace-less fashion. A church that practices church discipline in a biblical way, reflecting both grace and truth, visibly expresses its identity as God's holy temple within which the Spirit of God dwells.

68 Ott and Wilson add their own set of marks, which encompasses many biblical themes (2011, Loc. 258): confession of Christ as Lord (baptism); witnesses to Christ (evangelism); remembrance and fellowship of Christ (Lord's Supper); Spirit of Christ (filling, fruit, gifts); love of Christ (worship, devotion), Word of Christ (preaching, teaching); family of Christ (fellowship, community); sacrifice of Christ (stewardship, service); suffering of Christ (faithfulness, perseverance).

Each set of marks certainly has something to teach us, highlighting legitimate themes of Scripture and applying them to the concerns of its particular context. Ultimately, churches in different cultures may elect to emphasize certain groups of biblical practices based on the specific challenges and temptations of their context to biblical compromise.[69] As churches are planted in new contexts, they should be free to develop their own marks, under Scripture, that will help them pursue and distinguish true biblical churches in their context. In doing so, however, they would be helped by learning from churches in other times and places, which helps illumine blindspots and provides added perspective. As these new churches develop their ecclesiology, this will in turn enrich established churches with new insights.

As the church of Jesus Christ takes fresh root in unreached Muslim lands, it would do well to learn from the church across time, while not simply mimicking foreign frameworks in new contexts.[70] The classical attributes and Protestant marks have proven valuable to the church throughout history, casting a vision for how the church should grow into its identity as the body of Christ. Handled with biblical care and cultural sensitivity, the attributes and marks of the church provide an important contribution to a biblical vision of the church.

Two final questions remain for us to address in our vision of the nature and identity of the church. These two questions focus on two relationships—how the church relates to salvation and how the church relates to the world.

The Church and Salvation

"*Outside the church, there is no salvation.*" So said North African bishop Cyprian of Carthage in AD 251, laying down an axiom which would be affirmed in various forms throughout church history (1885a, 12).[71] Such a statement raises critical questions for those seeking to multiply biblical churches in Muslim contexts. Does salvation require that one identify with and participate in some church? If a Muslim comes to faith in Jesus, but never identifies with the church in any sense, can he be saved? These questions take us to the relationship between salvation and the nature of the church.

---

69 For example, Mark Dever's 9 Marks ministry has developed a set of marks oriented around formation of a healthy church: preaching, biblical theology, the gospel, conversion, evangelism, membership, discipline, discipleship, and leadership (https://www.9marks.org/about/the-nine-marks/). It would be illuminating to explore which aspects of these nine marks are biblically universal and which aspects are particularly oriented towards addressing deficiencies particular to the North American evangelical church context.

70 Vanhoozer says it is not the precise terms and concepts from the historical tradition that are binding for the global church, but rather the underlying theological judgments they represent (2013, chap. 3, "Response to Michael Bird"). Van Gelder notes that because the church is an empircal, visible reality, all historical ecclesiologies were somehow influenced by and responses to the cultural and historical elements of that time. The goal of drawing upon historical ecclesiological formulations is to "affirm the key insights and teachings of previously formulated ecclesiologies without imposing a previous contextual understanding of the church on our context as if a direct correspondence were possible" (2000, 40). This is what I have attempted here.

71 The Latin phrase is *"extra ecclesium nulla sallus"* (Cyprian 1885a, 12).

Cyprian took a strong position, "He can no longer have God for his Father who has not the Church for his mother" (1885b, 6), which the medieval Catholic Church interpreted in terms of the church as the functional mediator of saving grace through the sacraments (Tennent 2005, 172).[72] The Reformers, while rejecting this understanding of sacramental grace in favor of salvation by grace through faith alone, retained the ancient link between salvation and the church. Echoing Bishop Cyprian, Calvin speaks of the church as the "mother" of believers, such that "away from her bosom one cannot hope for any forgiveness of sins or any salvation"; and "God's fatherly favor and the especial witness of spiritual life are limited to his flock, so that it is always disastrous to leave the church" (Calvin 1959, IV.I.1). Therefore, the church is the "external" means by which forgiveness of sins is received, such that "we cannot enjoy it unless we abide in communion with the church" (ibid., IV.I.22). Despite a different understanding of the sacraments, the Reformers, like the ancient church, affirmed an essential link between the church and salvation.

By contrast, some have observed that contemporary evangelicalism goes the opposite direction. By emphasizing individual conversion with no substantial role for the church, contemporary evangelicals tend to see only a remote relation between the church and salvation (Horton 2011, 711). Timothy Tennent has argued that the vision of the church in the insider paradigm reflects this weak understanding of the relationship between the church and salvation (2007, 215). The question of the church-salvation relationship is not merely theoretical; it carries immense practical implications for the role of the church in evangelism and discipleship.

A strong biblical vision of the church should do justice to the rich relationship between the church and salvation, neither underestimating nor overestimating the church's role (Horton 2011, 711). To that end, we must begin by affirming unequivocally, with the Reformers, that salvation is not mediated through the church but through Christ alone, received by faith alone. One's participation in the church neither adds nor subtracts merit from the work of Christ that accomplishes salvation for all who believe. The fundamental question is not whether one is "inside" or "outside" of the church, but whether one is "inside" or "outside" of Christ.

However, this does not mean the church is peripheral to salvation. As discussed previously, the church is an integral part of God's plan of redemption, a plan to redeem not just individuals but a people for himself (Gen 12:2; Rev 5:9–10). The intended object of salvation is a community—the church, which God has created and redeemed in Christ by the Spirit. The biblical pattern is that salvation involves immediate incorporation into the church (Acts 2:42), since salvation is inherently communal:

---

[72] The doctrine has been repeatedly affirmed by the official magisterium, including Pope Innocent III and Lateran Council IV (AD 1215), Pope Boniface VIII in his papal bull *Unam Sanctam* (AD 1302), and Pope Eugene IV and the Council of Florence (AD 1438–45); cf. "The Popes on Extra Ecclesiam Nulla Salus," Slaves of the Immaculate Heart of Mary website, January 31, 2005, http://catholicism.org/eens-popes.html. However, Pope Clement XI denied the Jansenist proposition that there is no *grace* outside the church (*extra ecclesiam nulla conceditur gratia*) (Schaff 1919, chap. 4, "*The Papal Bulls Against the Jansenists*," cf. n 205).

> Every Christian has his life in Christ only as a member in the body of Christ. He shares in the life of Christ only by sharing it with all His people. The new birth, the new man in Christ, is a social reality. The ego which is crucified with Christ is the independent, self-sufficient ego. The life of Christ in the believer is a corporate life in which he can only share by sharing it with all. (Newbigin 1988, 131-32)

Entering into fellowship with the local church may not be a requirement for salvation, but it does not seem to be merely optional. It is simply the natural and right recognition of the nature of salvation: "To be saved by God is to be saved in and into his church" (Jenson and Wilhite 2010, 189)

The church also plays an instrumental role in bringing people to salvation and sustaining saving faith. God uses the church and its members to evangelize the nations, as the church preserves, passes on, and proclaims "the faith once for all delivered to the saints" (Jude 3). Once saved, the church plays a critical role in nurturing and spiritually forming believers as they "work out their salvation" in sanctification and persevere towards the goal of final salvation—discipleship happens in community (cf. Volf 1998, 163–78).

In the final analysis, we should reject "Outside the church, there is no salvation" as an extreme and erroneous statement. However, there is a softer sense in which it is true (Jenson and Wilhite 2010, 189), because all who experience salvation experience it as part of the body of Christ. Once the Spirit joins believers to the body of Christ through faith, participation in the church is simply an outward manifestation and expression of their new spiritual identity. Furthermore, although salvation is mediated only through Christ, the body of Christ is a divinely ordained instrument in the hands of the Spirit to make disciples and nurture them into the fullness of God's saving grace.

The role of the church in bringing the nations to Christ leads us to the final theme of our biblical vision of the church: the relationship between the church and the world.

The Missional Nature of the Church: The Relationship between the Church and the World

The church does not exist in a vacuum, but rather in the warp and woof of the world. How should we understand the nature of the church in relationship to the world in which it lives? This question is of particular concern with regard to insider movements, as well as for all seeking to multiply churches in Muslim contexts. How should biblical churches relate to the cultures, governments, and other human structures around them? To what extent ought biblical churches to be embedded in the structures of the world? Can the church be the salt of the earth without losing its saltiness? Our answers to these questions have implications for how we envision the church taking root in Muslim contexts, as well as how we appraise the insider paradigm.

The church-world relationship is characterized by a biblical tension that frames the church's identity in the world. (1) The people of God are a holy, set-apart nation, fundamentally "other" in the world, born from above, and strangers on the earth.

(2) Simultaneously, the people of God are a kingdom of priests *for* the world, participants in the mission of God in the world. This dual identity with relation to the world is encapsulated by the two phrases "holy nation" and "kingdom of priests" (Ex 19:6; 1 Pet 2:9), and it is confirmed by Jesus' statement that his disciples are "not of this world" and yet sent into the world (John 17:16–18).[73] The church is a company of exiles and sojourners living with eternal purpose in an unbelieving world (1 Pet 1:1, 17; 2:11–12).

But it is not enough to simply affirm both sides of the "holy nation" / "kingdom of priests" tension; we must also recognize that these two truths hang together. Israel's mission as a "kingdom of priests" was to be carried out precisely by being a holy nation. By living as a holy, set-apart community, Israel would display the wisdom and knowledge of the Lord to the surrounding nations (Ex 19:6). When Israel failed to be "set apart," it was unable to fulfill its priestly duty of ushering the nations to God. In Christ, this program was revived and passed on to the church, called to proclaim God's excellencies to the nations *as a holy people* living honorable, Christlike lives among the lost (1 Pet 2:9–12).

In this light, missiologists and theologians have reconfigured our understanding of "mission" as not merely an activity of the church, but as part of the essential nature of the church (Newbigin 1954, 163; Van Engen 1991; Van Gelder 2000, 31; Guder 2005, 116; Allison 2012, 103; Horton 2011, 715). The mission of the triune God (*missio Dei*) precedes the church, brings the church into existence, and then continues in and through the church, "God's missionary people" (Van Engen 1991, 17). The missional identity of the church can also be seen as an extension of the attributes of *apostolicity* (sent-ness; continuing the apostolic mission) and *universality/catholicity* (expressing Christ's universal reign) (Van Engen 1991, 76). But it can also be seen as the means of the church living out its essential identity in and for the world, thus recasting the four classical attributes into "adverbs which describe the missionary action of the Church's essential life in the world" (Van Engen 1991, 68). The one, holy, catholic, and apostolic church is thus a unifying, sanctifying, reconciling, and proclaiming force in the world (Van Engen 1991, 68).

Another way to conceive of the missional nature of the church is in terms of the church "gathered" and the church "scattered."[74] As the apostle Peter teaches, the church in this age is more than a "gathering," it is also a "diaspora" of exiles and strangers, scattered throughout the nations, called to bear witness to the excellencies of Christ in word and deed (1 Pet 1:1, 2:9–12). On the last day, the full people of God will gather together in the New Jerusalem, enjoying perfect fellowship with God and one another in the new creation, never to be scattered again (Rev 7:9–17, ch. 21–22). In this age, however, the church is not called to remain permanently in its gathered state; it is not to permanently cloister itself together, isolating itself

---

[73] David Mathis suggested revising the slogan "in, but not of" the world to "not of, but sent into" the world, based upon the emphasis of Jesus' prayer in John 17 (Mathis 2012).

[74] I'm not sure where I first heard this concept of the church "gathered" and "scattered."

completely from the world. Rather, the church gathers together to worship God and be filled up, and then scattered and sent back into the world as the salt and light of Jesus among the nations.

An important factor in the church's missional identity in the world is the reality of the kingdom of God. Van Engen fleshes out the church's missional identity by clarifying the relationship between church, kingdom, and world. The kingdom, or reign, of Christ, has at least three dimensions or spheres: Christ reigns in the church (R1), over all creation (R2), and over spiritual authorities (R3). While his dominion encompasses all three, Christ reigns in a special way among his people (R1), because "uniquely in them Christ rules as Head of the body, the church" (Van Engen 1991, 10).

Understood this way, the church on mission is essentially the expansion of "R1 authority" into "R2 territory" through "the conversion or translation of people from being unwilling subjects to willing subjects of the King" (Van Engen 1991, 110). While the kingdom is the goal of the mission, the church is a central vehicle in the mission:

> The total development of the missionary Church then aims at realizing the kingdom by pushing outward the primary sphere of Christ's rule—local missionary churches incarnated in a particular time, place, and culture. The Church, not the kingdom, is the Bride of Christ (Eph 5:25–27). The Church, not the kingdom, is the New Jerusalem (Rev 21). The Church, not the kingdom, is composed of those who have washed their robes in the blood of the Lamb (Rev 7:14), whom Christ will present without spot or wrinkle (Eph 5:27; Jude 24). So in this "time between the times" we focus on the Church because we understand that when we build missionary congregations we are already participating in our final goal, the coming of the kingdom (cf. Col 1:13–20). (ibid., 112)

Van Engen's clarification of the relationship between the kingdom and the church has important implications for the kingdom theology of the insider paradigm, to be discussed later. For now, Van Engen's discussion further underscores the reality the church is missional by nature; it exists because of mission, and mission is part of its essential identity as the church.

The church-world relationship can be summed up, therefore, in the ideal of the church as a "kingdom community," which describes people whose "essence is found first in their relationship to the King, Jesus Christ, and second in their obedience to the will of the King explicitly stated in the Scriptures" (Ott and Wilson 2011, Loc. 396). But what do kingdom communities look like?

> Kingdom communities are formed of people who are born of the Spirit, who enter God's kingdom with childlike faith, and who are poor in spirit. They are characterized by the values of the Sermon on the Mount. They strive for personal holiness. They know that they may experience suffering and tribulation in this world, but they live in the hope that the fullness of the kingdom will appear when Christ returns. Kingdom communities become a transforming, countercultural witness and movement having an impact on persons, families, communities, cities,

and nations. The power of the gospel becomes active in them, and they become the salt of the earth and the light of the world. (Ott and Wilson 2011, Loc. 396)

This description of kingdom communities draws together many strands of Scripture and captures the biblical relationship between the church and the world. It balances the priestly mission of the church with the calling to be a holy, set-apart people—which stand or fall together. Biblical churches should strive toward this vision of being a kingdom community in its particular setting with a transformative, countercultural impact on their communities and nations.

Conclusion

If our goal is the multiplication of biblical churches, we must have a clear understanding of what we are multiplying—a vision of our "end game." Clarifying "church" is absolutely critical in defining the goal toward which we should pray, strategize, and labor. This is all the more crucial when aiming to see churches planted among Muslims, who have complicated baggage in regard to Christians and traditional churches. The insider paradigm provides one approach to reproducing ecclesial communities among Muslims, and this model cannot be properly evaluated without a strong baseline for what the church is, essentially. Without such a baseline, we cannot distinguish between what is peripheral and what is central, between "the cultural" and "the biblical." A strong, robust definition helps us avoid both an excessively high bar and an overly low bar for defining the biblical church.

This chapter highlighted six important dimensions of the nature and identity of the church.

- The **core essence** of the church, in all of its forms, is defined by its unique redemptive relationship to the triune God. The church is the people of God—the community chosen by the Father, redeemed in Christ, and sealed by the Spirit.
- The church is both **local** and **universal**—a global, multiethnic family united in Christ, scattered throughout the world in localized communities of believers who gather regularly for worship, truth, fellowship, and edification, in anticipation of the great ingathering of all God's people in the New Jerusalem.
- The church is both **visible** and **invisible**—a physical, observable fellowship that gives a partial glimpse of the church's full, glorious identity, a present reality in the heavenly places that will be fully revealed in the New Jerusalem, a reality that far outstrips all present expressions of the visible church.
- The church is **one, holy, catholic, and apostolic community**, and it is called to aspire to live out this identity in its visible fellowship. The identity of the true church is tangibly expressed and cultivated through formative, biblical practices of abiding in the **Word, baptism, and communion.**
- The church is the company of **the saved** and an important instrument for the **salvation** and spiritual formation of disciples of Jesus.

- The church is **missional**, set apart from the world as a holy people and sent into the world as a kingdom of priests to bring the nations under the reign of King Jesus and into his kingdom community.

These six points, along with the biblical narrative and images of the people of God, form the baseline of a robust, biblical vision of the church, summarized in the table below. Altogether, this framework highlights distinct strengths and weaknesses in the insider paradigm, which will be discussed in turn. Before doing so, however, one more piece must be put in place, which is the question of the church and contextualization.

Table 2. Dimensions of the Biblical Identity of the Church

Core Essence of the Church	*The Redeemed People of the Triune God* • Chosen and Adopted by the Father • Body of Christ, Fellow Heirs with the Son • Temple and Dwelling of the Spirit

Local and Universal Church	*Local Church*
	1. Saved, Baptized Believers in Jesus
	2. Identifying Together as "ekklēsia"
	3. Regularly Gathering as "ekklēsia"
	4. Biblical Patterns of Community:
	  • *Worshipping God in Christ*
	  • *Testifying to and living out the **truth** of Christ*
	  • *Authient **fellowship** in Christ*
	  • *Spirit-guided **edification** of the Body*
	5. Led by Biblical Elders
	
	Universal Church
	1. Global, Multicultural Family of God
	2. Anticipation of Eschatological People of God

Visible and Invisible Church	*Visible Nature of the Church*
	• Visible, Observable Local Community
	• Visible, Observable Familial Ties with Universal Church
	  - Communication
	  - Partnership
	  - Visits/Hospitality
	  - Consultation/Consensus
	  - Sharing Resources
	• Partial, Imperfect Glimpse of Fullness of the Church
	  - Mixed company of believers and not-yet-believers
	  - Shortcomings in church fellowship
	
	Invisible Nature of the Church
	• The full glory and spiritual reality of the church in the heavenly places, already true and not yet fully manifested
	• The full membership of the body of Christ, known only to God
	• Invisible church partially visible in the present visible church, fully revealed in the new creation

INSIDER CHURCH

Attributes and Marks of the Church	*Classical Attributes*		
	In Christ, the Church is...		*The church is called to be...*
	one body, one in Spirit	**One**	one in reconciled fellowship
	God's holy temple	**Holy**	holy in all of life
	a universal body	**Catholic**	in community with the wider church
	founded on the apostolic teaching	**Apostolic**	faithful stewards of the apostolic truth and mission
	Protestant Marks		
	Word—regular, faithful communication and response to the essential truth about Christ in the Old and New Testament Scriptures		
	Sacraments/Ordinances—rituals that express and cultivate the core identity of the church		
	Baptism—joint testimony of Christ, the baptized, the baptizer, and any witnesses, to a new believer's repentance and faith in Jesus, cleansing from sin, identification with Christ in his death and resurrection, new life in Christ, and incorporation into the body of Christ		
	Lord's Supper—community meal commemorating the inauguration of the new covenant in the death of Christ and ongoing participation of the church in the body and blood of Christ		
Salvation and the Church	• Salvation is a community-creating event, leading to immediate incorporation into the body of Christ spiritually, and ideally into a visible church. • Justification is by grace through faith and does not require membership in a church, but the church plays an important instrumental role in bringing people to saving faith, as well as nurturing sanctification and perseverance in the faith.		
The Church and the World	• Missional, kingdom community • "Holy nation" set apart from the world: "royal priesthood" for the world • Gathered for worship as "family"; scattered for mission as "exiles and sojourners"		

CHAPTER THREE

Contextualizing "Church"

We were seated before four Asian men—an imam, a jihadist, and two Muslim Brotherhood disciples. They told remarkable stories of encountering Christ's forgiveness and experiencing transformation. Now they were involved in leading an extensive network of BMBs in their nation.

Because of their deep Islamic background, these men offered a unique perspective on the challenges of multiplying and sustaining churches in a Muslim society. How do new believers preserve their witness to the gospel without disrespecting Islam? What do they do in Ramadan, and how do they use the Qur'an? What identity labels do they affirm and what labels do they reject? How do their churches maintain a low profile and yet be consistent enough to provide meaningful accountability and growth?

These kinds of questions take us to the interface of the biblical church and cultural context. Defining the biblical nature of the church is foundational. But how does the biblical church relate to its social, cultural, and religious context? How does the church remain *the church* in a new cultural idiom?

These questions have been at the heart of the insider debate for years. Can a highly contextualized, "insider church" embrace Islamic customs, rituals, and identity-markers without compromising its biblical identity as the church? How should church planters advise emerging churches in such decisions?

Part of the challenge has been the diversity of views on the nature of legitimate "contextualization." Insider advocates at have times presented insider movements as representing appropriate, high-level contextualization (Travis 1998a, 1998b), while critics have charged them with crossing the line into syncretism (Parshall 1998). Still other insider advocates have sought to either separate contextualization from insider movements (Lewis 2007, 76), or advocate abandoning the "contextualization" paradigm altogether (Dyrness 2016, Loc. 108). Such disagreement on the meaning and parameters of appropriate contextualization surely contributes to the multiplicity of views on insider movements.

To clear the ground for an assessment of insider ekklēsia, it is important to clarify how ekklēsia relates to culture, and what counts as legitimate, authentic contextualization.

Recovering Contextualization

Some contend that contextualization has outlived its usefulness and should be replaced by other models. DMM practitioners have at times argued for a shift from contextualizing to "de-contextualizing" the gospel—minimizing foreign cultural baggage and presenting Jesus as "a-culturally" as possible.[75] The goal is for seekers and believers to discover God's truth for themselves and to self-contextualize the gospel, interpreting and obeying Scripture from within their own cultural framework.[76]

Others have argued for a paradigm shift from contextualization to a more multi-directional, dialogical model of interreligious encounter of mutual learning that accounts for the presence and activity of God in human religions (Dyrness 2016, Loc. 108).

These suggestions to move beyond "contextualization" are attractive for some wary of "contextualization wars." However, such proposals have too often critiqued caricatures of contextualization, rather than contextualization as it is espoused by its best proponents. Rather than move beyond contextualization, I propose we should define it properly and understand it biblically. When we do so, contextualization provides a useful, resilient framework for understanding the complex way that the church should interface with biblical cultures.

---

75 "As I prayed for this person, I realized that I had to find a way to minimize my cultural representation of Jesus. This is quite different from dressing Jesus up in a way that would be acceptable to another culture. How can I ever know another culture well enough to dress Jesus up to meet their expectations, wants, and needs? I cannot. But I do know my own culture, and if I am honest with Scripture and critical in my thinking and planning, I can present Jesus in a near-acultural way that can be assimilated and transformed into a cultural model by the ones God has chosen and prepared. I have learned that God has prepared men and women in every culture who can meet those who love Jesus from another culture, learn to love Jesus from them, strip away the cultural baggage attached (which we can minimize), and present Jesus to their own culture in a loving and caring way that results in lives changed and the Kingdom enlarged" (Watson and Watson 2014, Loc. 327).

76 Practically speaking, this means the local disciple-maker will refrain from explaining or interpreting the Bible, but focus on asking questions and getting local people to interpret the Bible for themselves and obey it, according to the Watsons' model.

Every term has a history, and "contextualization" is no exception. Our own definitions of terms should not ignore the ways such terms have been used previously, as well as their relationship to similar terms. Two concepts in particular rise to the surface as important precursors that shed light on the emergence of the concept of contextualization: *indigenization* and *inculturation*. A brief look at these two terms provides the prelude to my own definition to follow.

The "Indigeneous" Church and "Inculturation"

Originally describing "a plant or animal native to an area" (Terry 2000, 483), "indigeneous" was adopted by Henry Venn and Rufus Anderson in the mid-nineteenth century to describe the ideal of churches that "fit naturally into their environment" (Terry 2000, 483), rather than being culturally exotic or dependent on an outside body (Hodges 1979, 6, 13). Venn and Anderson coined the renowned "three-selfs" (supporting, governing, propagating), later criticized as too superficially focused on relationship with the sending church. While some proposed adding more "selfs,"[77] others advocated for a more dynamic vision, such as the one expressed in this classic statement:

> When the indigenous people of a community think of the Lord as their own, not a foreign Christ; when they do things as unto the Lord meeting the cultural needs around them, worshipping in patterns they understand; when their congregations function in participation in a body, which is structurally indigenous; then you have an indigenous Church. (Tippet 1979, 64)

Such a vision moved toward a greater focus on the social and cultural structures of the church, which relates in important ways to another key term that would emerge to prominence.

When evangelicals were speaking of "indigeneity," Roman Catholics were speaking of "inculturation."[78] A combination of the social science concept of "acculturation" and the theological concept of "incarnation,"[79] inculturation comprehensively included "the gospel, Jesus Christ, the faith, the people" (Bate 1994, 94–98). A widely referenced definition is that of Pedro Arrupe:

> Inculturation is the incarnation of the Christian life and the Christian message in a particular cultural context, in such a way that this experience not only finds expression through elements proper to the culture in question (this alone would be no more than a superficial adaption), but *becomes a principle that animates, directs and unifies the culture, transforming and remaking it so as to bring about "a new creation."* (Arrupe 1978, 173; quoted in Gallagher 1996, 178; emphasis added)

---

[77] Paul Hiebert added self-theologizing (1985, 195–96); Alan Tippet added self-imaging, self-functioning, and self-determining (1979, 61–64); and David Garrison added self-correcting and self-feeding (2010).

[78] The term "inculturation" was used as early as 1973, when Linwood Barney, a Christian and Missionary Alliance anthropologist defined it as "that process or state in which a new principle has been culturally 'clothed' in meaningful forms in a new culture" (Barney 1973, 57; quoted in Priest 2013, 300). The term arose to prominence, however, in Roman Catholic circles as a result of a 1974–81 theological consultation by the Jesuits (Bate 1994, 93).

[79] Cf. Schreiter 1985, *Constructing Local Theologies*, 5; cited in Priest 2013, 300.

Invigorated by a theology of incarnation and new creation, inculturation moved beyond *indigeneous expression* within the culture to *transformation* of the local culture—which paved the way for the emergence of contextualization.

Contextualization

As "inculturation" arose to prominence in Roman Catholic Jesuit circles, the term "contextualization" emerged at the World Council of Churches, where it was first used in 1972 by Taiwanese theologian Shokie Coe (Moreau 2012, 406),[80] who intended it "to convey all that is implied in the familiar term *indigenization*, yet seek to press beyond for a more dynamic concept which is open to change and which is future oriented" (Coe 1976, 21; Priest 2013, 301–2).

After some initial skepticism, "contextualization" eventually gained broad acceptance among evangelicals, who sought to define it within a biblical framework (Hesselgrave and Rommen 1989, 33; Hayword 1995, 135). The preference for "contextualization" over "indigenization" did not indicate a fundamentally new paradigm (Priest 2013, 302), as the two terms are sometimes used interchangeably (Padilla 1979, 307; Kraft 2005, xxv).[81] However, contextualization was a fresh term that pushed evangelicals beyond discussions of the relationship between sending and receiving churches into a greater focus on the relationship between the gospel and culture (Lausanne Committee for World Evangelization 1978, 23; Hiebert 1989, 103; Hayword 1995, 135; Gilliland 2000, 226; Chang et al. 2009, 199–200).

There is no universally agreed upon definition of contextualization (Hesselgrave and Rommen 1989, 35; Gilliland 2000, 225); David Bosch has called it a "blanket term for a variety of theological models," ranging from socioeconomic political theologies to indigenization/inculturation models (1991, 420–21). Evangelicals define and practice contextualization in numerous ways, as seen in Scott Moreau's maps of multiple evangelical models of contextualization (Moreau 2010, 169–71, 173–92).

Like inculturation, contextualization is a comprehensive term that refers not only to the gospel and theology but to everything in the church and the Christian life (Moreau 2012, 408; cf. Gilliland 1989, 27; Schineller 1996, 109–10). As Hesselgrave and Rommen put it,

> Contextualization is both verbal and nonverbal and has to do with theologizing; Bible translation, interpretation, and application; incarnational lifestyle; evangelism; Christian instruction; church planting and growth; church organization; worship style—indeed with all of those activities involved in carrying out the Great Commission. (Hesselgrave and Rommen 1989, 200)

---

80 The concept was discussed in the Theological Education Fund publication *Ministry in Context* (Gilliland 2000, 225).

81 Eitel seeks to integrate and distinguish the two concepts, calling "indigeneity/accommodation" the "external momentum" (i.e., the missionaries) and "contextualization/inculturation" the "internal momentum" (i.e., local people self-theologizing) (1998, 303–4). Genuine indigeneity (external), says Eitel, should *lead* to contextualization (internal) (ibid., 311).

The contextualization of the church is just one integral part of a comprehensive process by which the gospel and the whole life of faith take root within a particular culture.

The concept of contextualization integrates biblical and anthropological ideas to clarify the relationship between gospel and culture, taking into account the social and cultural structures of society so as to remove any unnecessary cultural offense (Hiebert and Meneses 1995, 19). Hiebert lays down three axioms that define the way the gospel relates to cultures: (1) the gospel is distinct from any one culture, (2) the gospel must always be expressed in cultural forms, and (3) the gospel calls all cultures to change (Hiebert 1985, 52–56).

Hiebert defines culture as "the more or less integrated system of ideas, feelings, values and their associated patterns of behavior and products shared by a group of people who organize and regulate what they think, feel, and do" (Hiebert 1985, 30). It is clear from this definition that what we typically mean by "religion" can be very much a part of culture, and certain cultures can be more explicitly religious than others (e.g., Muslim cultures).

Contextualization is implied in the nature of the church. The "catholicity" or universality of the church implies that the church can and should be expressed in every culture (Van Gelder 2000, 41; 2007, 34), and the missional nature of the church implies that the church should participate in God's mission to take shape in other cultures (ibid.). The nature and purpose of the church is unchanging, but the "organizational reality" of missional churches should be adapted to their particular contexts (ibid.).

Every ecclesiology is "contextual," but the goal is to develop a "missiological ecclesiology" which intentionally draws the church into the mission of God in its context (Van Gelder 2000, 37–41). A "missional church" seeks to "break the missional code," which is to "recognize that there are cultural barriers (in addition to spiritual ones) that blind people from understanding the gospel…. Discerning Christians discover those relevant issues and break through the resistance—so that the name and reality of Jesus Christ can be more widely known" (Stetzer and Putman 2006, 5).

In light of the history of the term, I propose the following working definition of contextualization: *Contextualization is the intentional, ongoing process by which the gospel, biblical faith, and the church of Jesus Christ are expressed in human cultural and social settings, such that the underlying worldview, as well as the social and cultural structures are transformed and redeemed by the gospel and the kingdom of God* (adapted from Hiebert and Meneses 1995, 370, 374–75).[82]

---

[82] A more comprehensive and less "church-centric" definition would be that of Craig Ott, who defines contextualization in his graduate course on the subject as *"the dynamic, ongoing process of communicating, reflecting upon and living out the Christian faith in ways appropriate to a given culture and consistent with biblical teaching."*

Transformation of culture is not something that happens all at once, and culture is constantly changing, which means that contextualization is an ongoing process. It is a comprehensive process which involves the whole church, as many actors play a role in the communication, translation, and application of biblical faith to the structures and values of culture. Furthermore, contextualization takes place within cultural settings but does not leave cultures unchanged—it brings Christ's "new creation" to bear on a particular social and cultural setting.

Defining what we mean by "contextualization" is important, but we must also clarify what counts as authentic, legitimate contextualization of the church. For that we turn to the Scriptures, which provide clear principles and precedents for the dynamic relationship between the people of God and their surrounding cultural and religious environments.

The Contextualization of the People of God in the Old and New Testaments

A biblical word search on "contextualization" comes up empty, but a close reading of Scripture reveals the way the people of God, from Abraham to the church, have always existed in dynamic relationship with their cultural and religious contexts. Whether speaking of Israel in Ancient Near Eastern (ANE) culture or the church in first-century Jewish and Greco-Roman cultures, a consistent set of principles and precedents can be observed that provide a clear basis for defining the parameters of authentic, biblical contextualization of the church today (cf. Conn 2000, 481).

Old Testament: The Contextualization of Israel in the Ancient Near East

The contextualization of the people of God began with the formation of Israel in the ANE cultural and religious context. Three key patterns can be observed regarding the relationship between Israel and its ANE context which set the trajectory for contextualization of the church in the New Testament: cultural congruence, cultural divergence, and the problem of syncretism.

(1) **Cultural Congruence**

The theological identity of Israel as the people of God was expressed and developed very much within ANE culture and society, resulting in a large degree of continuity with ANE culture. A number of familiar ANE forms were adopted to express Israel's identity as God's people, beginning with their basic form as a "nation among the nations," which was a "political unit with a common land, language, and government" (Wenham 1987, 275; cf. Hamilton 1990, 371). The identity-forming event of the exodus resembles other ANE stories of a nation being delivered from subjection to a king and brought into subjection to a god (Walton et al. 2000, 94).

One of the most significant ways of expressing and defining Israel's identity as God's people was shaped profoundly by the ANE culture—the covenant-treaty (Hebrew, *berit*; Glasser 1989, 40). The Mosaic covenant is likely a fusion of an ANE Hittite suzerain-vassal treaty and ancient law codes from the second millennium BC (Gallagher 2005, 140; Dillard and Longman 1994, 98–99; Walton et al 2000, 172).

The ordinary nature of ANE covenants ensured that the identity of Israel as the covenant people of God, unique as it was, was not altogether foreign, but relatable and understandable in the ANE context (Gallagher 2005, 140).

It should be noted that this cultural continuity also included what could be called "religious" ANE elements. One example is the terminology for the God of Israel, who is sometimes called "El," a word also used for the Canaanite high god (Talman 2015c, *UIM,* Loc. 4479). Another example is the ANE religious elements which are included in the lawful worship of Israel, such as sacrifices and burnt offerings (Lev 1–6), the use of sacred places, such as altars (Gen 12:8; Ex 27:1–8), and temples (1 Kings 6).[83] As God revealed and shaped the identity of his people, he made use of religious terms, forms, and practices which would have resonated meaningfully with people of the ANE.[84] Israel's relationship to its ANE cultural and religious context is clearly marked by an element of cultural congruence, a key theme that continues into the New Testament.

(2) Cultural Divergence
In addition to congruence with context, the Old Testament clearly reveals an unmistakable element of divergence in the relationship of God's people to their cultural and religious context. The divergence begins with Abraham, who was called out of his family, nation, and worshiping community, not to reform an existing nation, but to start a completely new nation that would worship and follow Yahweh (Gen 12:1; Josh 24:2–3; cf. Acts 7:2–4).

Israel was a "nation among nations," but it was more than that—it was a holy nation, set apart from other peoples belonging to God. Despite some cultural resemblance to other nations, Israel was clearly distinguished as the people among whom God's presence dwells (Wells 2000, 56). Its identity did not ultimately come from the surrounding ANE culture, but from *Yahweh*, since to be "holy" is to be "other," to be like *Yahweh* (ibid., 96–97), to live a common life that embodied the holy character of God (Hartley 2003, 425).

This "set-apart" identity of Israel as the special people of the holy God was to be expressed and maintained through obedience to the Torah, which included specific and detailed instructions regulating all aspects of personal, social, and religious life, providing daily reminders of their separation from the unrighteous aspects of the surrounding culture (Wright 2006, 257). Israel's identity may have been expressed in ways that resonated with the ANE culture, but at a core level they were called to be *unlike* the surrounding culture—to be a distinctive, holy nation of priests bearing witness to the living God in their cultural context (Ex 34:10–16; Deut 7:1–6).

---

83 For example, Solomon's sacrifices and burnt offerings to foreign gods (1 Kings 11:8); altars of foreign gods (2 Chr 33:15); the temple of Dagon (1 Sam 5:2).

84 Harley Talman discusses this Old Testament theme in terms of an "attitude of absorption" and openness toward non-Israelite religions (Talman 2015c, Loc. 4452). He gives several other examples, and then sums up this particular theme: "Thus we have seen much evidence of an Old Testament attitude of appropriation of positive elements in pagan religions. This seems to reflect Yahweh's desire to communicate his message with maximum impact by using ideas, terms, forms, and elements that were already familiar to the audience" (ibid., Loc. 4528).

This discontinuity of Israel with its context necessarily implied a clear religious, theological discontinuity—Israel is distinct because its God is distinct. Because of its unique God, Israel was called to separate itself from the religious systems and practices of its ANE neighbors and engage in unique and distinctive worship prescribed by *Yahweh*. The presence of select familiar ANE religious forms in Israelite worship provided an element of understandability in an ANE religious context, and yet there was a clear and profound divergence, both in the object of their worship (*Yahweh*, and not idols or the many other gods) and in the manner of their worship (through prescribed sacrifices in the tabernacle/temple, not through unauthorized worship practices).[85] Whenever Israel breached this prescribed discontinuity, blurring the lines between God's prescribed worship and the worship practices of the nations, there were serious consequences, which leads us to our third key theme.

(3) The Problem of Syncretism

A recurring theme in the Old Testament is the repeated failure of Israel to live out its calling as a holy, priestly nation, succumbing to the danger of what has been called "syncretism," or an inappropriate mixture of biblical faith and practice with anti-Scriptural ideas, practices, or worship (Moreau 2000, 924). Syncretism was prohibited in the first two commandments (Ex 20:3–6)—the first addresses mixing the worship of *Yahweh* with worship of other gods, while the second addresses mixing lawful with unlawful worship of *Yahweh*. This expectation is reiterated throughout the Torah, which calls God's people to exclusive and wholehearted love for *Yahweh* alone (Deut 6:5).

The Israelites, however, repeatedly disobeyed this command throughout their history: (1) they combined *Yahweh* worship with Canaanite Ba'al and Ashtoreth worship (Judg 2:13; 1 Sam 7:4); (2) they incorporated unauthorized rituals of priesthood and temple (1 Kings 12:25–33); (3) they engaged in pagan religious practices specifically outlawed in the law, such as human sacrifice, divination, and superstition (2 Kings 17:17); and (4) they engaged in specifically outlawed ethical practices, such as sexual immorality and oppression of the poor (Amos 2:6–8).[86] The result of this syncretism of belief and practice resulted in Israel losing its distinctiveness as a people, becoming "just like" the other nations, and therefore leading to the exile, the reversal of the exodus (2 Kings 17:7–23).[87]

---

85 Harley Talman captures these two themes of cultural continuity and cultural discontinuity in terms of a dual Old Testament attitude of "absorption" and "rejection" of non-Israelite religions (Talman *2015c*, Loc. 4529).

86 One of the weaknesses of Dyrness' discussion of attitudes toward religion in the Old and New Testaments in chap. 3 of *Insider Jesus* is that he virtually ignores the first three of these items, focusing almost exclusively on the fourth item: the ethical failures of Israel. (Though he mentions Ba'al worship, he reduces this too to a failure of ethics, not a failure of worship [2016, 933]). Dyrness then reaches this puzzling conclusion: "With significant exceptions, God shows a remarkable tolerance toward other religions in the First Testament" (ibid., 916). Such a conclusion is difficult to square with the full scope of Old Testament theology, not least the explicit, repeated divine polemic against idolatry and unauthorized religious practices (for religious, not just ethical, reasons) in every part of the Hebrew canon.

87 Talman is right to say that God's critical attitude of "rejection" of other religions also applied to Israelite religion when it fell below his standards (Talman 2015c, Loc. 4553).

The relationship between Israel and its surrounding cultural and religious context, therefore, reveals these three themes of cultural congruence, cultural divergence, and the ever-present problem of syncretism. Each of these themes are continued forward into the New Testament, shaping the way the church interacts with its first-century—and contemporary—contexts.

The Contextualization of the Church in Jewish and Greco-Roman Cultures
The ways in which the early church engaged and interacted with its cultural context are foundational to giving us biblical parameters for contextualizing the church today. The same dynamics at work in Old Testament Israel are also present in the New Testament church.

Cultural Congruence with First Century Culture

Like Israel before it, the church absorbed and utilized several cultural forms and social structures from its context in various ways. First, we have already discussed how Jesus' vision of the church drew upon the Mediterranean strong-group model of the family familiar in the first century (Hellerman 2009, 64, 71). Jesus' use of home/house gatherings as a key venue for discipling his followers further solidified the connection between Jesus' community and the family structure (Gehring 2004, 46–47).[88]

Related to this is the ancient Greek *oikos* (household) structure, which also played a role in shaping the identity of the early church. Scholars have observed how central this structure was to the early Christian community (Stegeman and Stegeman 1995, 277; Gehring 2004, 94); the early custom was gathering "house-to-house," likely in private homes owned by Christian benefactors (Blue 1994, 124–25, 189). The *oikos* structure facilitated the church retaining an integral connection with the culture:

> With the integration of the "house" into the church, a very important principle became fruitful for missional outreach. The believers remain ... in the world and consider themselves obligated to the historical and created social stations through which life in this world is sustained ... (1 Cor 7:20–24). Because they live together *with* other people *within* the social order and according to its rules and yet they live *differently* than the others, they become witnesses—through their words, their life, and their suffering. (Goppelt 1962, 60–61; quoted in Gehring 2004, 228).

The Greek *oikos* and Mediterranean family structures served therefore as two complementary cultural structures used by the early church to express its theological identity as the family and household of God.

To this I would add that the reason for such a rejection is that Israelite religion had departed from God's law and become syncretistic, accepting unlawful religious practices from the nations and mixing, or assimilating, them into its own religious system.

88 Jesus' understanding of the church as the true family of God "was illustrated all the more clearly because he was often in or in front of the house of Peter as he taught on the subject. Everyone could see how he and the disciples lived together. Jesus not only spoke theoretically of this new family of God; he called real people together and he 'lived among them.' Nowhere was this more evident than in the house of Peter at Capernaum" (Gehring 2004, 47–48).

A third contemporary social structure which shaped the church was the *religious voluntary association*. There were voluntary associations of various kinds (religious and nonreligious), but the voluntary *religious* association was a part of a broader cultural trend at that time in which people, disenchanted with traditional religions (whether Jewish or Greco-Roman), formed voluntary groups seeking nontraditional forms of religion (e.g., Qumran, Jewish synagogues, Greco-Roman mystery cults, etc.; cf. Banks 1980, 17–20; Ascough 2002).

The early churches planted by Paul and the apostles resembled such associations; and therefore, "Paul's communities must be seen in retrospect as part of a wider movement towards spontaneous association of individuals in society, and as a parallel development to the religious fellowships that were growing in popularity within Judaism and Hellenism during that period" (Banks 1980, 22). By gathering in ways which resembled other voluntary gatherings outside traditional religious structures, the early churches were in a form which was culturally recognizable and even familiar.[89]

Two other contemporary social structures which the New Testament authors drew upon to describe the identity of the New Testament church were the *polis* (city-state) and the idea of a *universal brotherhood/commonwealth*. The church is sometimes imaged as a heavenly *polis* (Phil 1:27; 3:20; Acts 23:1) or heavenly Jerusalem (Gal 4:26; Heb 11:10; 12:22–23; 13:14; Rev 21:2), and various metaphors for the church can be seen to have political dimensions, such as body of Christ, temple of God, and ekklēsia (Stegeman and Stegeman 1995, 286–87).

The concept of *universal brotherhood/commonwealth*, on the other hand, was a social concept that transcended the polis. This ideal emerged in the culture of the time as a vision for a kind of worldwide community which would unite different kinds of people together as one. Such an ideal has clear resonances with the New Testament vision of the church as a universal community and a new humanity (Banks 1980, 15–16).

The Mediterranean family, the oikos, the voluntary religious association, the polis, and the universal brotherhood—these are all examples of contemporary social structures which influenced the identity and cultural shape of the New Testament church. The church cannot be reduced to any one of these social structures, but rather includes elements from all of them in its theological expression of community, which made the church an attractive community in the first-century world:

> This means that, psychologically speaking, Paul's approach [to Christian community] had a decided advantage over its first century competitors, since it offered so much more than any of them and offered things which elsewhere could only be found by adhering to more than one religious group. (Banks 1980, 49)

---

89 As Gehring says, "The Christians also chose a socially and legally accepted form for their religious assemblies. In particular, the example of the mystery cults illustrates 'how natural it would have been in those days for others in society to view and to accept the Christians as another religious association'" (2004, 291).

Such a holistic combination of cultural forms of community was not likely an intentional missional strategy (Banks 1980, 49–50)—though inspiration of the Spirit certainly played a role. However, as the apostles planted and developed churches, they naturally drew upon the variety of cultural resources within that context, resulting in a robust and culturally rich idea of community.

Cultural congruence can be observed in both Israel and in the church. But the early church did not simply conform and assimilate to the culture of either Palestinian Judaism or Greco-Roman society (or even a combination of the two), but expressed its identity in countercultural ways that challenged, critiqued, and transformed elements from the surrounding cultures, introducing an element of divergence.

Cultural Divergence

The New Testament church diverged from its context in a variety of ways, and one example is in the area of ethics. The early church clearly challenged the prevailing ethics of Greco-Roman society in areas such as sexuality, temple prostitution, and fair treatment of slaves.[90] Jesus challenged aspects of the prevailing Jewish ethical standards related to ceremonial cleansing (Matt 15:1–20), Sabbath observance (Matt 12:1–8), and eating with known "sinners" (Luke 6:29–32). In the early Christian movement, when Christ-following Jews ate with their Gentile brothers in Christ, they broke with prevailing Jewish culture of complete separation from the Gentiles, a profound development for the nature of the church (Acts 10; Gal 2:11–14).

Another example of cultural divergence is the way Jesus employed the Mediterranean family structure to counterculturally subvert the values of loyalty to natural family. In making his disciples a surrogate family, Jesus reconstructed their social identity around himself, with loyalty to Jesus taking precedence over natural family ties. As in Muslim cultures today, such a notion would have been profoundly countercultural and shocking in the first-century Jewish context (Hellerman 2009, 64, 71; France 2007, 330; cf. Matt 8:21–22; Luke 9:59–62; 12:51–53; 14:25–27).

The use of *oikos* structures also reflect cultural divergence, as they were not simply adopted wholesale, but were also adapted and transformed, as seen in the household (*oikos*) codes, which reflect countercultural relationships between husbands and wives, masters and slaves (Eph 5:22–6:9; Col 3:18–4:1). The equality and unity in the church regardless of ethnic group and social class challenged the hierarchy of the traditional oikos (cf. Gal 3:28; Eph 3:28–29; Col 3:11)—even slaves and barbarians, normally at the bottom of the hierarchy, are elevated to equal status in Christ (Col 3:11; Phlm 16–17; Gehring 2004, 294).

The voluntary religious association is another example of a familiar structure which enabled the church to both "fit in" culturally and to distinguish itself,

---

90 I am grateful to Craig Ott for sharing this insight with me.

"simultaneously establish[ing] a sense of place within local culture or society while also forming a basis from which to assert distinctiveness and even preeminence (for the group or its God)" (Harland 2003, 12). An outsider would have seen the church as a very *peculiar* voluntary association, a group opposed to the Roman pantheon which "insisted that only their god and no one else's was deserving of recognition or honor" (ibid.). Like the family and the oikos structures, the voluntary religious association enabled churches to develop an identity that was both familiar *and* unique—both at home in the culture and yet distinct from it.

A final point of divergence to note is the church's choice of the word ekklēsia rather than *sunagoge* to denote church gatherings, indicating a growing awareness that the Christian communities were distinct from normal Jewish gatherings. In a variety of ways, the New Testament church transformed first-century cultural forms in a mixture of convergence and divergence.

The Problem and Presence of Syncretism

As in Old Testament Israel, syncretism was a danger for the New Testament church (Moreau 2000, 924). Paul warns Gentile believers against syncretism when he calls them to flee idolatry (1 Cor 10:14–22). The warning to believers being "unequally yoked together with unbelievers" (2 Cor 6:14) likely spoke against participating in the Greco-Roman and mystery cults: "The Corinthian believers must not be joined with the Corinthian 'unbelievers' in the cultic life of the city, but rather 'come out' from among them" (Barnett 1997, 342, 345).

Not only Gentiles, but also Jews, were in danger of syncretism. The letter to the Hebrews likely addressed Jewish believers who were in danger of retaining Jewish heritage and religious institutions rendered obsolete by Christ and new covenant faith. Paul's letter to the Galatians contains strong warnings against syncretistic beliefs and practices that threaten the essence of his gospel: specifically, combining belief in Jesus with the contemporary Jewish belief and practice that justification before God required circumcision and law-keeping (Gal 5:2–6); adding these to biblical faith resulted in "a different gospel" (Gal 1:6).

The letter to the Colossians addresses syncretisms Jewish and pagan. Paul warns the Colossian church against mixing their faith in Christ with any Jewish or Gentile elements that would subvert or downgrade the sufficiency and supremacy of Christ (Col 2:8–11), whether Jewish rituals or various superstitions (Col 2:16–29). The danger of syncretism motivated Paul to earnestly pray for and exhort believers to distinguish truth from man-made error in maturing faith in Christ (Col 2:1–7).

The New Testament warnings against syncretism, as in the Old Testament, are rooted in the expectation for God's people to "be holy, as I am holy" (1 Pet 1:16). While Israel lived as a territorial nation under a detailed legal system, the church lives as "strangers and aliens" scattered throughout the nations, displaying God's holy character and the Spirit's sanctifying presence in their conduct among the lost (1 Pet 1:1; 2:11–12). The syncretism of Christ and Belial, of light and darkness, have no place within the church, God's holy temple (2 Cor 6:14–7:1).

Authentic Contextualization of the Church

The three themes outlined express biblical principles for contextualizing the church in such a way that preserves its distinct identity and avoids the danger of syncretism. Each of these three biblical themes have been reflected in evangelical discussions of indigeneity, inculturation, and contextualization.

Missiological Concerns for Clarifying Authentic Expressions of the Church

Indigenous church advocates recognized the danger of an "absolute indigeneity" in which the church is so native that it loses its Christian identity. The goal should never be complete indigeneity, which "would in appearance, functioning and meaning be no different than the rest of culture" (Kraft 1979, 88–89). The adjustment to culture involved in indigenization "does not have to be pleasing to that culture, but it does have to be understandable…. The exclusiveness of the Nicene position, for example, must have been highly displeasing to Gnostic culture, but it was beautifully clear" (McGavran 1975, 55). The *desirable goal* of truly indigenous churches is clearly distinguished from the *undesirable outcome* of churches that have so conformed to the culture that they have lost their true biblical identity.

Inculturation proponents likewise have sought to distinguish authentic from inauthentic expressions of the church, in terms of distinguishing inculturation from "culturalism":

> Inculturation of a religion into many cultures assumes that the religion in question *retains its essential identity*. If a religion is radically transformed through its contact with a culture, then we are not speaking of inculturation, but of culturalism—the absolutization of culture, or at any rate, in a given instance, the triumph of culture. (Shorter 1999, 42; emphasis added)

While the use of "religion" is somewhat ambiguous, it is clear that the danger of "culturalism" is essentially the same as "total indigeneity." Michael Gallagher elaborates further, advocating for a balance:

> Sometimes the term "inculturation" is so identified with a positive Incarnation-emphasis that it can come to mean the entry into cultures without much reference to the necessity of transformation. This can be due to a lack of "critical analysis" and an "over-estimation of culture." It seems wiser when "inculturation" is taken to include both these horizons— of Incarnation and Redemption, of insertion and conversion. (1996, 178)

The danger to be avoided is of the church being swallowed up and transformed by the culture rather than being a redemptive, transformational presence in culture.

Missiological discussions of contextualization have also reflected this concern by distinguishing contextualization from *syncretism*. The danger to be avoided is that "the human situation and culture of peoples so dominate the inquiry that God's revelation through the Bible will be diminished" (Gilliland 2000, 227). The term *syncretism*, some have observed, can be used as a "power word" by those in the West to exercise domination over others while remaining oblivious to the syncretism in the Western church, since "No church in any culture is free of the accretions of culture, and none of us is as objective in seeing syncretism in our own culture as we like to think we are" (Moreau 2000, 924; Heideman 1997, 37, 48). But this calls not for avoiding the concept altogether, but rather greater humility, clearer biblical thinking, and multicultural hermeneutical communities that can facilitate a broader application of the concept to *all* cultures, including that of the missionary (Moreau 2000, 924).

Tippet defines syncretism as "the union of two opposite forces, beliefs, systems or tenets so that the united form is a new thing, neither one nor the other (1975, 17). While some see syncretism as a neutral concept that can be positive or negative (Schineller 1992, 50), its more common usage is of a negative phenomenon which is to be distinguished from the positive phenomenon of authentic contextualization (Tippet 1975, 27; Lausanne Committee for World Evangelization 1978, 28–29; Hiebert 1985, 185; Sanchez 1998; Moreau 2000, 924; Ott and Wilson 2011, Loc. 2479).

While sometimes limited to compromise with only the "essential core of the gospel," syncretism is better understood in terms of compromise to "the whole of Scripture," since "the entire biblical corpus and all that Scripture is intending to communicate is essential, basic, and critical" (2010, 115). In other words, syncretism is a subversion of Christian beliefs by an unbiblical worldview (Hiebert and Menses 1995, 253).

Syncretism can result in "cultural captivities" that subvert the biblical nature of the church:

> If the church today loses its battle against being a religious club or a corporation, it will be or it is in danger of becoming just another human organization captive to its times. If the church wants to reach the city, it must first be the church in the biblical sense of that term—a place where Christ is in the midst and the Holy Spirit is present in holiness and power. (ibid., 349–50)

Cultural structures are not merely neutral matter for the expression of the church; they can also reflect unbiblical beliefs and values that can potentially undermine the biblical nature of the church.

Missiological thinking on indigenization, inculturation, and contextualization reflects and confirms the biblical concerns in the relationship between God's people and their cultural context. The desirable goal is legitimate indigeneity/inculturation/contextualization, and the undesirable outcome is total indigeneity/culturalism/syncretism.

What Contextualization Is Not: Avoiding Opposite Errors

One way of clarifying the parameters of authentic contextualization is by defining what contextualization is *not*. Authentic contextualization can be distinguished from two errors: (1) presenting the gospel and biblical truth in "foreign clothing," and (2) the inclusion of elements of the local culture which "alter or eliminate aspects of the message upon which the integrity of the gospel depends" (Hesselgrave and Rommen 1989, 1).

But the dangers are more subtle still. Legitimate or "critical" contexetualization avoids two trends that characterized earlier eras in missions: *non-contextualization* and *uncritical contextualization*. Non-contextualization, dominant in the 1800–1950s era of Protestant missions and associated with colonialism, is the complete rejection of traditional non-Christian cultures, which can result in a culturally foreign church as well as syncretism with old beliefs/practices going "underground" when not addressed by the theology of the missionary (Hiebert 1987, 104, 106). In the mid-twentieth century, anti-colonialist reaction to non-contextualization emerged, leading to uncritical (or "naïve") contextualization, characterized by an uncritical affirmation of traditional non-Christian cultures, resulting in a syncretism with unbiblical values and compromise of the gospel (ibid., 108–9; cf. Hiebert 1985, 152–56).[91]

What Contextualization Is: The Positive Goals of Contextualization

Naming the dangers to avoid is an important starting place, but it is not yet sufficient for clarifying authentic, biblical contextualization. Unless the positive goals are specified, contextualization is reduced to a precarious balancing act of avoiding dangers rather than a positive, substantive pursuit of a biblical goal. Simply put, authentic contextualization, in the first instance, is communication of the gospel and truth of Christ in a way that is faithful to divine revelation and meaningful to its context (Sanchez 1998, 332–33; Hesselgrave and Rommen 1989, 200; Eitel 1998, 312).

An authentic contextualization of the *church*, then, must be both *faithful* to biblical ecclesiology and *meaningful* within its sociocultural context. Contextualization of the church begins with meaningful and relevant communication of biblical truth, including the gospel and the nature of the church. Furthermore, the symbols, signs, and way of life adopted by the church continue to communicate—both to the members of the church and to the outside world—important things about the nature and identity of this community, the kind of people they are, and the character of the God they worship.

---

[91] In some ways, Dyrness' reaction against evangelical contextualization in *Insider Jesus* echoes aspects of the anti-colonialist reaction against the era of "non-contextualization." An anti-colonialist thrust can be detected in Dyrness' argument (colonialism is mentioned in one form or another a full twenty-five times); and he is mostly affirming, and rarely critical, of the value of human religions. Thus, while Dyrness attempts to move beyond contextualization, his proposal may be actually hearkening back to an earlier, reactionary era that misses the more balanced perspective of "critical contextualization," which is neither totally rejecting nor totally affirming of cultures/religions.

However, contextualizing the church is more than communication; it also involves the creation and formation of a body of believers within a cultural context (Hiebert and Meneses 1995, 370). Therefore, the communication model of contextualization as "authentic" and "meaningful" communication should be supplemented with additional perspectives.

One of these perspectives is Hiebert's model of *critical contextualization*. Rather than wholesale rejection of culture (non-contextualization) or wholesale affirmation of culture (uncritical contextualization), the goal is a critical, biblical response by the indigenous church to the symbols, beliefs, and practices of its culture. Not something the missionary does for the church, critical contextualization is undertaken by the indigenous church as an act of "self-theologizing," though the missionary can facilitate this process and contribute in constructive ways.

Hiebert envisions a process whereby the indigenous church first carefully analyzes the function and meaning of a particular cultural/religious issue or form, and then studies the Scriptures for relevant biblical teaching, which acts as a grid through which the church critically assesses how it will engage this particular form (1987, 109–10). The indigenous church can elect to preserve, reject, or modify the cultural form, substitute it with something from the Christian heritage from another culture, or create a totally new Christian symbol (ibid., 110). Careful attention must be given to the complex and varied ways that form and meaning are related in different cultural symbols, in order to determine whether the symbols can be appropriately used or repurposed with Christian meanings (ibid., 108–9).

Each particular local church has the authority to make its own contextual decisions, but they should not do so in isolation from the global church, which provides a multicultural hermeneutical community as a check that can illumine cultural blind spots (Hiebert 1987, 110). Therefore, authentic contextualization of the church should be understood as *an intentional, ongoing, critical engagement of the indigenous church with their local culture under the authority of Scripture in conversation with the global church.*

Another perspective which helps to clarify the nature of authentic contextualization of the church is Andrew Walls' indigenizing and pilgrim principles (1982; cf. Bosch 1991, 455; Ott and Wilson 2011, Loc. 2479). These two principles are inherent in the gospel, creating a tension within which legitimate contextualization of the church takes place. The *indigenizing principle* is rooted in the fact that Christ accepts us as we are—along with our cultural and social identities and situations—which makes the church "a place to feel at home" (Walls 1982, 97).

The *pilgrim principle* is rooted in the fact that Christ accepts people "in order to transform them into what He wants them to be" (ibid., 98). The effect is that

> the Christian inherits the pilgrim principle, which whispers to him that he has no abiding city and warns him that to be faithful to Christ will put him out of step with his society; for that society never existed, in East or West, ancient time or modern, which could absorb the word of Christ painlessly into its system. (ibid., 98–99)

Taken together, these two principles have important implications for the church's familial and societal relationships:

> The Christian has all the relationships in which he was brought up, and has them sanctified by Christ who is living in them. But he has also an entirely new set of relationships, with other members of the family of faith into which he has come, and whom he must accept, with all their group relations (and "disrelations") on them, just as God has accepted him with his. Every Christian has a dual nationality, and has a loyalty to the faith family which links him to those in interest groups opposed to that which he belongs by nature. (ibid., 99)

That is, the indigenizing and pilgrim principles *affirm* and *sanctify* the cultural identity of the church, as well as *transform* and *transcend* it through membership in the body of Christ. Walls fleshes this out in an important passage, worth quoting at length, which draws together the biblical theology of the church and the cultural contexts in which the church exists:

> The Christian is given *an adoptive past*. He is linked to the people of God in all generations (like him, members of the faith family), and most strangely of all, to the whole history of Israel, the curious continuity of the race of the faithful from Abraham. By this means, the history of Israel is part of Church history, and all Christians of whatever nationality, are landed by adoption with several millennia of someone else's history, with a whole set of ideas, concepts and assumptions which do not necessarily square with the rest of their cultural inheritance; and the Church in every land, of whatever race and type of society, has this same adoptive past by which it needs to interpret the fundamentals of the faith. The adoption into Israel becomes a "universalizing" factor, bringing Christians of all cultures and ages together through a common inheritance, lest any of us make the Christian faith such a place to feel at home that no one else can live there; and bringing everyone's society some sort of outside reference. (ibid.)

Faith in Christ not only brings us into the global body of Christ, but it also gives us a new history, bringing us into the identity-defining narrative of the people of God discussed in chapter 1. The biblical narrative of the church is therefore crucial for putting all churches, in all their cultural diversity, onto a level playing field, placing every local church into the community and story of the people of God, from Abraham to Israel to the church. This fact, Walls reminds us, means that every church will be out of step with its culture to *some* degree, while simultaneously being indigenous to that culture.[92]

---

[92] Duerkson and Dyrness critique Walls' indigenous/pilgrim principles for two reasons. First, they argue that these principles assume "that the church somehow exists above and apart from culture. Instead, we contend that the church can never transcend its culture. … even those churches that have sought to counter culture do so using existing cultural categories!" Second, they argue that the relationship between church and gospel/church is more complex than simply avoiding two poles (2019, 59-60).

However, Walls is not seeking to simplify the church's relationship to culture in terms of two opposing poles; rather, he is highlighting two paradoxical realities that are in tension, two impulses which by themselves could lead to unhelpful extremes, but held in tension, balance out one another. Furthermore, it is far from evident that Walls is assuming

INSIDER CHURCH

Critical contextualization and the indigenizing/pilgrim principles provide appropriate capstones to a framework for an authentic contextualization of the church. We can sum up authentic contextualization of the church as follows: *Following the biblical patterns of contextualization of Israel and the church, authentic contextualization avoids the twin dangers of cultural foreignness and syncretism by faithfully reflecting the biblical nature and purpose of the church in ways which are meaningful to the local context; which critically engage with and transform the beliefs, practices, and symbols within the culture; and which reflect the indigenous-pilgrim character of the people of God.*

We have now defined the meaning and parameters of authentic, biblical contextualization of the church, which give guidelines for the way the biblical church takes shape in and transforms its cultural context. This provides a crucial part of the framework for assessing various strategies and approaches for multiplying churches in Muslim cultures, such as the insider paradigm.

Having outlined the biblical nature of the church and the way the church takes shape in cultural contexts, it is time to take a fresh look at the insider paradigm in light of the biblical vision in order to assess how it both helps and hinders the development of biblical churches in Muslim cultures.

---

the church "exists above and apart from culture" or can "transcend its culture." Walls' indigenizing principle clearly affirms the cultural rootedness of the church. The pilgrim principle, does not imply that the church can "transcend" its culture, but rather that *every biblical church has at least two points of reference outside its culture which makes it, to some degree, out of step with its culture, qualifying its indigeneity.* The two points of reference highlighted by Walls are (1) believers in the universal body of Christ from other cultures, and (2) the "adoptive past" of the history of Israel and the people of God in Scripture. These outside points of reference provide an important reminder and check against the danger of a full, absolute indigeneity.

PART TWO

*Toward a Fresh
Appraisal of
Insider Church*

CHAPTER FOUR

Clarifying Insider "Ekklēsia"

In the middle of the COVID-19 lockdown, Ahmad was devouring the Word. By government orders, we were confined to our homes, so we started studying the Bible together on WhatsApp calls. Despite the poor Internet quality, Ahmad persevered, discovered new truths about God, and committed himself applying and sharing the story. As we were finishing, Ahmad interjected, "Hey, next time I need your advice on some things. How do Christians pray? And how do I fast? And should I stop going to the mosque? And how do I talk about my faith to people?"

Ahmad was wrestling with how his newfound faith should take shape for him in his Muslim milieu. The way that cross-cultural workers answer such questions—the advice given, the options presented—is shaped by our assumptions about what is (and what is not) helpful for disciples and emerging churches as they grow to maturity and fruitfulness. It is also shaped by our underlying theology of the nature of the church and how the church takes shape in various cultures.

The insider paradigm includes a particular set of assumptions and implications regarding the nature of the church. Some of these positively and creatively express the biblical nature of the church, while others undermine and fall short of it. A responsible approach to multiplying biblical churches among Muslims ought to learn from both the strengths and weaknesses of the insider paradigm.

To do so, however, requires an accurate understanding of the particular ecclesiological assumptions and implications of the insider paradigm in the first place. Too often the debate over insider movements has been driven by mischaracterization and straw-men arguments, increasing misunderstanding and suspicion and entrenching people more firmly into their sides. A better way forward is to recognize that as brothers and sisters in the body of Christ and fellow laborers in the Lord's field, we ought to take the time and effort to listen and understand one another charitably and accurately. Then we will better understand whether we actually disagree, and if so, where precisely the points of disagreement are, enabling us to discern potential pathways toward mutual understanding and consensus. This is the intended spirit and purpose of this chapter (and the next) in describing and evaluating the vision of the church in the insider paradigm.

The insider paradigm broadly supports and affirms "insider" identity and movements, which typically refer to Jesus' followers retaining or remaining in the "socio-religious" identity of their birth—i.e., identifying as "Muslim followers of Jesus." In addition, the insider paradigm has often supported ongoing participation in key Muslim rituals, modifying and reinterpreting such participation in a way that is viewed as compatible with a vital faith in Christ (e.g., ritual prayer, mosque worship, Qur'an reverence, confessing prophethood of Muhammad).

In this chapter, I attempt to outline, as straightforwardly and fairly as possible, the ecclesiological outlook of the insider paradigm as described by its chief architects and leading thinkers in their prolific writings.[93] Insider advocates come from a variety of ecclesial backgrounds and perspectives, and they do not all agree on every aspect of ecclesiology.[94] However, decades of collaboration have given rise to a recognizable ministry paradigm, and this paradigm includes a particular set of commitments and perspectives on the nature of the church—a vision of ekklēsia for insiders—that challenges traditional perspectives in significant ways.[95] The present chapter describes this vision, while the next evaluates it in light of the biblical vision of the church.

The particular vision of ekklēsia in the insider paradigm will be outlined from the perspective of the following key issues, which have been addressed previously, and the next chapter will revisit each one to highlight its strengths and shortcomings.

---

[93] It is important to state that not every missionary who claims the insider banner practices the "insider" paradigm in ways which are consistent with the way the paradigm is articulated by its leading missiologists.

[94] I'm grateful to both Don Little and Kevin Higgins for alerting me to this in personal communication. As just one example, Duerkson and Dyrness, authors of *Seeking Church*, hail from the Mennonite Brethren and PCUSA churches, respectively (2019, 2).

[95] *Understanding Insider Movements* is a case in point, a testimony to this collaboration and a standard resource for understanding the insider paradigm. Talman himself freely speaks of the "insider paradigm" in chap. 2 of *UIM*, entitled "The Historical Development of the Insider Paradigm."

Each of the following categories represents an important dimension of the nature of the church, and each provides a window into the unique contours of insider ekklēsia:

- biblical story and themes
- core essence of the church
- local and universal church
- visible and invisible church
- attributes and marks of the church
- relationship between the church and salvation
- relationship between the church and the world

Biblical Narratives and Themes for Insider Church

The insider paradigm highlights various themes and parts of the biblical narrative to undergird its vision of ekklēsia for insiders. The particular themes and passages emphasized, and the way they are applied to insider movements, are foundational to the insider perspective on the nature of the church.

Old Testament: Inside and Outside the People of God

There are a few Old Testament themes that insider advocates appeal to in developing an ekklēsia for insiders. Charles Kraft argued that the Old Testament people of God, in the form of people "born involuntarily into extended kinship groups," is a more suitable form for Muslims than the "voluntary association" form of the Greco-Roman church (1979, 115). Woodberry, on the other hand, suggested that the theme of "the faithful remnant," first in Israel and then among the nations, holds potential for illuminating insider ekklēsia (2007, 26).

One commonly referenced theme relates to Old Testament figures who seem to worship the true God without joining the covenant community of Israel (Talman 2015c, Loc. 4583). The most cited individual is Naaman the Syrian, who converts to belief in *Yahweh* as the one true God, and yet returns to his homeland having received pardon (or permission) from Elisha for bowing before a pagan god when accompanying his master to the temple (2 Kings 5; Baeq 2010; Talman 2015c, Loc. 4596–4636).

Other examples cited are Melchizedek (Gen 14:18–20; Heb 7:1–10), Abimelech (Gen 20), Jethro (Exod 18), and the queen of Sheba (1 Kings 10:1–13; Talman 2015c, Loc. 4583), considered Old Testament precedents of believers who worship God but remain inside their "socio-religious" community.[96] As such, they are seen as precursors to the "non-proselyte conversion" in the New Testament, as well as a paradigm to a church of insiders following Jesus within Muslim identity and community.

---

96 See Harley Talman's "The Old Testament and Insider Movements" in *Understanding Insider Movements*, which focuses on the issue of an Old Testament theology of religions and non-proselyte conversion (2015c).

These Old Testament themes, however, are not as significant in the insider paradigm as the several New Testament themes used to undergird insider ekklēsia.

Insider Church and the Kingdom

No theme is more pervasive in the insider paradigm than the theme of the kingdom of God. In many ways, a theology of the kingdom, and the kingdom parables, provide the overarching biblical and theological framework for the insider paradigm as a whole and for its vision of ekklēsia in particular.

Insider advocates see the theology of the kingdom as putting "church" in proper perspective. Jesus did not come to found the institutional "Christian church" or start a new religion; he came to inaugurate the kingdom, an expansive reality which transcends the established church and can spread in the midst of non-Christian religious communities.

The theology and parables of the kingdom are seen as reframing a traditional view of the church, offering a new "kingdom paradigm" of church planting. Whereas the traditional paradigm is framed by "conflict of religions" and denominationally "separatist" ecclesiology, a "kingdom paradigm" understands the kingdom to transcend denominations and religious communities: "The Kingdom of God includes the Church, but is bigger than the Church. The Kingdom refers to the whole range of God's exercise of His reign and rule in the universe. This includes religions" (Higgins 2009, 87; cf. Taylor 2015, Loc. 4371).

The parables of the kingdom—especially the yeast in the dough—shift the focus from "church planting" to "kingdom sowing" in the insider paradigm (Travis and Woodberry 2010). The former represents a more Western, organizational, and institutional concept of the church and the latter expresses a more dynamic, organic view of the church:

> The church, when understood from a Kingdom perspective, is not so much a congregation, as it is *a movement, a life, an organism, a seed*. According to Jesus' metaphors, the church lives and grows amidst all sorts of other things: weeds, rocks, and dough. (Higgins 2015, Loc.5404, emphasis added)

This organic view of the church, shaped by the imagery of the parables, is extended to imply that Jesus himself expected, and taught us to expect, an ekklēsia which could take shape "within the religio-cultural world of the Muslim community" and would "include Islamic places and patterns of worship" (ibid., Loc. 5421).

This understanding and application of the "kingdom" theme will be evaluated in the next chapter, but there is no mistaking that it is a hugely influential component of the biblical framework for an insider church, reframing the nature of ekklēsia as a community that can take shape within, and spread among, non-Christian "socio-religious" communities. Another critical building block for insider ecclesiology is the Jesus-movement as it unfolds among the Jews and Gentiles in the book of Acts.

The Jerusalem Church as First Insider Church

For insider advocates, the first church was an "insider church." The first Jewish believers in Jesus did not intend to form a separate religious community, but rather formed a sect within Judaism called "the Way" (cf. Acts 9:2; 19:9). While they gathered with other Christ-followers, they still identified as Jews, followed Jewish laws, and continued in temple prayers at a time when temple leadership was officially opposed to faith in Jesus (Higgins 2015b, Loc. 5623). For insider advocates, this provides a clear biblical precedent for contemporary insiders who gather together with other believers and yet continue to pray in the mosque and identify as Muslims (Travis 2000, 53).

This understanding leads to a reframing of the nature of ekklēsia as "a movement within the social and religious life of the Jewish people" that "took structural or formal expression as it met in separate homes or public gatherings *and* as its members continued in the Temple and the synagogue" (Higgins 2006, 118; emphasis in original; cf. 2009, 78). Thus, "They did not cease to be the church in the Temple worship, and they did not cease to be Jewish in the home meeting" (ibid.). The dual identity in the first church is taken as a basis for affirming the legitimacy of insider ekklēsia which combines ecclesial and "Muslim" identity, believing fellowships and mosque worship, as potentially reconcilable.

In addition to finding support for insider ekklēsia in the early Jesus-movement among Jews in Jerusalem, the insider paradigm finds support in the Gentile church, particularly in light of the Jerusalem Council in Acts 15.

Insiders, the Gentiles, and the Jerusalem Council

Acts 15 plays a critical role in the biblical framework for insider ekklēsia, and many parallels are drawn between the Jerusalem Council and the contemporary insider controversy. The inclusion of the Gentiles in God's people was a new, surprising work of God initially resisted by the church, but eventually accepted through Spirit-led consensus and consultation. Similarly, insider advocates contend, it is important to recognize that God is doing something new and surprising in our day to include Muslims in the church "*as Muslims.*" Just as the apostles did not require the Gentile believers to be circumcised and keep the law and therefore become Jews, so today the church should not require Muslim followers of Jesus to become "Christians" or adopt a "Christian identity." If Gentiles are able to be saved and follow Jesus by faith *as Gentiles*, without becoming Jews, then Muslims can be saved and follow Jesus by faith *as Muslims,* without "becoming Christians."[97]

The result of the Jerusalem Council is a "bilateral ecclesiology" for Jews and Gentiles (Talman 2015, Loc. 6093)—or "multilateral ecclesiology" for all nations (Talman 2015, Loc. 6109)—with a Jewish church following the Jewish law and a

---

[97] Talman sees this as the New Testament counterpart to the "non-proselyte conversion" in the Old Testament discussed previously (Talman 2015c, "Old Testament and Insider Movements," Loc. 4780).

Gentile church free from it. However, the fact that the council required Gentiles to follow a limited number of Jewish laws for the sake of unity with the Jewish church implies that insider fellowships may eventually need to adjust their practice of church in order to express unity with the wider body of Christ (Woodberry 2015a, Loc. 5978–5996).

Thus both the Jewish Jerusalem movement and the Gentile movement in Acts are taken as paradigmatic for insider ekklēsia, albeit in different ways. The early Jewish church is viewed as a paradigm for the *positive* idea of ekklēsia remaining in its natural "socio-religious" culture and community, while the Gentile church (and the Jerusalem Council decision) is taken to be a paradigm for the *negative* idea that biblical ekklēsia does *not* require adopting a foreign "socio-religious" identity and culture.

The paradigms in Acts of the early Jewish and Gentile movements are an important part of the biblical framework for insider ekklēsia, and the following chapter offers a critical assessment of their legitimacy. Now I turn to another important New Testament theme that undergirds insider ekklēsia, which is the theme of the household/oikos.

Insiders in Household/Oikos Churches

The concept of "house/household" in the New Testament (oikos in Greek) has particular relevance in shaping insider ekklēsia. Drawing upon the theme of household conversions in the book of Acts, the insider paradigm promotes an "oikos model" of church in which the family network itself *becomes* the church. This is set in contrast to the "Western aggregate model" of church, in which ekklēsia takes the form of a conglomeration of individual believers gathered into a new society separate from (and potentially a threat to) existing family networks. With minimal disruption to the natural family, the household/oikos model enables new believers to remain within their community network, thus facilitating a potential insider movement, as well as fulfilling the Abrahamic promise of blessing for all families of the earth (Lewis 2007, 75–76; 2010, 34).

As later discussion shows, the oikos theme and family networks play a significant role in insider ekklēsia in ways that both contributes to and falls short of the full biblical nature of the church. In addition, the insider paradigm also draws upon the body of Christ theme in its vision for insider ekklēsia.

Insiders and the Body of Christ

The "body of Christ" theme plays an important role expressing insider ekklēsia that is outside the existing Christian community and inside Muslim community and identity. Insider advocates highlight the way the "body of Christ" focuses on the spiritual connectedness of believers to Christ and to one another rather than membership in a particular ecclesial body (Travis et al. 2006, 124; Higgins 2006, 118–19; Duerkson and Dyrness 2019, 117). Membership in the body of Christ does not require "joining a church," identifying as "Christian," or rejecting one's membership in the Muslim *umma*. Rather, it is a spiritual identity effected by God when one believes in Jesus, and it can be expressed in fellowship with other believers as well as in other social and religious spheres of daily life (Higgins 2006, 118–19). These local insider expressions of the body of Christ can develop visible forms and structures for their community life, and their identity as members of Christ's body does not exclude membership and participation in another religious community (Higgins 2006, 118–19). The body of Christ, like the kingdom of God, transcends religious communities (Travis and Woodberry 2015).

Other New Testament Themes

A number of other biblical themes are occasionally referenced in the insider paradigm. One is the church as a *holy community of the Spirit*, which highlights "restored and restructured relationships" in the church that attract the outside world, without dividing the church from the world (Duerkson and Dyrness 2019, 120). Another theme is the *new creation*, which, along with the kingdom, is taken as central to God's purposes for the world, while the church is secondary and instrumental in participating in God's new creation project (Duerkson and Dyrness 2019, 150). The themes of garden, city, and temple can all be traced to a culmination in the new creation, when the church will be transformed into a new, unknown form, which makes all present ecclesial forms and structures provisional and temporary (ibid., 177–85).

The foundation of insider ekklēsia is a particular group of biblical themes and narratives given particular emphasis, interpretation, and application that creates the space for, and even encourages, insider expressions of church. This insider biblical theology, thoroughly evaluated in the next chapter, is foundational in shaping all remaining dimensions of insider ekklēsia discussed below, including the essential identity of insider ekklēsia.

Insiders and the Identity of the Church

The question of the essential identity of the church is at the heart of the insider controversy. If insiders retain the "socio-religious" identity of their Muslim community, then what is the identity of the church, and what sets it apart from the Muslim community? Insider-ministry advocates articulate their answers both negatively and positively—what the church *is* and what it is *not*.

First, insider advocates emphasize that the core essence of the church is not to be found in Western church institutions, traditions, or cultural expressions (Duerkson and Dyrness 2019, 71–72). Some insider advocates avoid using the word "church" in favor of other terms such as "Christ-centered communities" or "biblical ekklēsia" (Travis 1998b, 412; 2012, 241, n. 36). Higgins, who uses the word "church," explains concerns about this English word:

> I am convinced that hidden in the word "church" for many of us are concepts that are not entirely biblical, but are rather identified with our experience of church as independent, isolated, and self-contained congregations. We therefore run the risk of equating that experience with the essence of "church." (2015a, Loc. 5381)

Higgins argues that many people import their own (Western) congregational experience of church, which must be separated from the essence of the biblical church.

Second, the insider paradigm affirms that a Christian "socio-religious" identity is not a part of the core essence of the church. An ekklēsia does not need to identify as "Christian" to distinguish itself from its community, but can indeed retain Muslim "socio-religious" identity (Travis 1998b; Travis 2015a, Loc. 837). The "retaining of social and religious identity" is understood as "not leaving" one's family or religious community in which one was born and raised, but remaining in one's family *and* "socio-religious" community (ibid., Loc. 817–37). "Christian socio-religious identity" then, is clearly excluded from the essential identity of the church.

While insider-ministry advocates affirm that insider movements retain their "socio-religious" identity as Muslims, they also possess an "ecclesial identity," which requires at least three things. First, an ecclesial identity requires a community or fellowship of people who believe and follow Christ—a "Christ-centered community," the key constant for C1-C5 communities in the C-spectrum (1998a, 407; cf. also Parshall 1998, 405; Travis 1998b, 412). Duerkson unpacks this further in his article "Must Insiders Be Churchless?"

> A church, according to the New Testament, is first and foremost a locally identified group of believers who are committed to following Jesus and his commandments, and to doing this together.... A church is, quite fundamentally, a *community* that follows the commands and example of Jesus, including expressions of baptism and communion.... In the New Testament this idea of community is often expressed through kinship language and practices. The church is a family whose members care for each other in familial ways. (2012, 162; emphasis in original)

Duerkson develops further the notion of the church as a community centered on Christ, in terms of a commitment to follow Jesus and his teachings together as a family. This is understood as the essence of the "ecclesial identity" of the church, which is to be distinguished from its "social identity," which they continue to share with their Muslim family and community.

The ecclesial identity of the church for insiders is shaped by the kingdom of God. Rebecca Lewis highlights the essential identity of the church in her comparison between insider movements and church planting movements:

> So the main differences between "insider movements" and "church planting movements" lie in the nature of the "house churches" (pre-existing social networks turning to Christ rather than artificial aggregate groupings) and the social identity

of those involved (retained versus changed). In both movements the churches are not institutionalized, and the people in both movements share *a new spiritual identity as members of the Kingdom of God* and disciples of Jesus Christ. In the case of "insider movements," however, this new spiritual identity is not confused or eclipsed by a new social identity. (2007b, 76, n. 1; cf. Lewis 2015b, Loc. 12528–47; emphasis added)

Insider churches and "CPM" churches differ in form and social identity, while they share an essential identity as members in God's kingdom, which, significantly, does *not* require a new "social identity."

The ecclesial identity of the church is also defined in terms of the body of Christ. Kevin Higgins, in response to Tim Tennent's critique that insider movements fall short of a fully biblical ecclesiology, proposed the following definition of the essence of the church:

> *The Church is the Body of Christ, and the assembly of believers who have been saved by grace through faith.* The Church is therefore a creation of God in Christ through the Holy Spirit. It is not a human organization or institution, although clearly forms and structures do factor in as tangible ways in which this community expresses itself visibly. No human being can "make" a church or join the Church and as such, is called to live out their membership in the Body of Christ, the Church, as a full time lifestyle in every venue of life… . *One's identity as a born again member of the Body can and does overlap with one's identity in other spheres of life, including one's religious life.* (Higgins 2006, 118–19; emphasis in original; cf. 2015c, Loc. 12730)

Higgins' definition continues the insider theme mentioned previously of distinguishing the essence of the church from organizations and institutions, emphasizing the church as the body of Christ, and therefore a creation of God, not man. Rather than people "making/planting" or "joining" the church, it is God who creates the church and incorporates people into it; and human beings are to live out their membership in the world "as a full time lifestyle in every venue of life," an identity which can "overlap" with other identities, such as one's religious identity. Higgins further elaborates a theology of church which creates space for insider expressions of faith:

> I am suggesting here that the biblical definition of "church" does not necessarily refer to a "bounded" or "closed" set social grouping which prevents a member of His Body, the church, from also being a "member" of another social or even religious structure or expression. However, a clarification is needed lest I be misunderstood. On one side, I do see church as a closed set, for only those who are born from above and incorporated by the Spirit into His Body are members of the church! But as such, they are not thereby excluded from living in and among other social and religious structures as yeast in the dough. (Higgins 2006, 118; cf. Higgins 2015c, Loc. 12729)

Higgins argues that the theological boundaries of the body of Christ do not require believers to give up their membership in other social and religious structures; one can have dual membership. The essence of the church is found not in changing social and religious identity, but rather in the spiritual regeneration and incorporation of believers into the body of Christ by the Holy Spirit.

One way the essence of the church has been defined is in terms of the special presence and work of God relating to a particular community in its cultural context. While all social entities emerge through the interaction of individuals to one another, ekklēsia comes into existence when people within a particular cultural context relate to one another and to God in a special way (Duerkson and Dyrness 2019, 71–72). The biblical metaphors that express the nature or "theological ontology" of the church are taken to "express the special way God is present and working in and through these communities, despite their very diverse cultural expressions" (ibid., 108). Therefore, when insiders relate to one another and to God in a particular context in specified ways, ekklēsia "emerges" in that context.

It is clear that the insider paradigm presents particular ways of defining the core essence of the church that include insider communities as expressing the biblical church. These unique perspectives include clearly distinguishing the church from cultural forms and institutions, as well as separating the essence of the church from affiliating with a particular religious identity (Christian, Muslim, etc.). What is highlighted is the presence and work of God in creating the church by regenerating believers and uniting them to Christ's body, a reality which can take place among people who retain their "socio-religious" community identity as Muslims. These perspectives challenge our understanding of the church in positive ways, even as they raise some important concerns, both of which I will take up in the next chapter.

Besides the essence of the church, the insider paradigm has a unique perspective on defining the local church, as seen below.

Insiders in Local Ekklēsia

From the beginning, insider advocates have affirmed the importance of local fellowships or "Christ-centered communities." Some defining features of local ekklēsia and "church life" can be discerned.

The Basic Features of Local Ekklēsia in the Insider Model

The vision for the local church in the insider paradigm can be summarized as follows: a *group of Muslims in a family/social network who commit to following Jesus together while remaining part of the Muslim community as "socio-religious" Muslims.* There are four key components of this definition: (1) belief in and discipleship to Jesus, (2) Muslim family/social networks, (3) ongoing participation in the Muslim community, and (4) commitment to one another.

Fundamental to the local insider church is *commitment to follow Jesus*. Insider fellowships consist of people who believe in and follow "*Isa al-Masih*" (the Muslim name for Jesus)[98] as their Savior and Lord (Higgins 2009, 77; cf. Higgins 2015 Loc. 12730). Various insider advocates and missiologists give firsthand testimony to encountering and experiencing the sincere faith of insiders from such fellowships (e.g., Travis and Travis 2006).

While only those who believe and are saved are part of the body of Christ (Higgins 2015, Loc. 12730), insider advocates do not advocate separating out believers from not-yet-believers, so as not to disrupt the family network by creating a competing "believers-only" community, which leads to the second component: *Muslim social/familial networks* (Lewis 2007, 75–76). Rather than "planting" churches as new social units, insider advocates seek to "implant" churches in Muslim social networks, preserving these networks to allow the gospel to spread in the community along the lines of extended family and close friends (Talman 2004b, 8).

This insider "oikos" model of church is contrasted with the prevailing Western model of church as a "voluntary society," in which "people must be given freedom to join the community of Christ's followers by their own mature decision and should decide for themselves as adults to receive baptism" (Duerkson and Dyrness 2019, 50–53). This model, also known as the "believers church," is argued to have originated in the Anabaptist and free-church movements, having spread throughout the globalized world, and yet has been resisted in more communal-oriented societies, as those in Muslim, Hindu, and Buddhist nations.

The insider paradigm offers an alternative, advocating an "oikos" model that seeks to avoid "aggregate churches" of strangers, extracted from their families in a separate church structure (Lewis 2007, 75; cf. Lewis 2015b, Loc. 12587). In insider churches,

> Families and their pre-existing relational networks *become* the church as the gospel spreads in their midst. The God-given family and clan structures are thereby supported and transformed from unbelieving communities into largely believing communities. Decisions to follow Christ are more communal rather than individual. … The destruction of families and the creation of semi-functional, extracted, new communities of believers-only is thereby avoided, and the gospel continues to flow along preserved relational pathways. (Lewis 2015b, Loc. 12587)

The goal is to preserve, rather than disrupt, existing family networks. This means a different vision of ekklēsia, not as a competing community *outside* the family, but as a transforming community *within* the family:

> In "insider movements," therefore, there is no attempt to form neo-communities of "believers-only" that compete with the family network (no matter how

---

98 *'Isa al-Masih* is "Jesus the Christ" in Islamic Arabic. Arab Christians, however, refer to Jesus as *Yasua' al-Masih;* and most of the Bible translations, liturgy, and Arabic worship songs use *Yasua'*, not *'Isa*. However, some contextualized Bible translations, as well as some contextualized movements in the Arab world, use 'Isa.

contextualized); instead, "insider movements" consist of believers remaining in and transforming their own pre-existing family networks, minimally disrupting their families and communities. These believing families and their relational networks *are* valid local expressions of the Body of Christ, fulfilling all the "one another" care seen in the book of Acts. (Lewis 2007, 75–76)

Preserving and staying within Muslim social and familial networks is a key emphasis in this particular insider model of local ekklēsia.

In addition to seeing the church take shape in existing Muslim familial/social networks, the local ekklēsia for insiders includes a third component: *ongoing membership or participation in Muslim community identity and/or practices.* When Rebecca Lewis distinguishes local "insider" churches from those in "church planting movements," she highlights two key factors: (1) remaining in family networks, and (2) remaining "Muslim" in terms of "social identity" (Lewis 2007, 76, n. 1). When local believing families come to faith and become a local expression of the church, they do not renounce their Muslim identity or call themselves Christian. Rather, these local fellowships continue to see themselves as Muslims and identify as Muslims, remaining an ongoing part of the Muslim community, while also seeing themselves as part of the kingdom of God and the body of Christ (ibid.).

But maintaining a Muslim identity often requires ongoing participation in Muslim ritual practices (Travis 1998a, 411–15). Insider advocates have variously supported and defended one or more of the following practices: (1) ongoing participation in Islamic ritual prayer (*salāt*) at the mosque or at home, substituting biblical content for Qur'anic words (e.g., Uddin 1989, 267–72; Travis 1998b, 414); (2) affirming the full Islamic confession of faith (*shahada*) that there is no god but God and Muhammad is the apostle (*rasul*) of God, reinterpreting Muhammad's apostleship or prophethood in a more limited fashion (cf. Higgins 2004, 120–21; Brown 2006, 131; Talman 2014; Talman 2015b); and (3) retaining some ongoing ritual use of the Qur'an in private or corporate worship, reciting texts that support but do not contradict the Bible (cf. Uddin 1989, 267–72; Travis 1998b, 414; Brown 2006, 131; Travis and Woodberry 2015). Insider advocates do not argue that these are necessary to the insider paradigm, nor are they universal practices by all insiders. However, the insider paradigm has been used to defend these practices as biblically permissible ways for people to follow Jesus while maintaining Muslim identity.

In addition to the above elements, many insider advocates also include *commitment to one another* as a part of the core of the insider model of the local church. This can be seen in a number of the definitions of the local church by insider advocates, such as that of Duerkson:

> A church, according to the New Testament, is first and foremost a locally identified group of believers who are committed to following Jesus and his commandments,

and to doing this together…. A church is, quite fundamentally, a *community* that follows the commands and example of Jesus, including expressions of baptism and communion. (2012, 162; emphasis in original)

Part of the definition of the local church is togetherness and a common commitment to follow Jesus as a community. This same idea is expressed differently by Talman, who adopts a definition of church from the Ryrie Study Bible:

> A local church can be defined as "a group of professing believers in Christ who have been baptized and who have organized themselves for the purpose of doing God's will." … This shows us the need for contextualizing ecclesiology. Following Ryrie, I would maintain that the biblical absolute here is that of "organization to do God's will," but I would suggest that the form of that organization is not mandated. … Hence not only would a "Jesus mosque" be acceptable, but so might a movement within the Muslim community that is not determined by its place of public worship. (2004b, 9, 12, n. 18)

Seeking to distinguish "local church" from a specific worship location, Talman zeroes in on "organization to do God's will" as the essential component of the local church, which implies a common commitment or togetherness of a community of believers. Dyrness likewise says that "an incipient ecclesial form" is present wherever the purposes of Ephesians 4:11–16—members being built up to maturity in Christ—are being fulfilled, even imperfectly (2016, Loc. 2731).

The core of the insider model of the local church is therefore one in which discipleship to Jesus spreads throughout a Muslim family such that the family network itself becomes an expression of the local church, committed to following Jesus together while remaining within the Muslim community as "Muslims." In addition to this core description of the insider model of the local church, it is also important to look at the nature of the gatherings and community life of the local church in the insider paradigm.

Local Church Life in the Insider Model

Local gatherings of insider fellowships have been affirmed in the insider paradigm from the beginning (Travis 1998a, 408; William 2011, 70), and insider advocates provide various profiles and descriptions of these gatherings which illumine the nature of local ekklēsia in the insider paradigm. Local gatherings are often described as focusing on Bible study, prayer, and fellowship (Travis and Travis 2006; Dyrness 2016, Loc. 2731). However, such gatherings are not alternatives to prayers at the mosque, and the level of openness of such gatherings depends upon local circumstances, social skills of the believers, and response of the particular neighborhood (Travis and Woodberry 2015, Loc. 1481)

The majority of insider advocates affirm the importance of gathering together in local ekklēsia, but there are differences as to how structured and organized such gatherings should be. Some insider advocates, such as Rebecca Lewis, have suggested that the gathering of believers need not be planned and structured; it can be spontaneous and organic, as what happens in the course of natural family life. In the "oikos/household" model, believing families "do not need to adopt the meeting and program structures common in Western aggregate churches" (Lewis 2007, 75–76). Since the church simply *is* the family network, then the church can express itself in the context of the natural activities and relationships of family life.

The insider model of local church is depicted as a model of "church-in-process," an "emerging" church which contains aspects of the nature of the church if not yet fully expressing it (Travis 2000, 53, 59; Higgins 2006, 119). This emerging, in-process ecclesiology can be seen in the following definition of local ekklēsia from an insider perspective:

> *Every local "church" body is an expression of the Church body.* And every time believers meet together, they are an expression of the Body. Of course, not every gathering of believers contains all of the elements of all that the scriptures teach regarding "church." The primary marks of a mature expression of the Church include these functions from Acts 2:42–47: The church exists where there is apostolic teaching, fellowship, breaking bread (both as real meals, and the Lord's Supper), prayer/worship, the miraculous work of the Holy Spirit, radical generosity in community life, intentional gathering together (publicly in the "Temple," and as believers house to house), and the ongoing addition of new believers. (2006, 119; cf. Higgins 2015c, Loc. 12748; emphasis in original)

Higgins affirms that insider gatherings are, on the one hand, a real expression of the church, the body of Christ; and at the same time they do not yet reflect all the elements of the biblical church, which he equates with "a mature expression of the Church" (taken from the profile of the early church in Acts).

One way the emerging character of insider communities is described is by analogy to the Catholic perspective on Protestant churches, which affirms that the true church exists fully only in the Roman Catholic Church, while also affirming the presence of ecclesial communities and (Protestant) churches with elements of "sanctification and truth" that are not yet in full communion with the Catholic Church (ibid., Loc. 2678–94).

This developmental, in-process model of the church can be seen in at least two practical areas: sacraments/ordinances and elders. Many insider advocates affirm baptism and/or the Lord's Supper in their explanation of the local church: some have emphasized baptism (Talman 2004b, 9), some communion (Higgins 2006, 119), and some both (Travis 1998b, 414; Duerkson 2012, 162). Those who are aware of insider movements indicate a varied practice among various movements:

> In some movements it seems to be a common practice to remember the sacrifice of Jesus for the forgiveness of sins during a meal shared together. Most Jesus-following Muslims practice some form of water baptism as well, not to indicate a change of

religious affiliation, but as a sign of identifying with Jesus, who has opened the way for the cleansing of sin and for new life in Him. Some Muslim disciples of Jesus who do not yet practice outward water baptism consider themselves to have been baptized spiritually because of their relationship with Christ, who baptizes with the Holy Spirit. (Travis and Woodberry 2015, Loc. 1516)

The practice of these two rites is thus not yet universal among insider movements, and if affirmed as essential to the local church, express an emerging, "in process" character of insider ekklēsia.[99]

The appointing of elders is another area where this developmental, in-process nature of the insider model can be observed. As with the ordinances, it appears that the appointment of elders has taken place in some, but not all, insider fellowships (Travis et al. 2006, 124; 2006, 119; cf. Higgins 2015, Loc. 12767). Some insider advocates emphasize appointing elders as essential to the nature or functions of a "mature church," with some churches not yet having arrived (2006, 119; 2009, 77; cf. Higgins 2015, Loc. 12767). Another perspective sees the "offices" of the church as reflecting functions of the church as a whole, which can develop into particular roles when the particular need arises; e.g., the ministry of *diakonia* (service), a function of the whole church, eventually required the development of particular roles in Acts 6:1–7 (Duerkson and Dyrness 2019, 126).[100]

Thus, we see that insider advocates generally affirm the appointment of elders as a biblical feature of mature churches, while also allowing time and space for emerging, immature churches to grow into mature, elder-led churches, allowing flexibility in terms of the timeframe and the particular style of leadership.

One key reason that the insider model provides considerable developmental space for local fellowships is because of the principled distance between insider movements and Christian churches. Insiders, by default, are often isolated from national Christians or churches (if there are any); and cross-cultural workers, or "alongsiders," are generally very careful about how involved they are with the community, ideally limiting their involvement to mentoring relationships with key insiders in the movement (Travis and Travis 2015, Loc. 10561). This means that growth and development from an "emerging, infant" church to a community that fully expresses the elements of the New Testament church may be a gradual process.

The contours of the insider model of the local church have now become clear. At its core, the church is envisioned as a group of Muslims in a family network who are committed to following Jesus together—expressing local church as a

---

99 In his case study of an insider movement in East Africa, Ben Naja found that 80 percent of the believers had been baptized (Naja 2015, Loc. 3445). He did not ask about the practice of communion.

100 "What are normative, then, are not the contingent forms these offices took in their first century setting (or in their later setting in church history); rather, the offices or functions developed as needed for the health and growth of the body, whatever culturally appropriate (and contingent) form they might take" (Duerkson and Dyrness 2019, 126).

family/community, while continuing to participate in the Muslim community "as Muslims." The community life of local insider churches is one which seeks to gather together in ways appropriate to the context for Bible study, prayer, and fellowship, as they seek to gradually grow and develop under the guidance of the Spirit into a full expression of a mature, biblical church, led by elders and practicing the sacraments.

The question to which we now turn is the issue of the relationship of these local insider fellowships to the larger body of Christ, the universal church.

Insiders and the Universal Church

By definition, Muslim insiders do not identify as Christians, and thus identify with the Muslim umma[101] over the "Christian umma," at least nominally (Talman 2004b, 8; Travis 2015a, Loc. 817). This raises the critical question of the role of the universal church in the insider paradigm. Insider advocates affirm the universal church as a *theological, spiritual reality*, while also acknowledging that insider churches face unique challenges in seeking to express this ideal in their context.

Insider advocates across the board affirm that insiders, and insider fellowships, are part of the universal church. All groups on the C1-C6 spectrum are affirmed as part of the larger body of Christ (Travis and Travis 2005, 402; Travis et al. 2006, 124). By virtue of faith in Christ, insiders are spiritually united by God to the body of Christ, making them members of the universal church (Higgins 2006, 118–19; cf. Higgins 2015, Loc. 12730). As Paul and Barnabas advocated for the Gentiles to be accepted by the Jerusalem church as full members of the church, so insider proponents advocate for insider believers to be accepted as part of the global family of God (Massey 2004; Bartlotti 2015, *UIM*, Loc. 2125).

It appears that many insiders, while not identifying as Christians, see themselves as a part of a larger community in Christ that transcends religious communities:

> Based on comments from Muslim followers of Jesus as well as colleagues who know these believers well, we can affirm that the great majority of Jesus-following Muslims view all people who are truly submitted to God through Christ, whether Christian, Muslim, or Jewish, as fellow members of the Kingdom of God. The presence of the Spirit of God in both born-again Christians and born-again Muslims points to realities—the Body of Christ and the Kingdom of God—that go beyond socio-religious labels and categories. (Travis and Woodberry 2015, Loc. 1477)

Though Muslim followers of Jesus may distance themselves from Christians in name, they generally see themselves as spiritually connected with those Christians who are truly born again; and when Christians see the presence of the Spirit in the lives of insiders, they should similarly recognize them as part of the body of Christ. In insider ecclesiology, it is not religious affiliation that indicates whether or not one is part of the universal church; it is the presence of the Spirit of God in the life of the believer.

---

[101] The original meaning of Arabic *umma* is "nation" or "people," and it is primarily used to refer to the worldwide Muslim community—the "Muslim nation."

While affirming this spiritual reality, insider advocates acknowledge the practical limitations of insiders expressing the universal church visibly (Duerkson 2012, 165; Dutch 2000, 22), as connectedness and solidarity to one's Muslim birth community takes priority over visible identification with the non-Muslim believing community. Insider advocates acknowledge this shortcoming, while warning evangelical critics not to hold insiders to higher standards than what evangelicals themselves have been able to achieve, with their many denominational divisions and independent churches (Duerkson 2012, 165; Higgins, Jameson, and Talman 2015, *UIM*, Loc. 1716). For some, this deficiency is another part of the insider church's "emergent," in-process character (2016, Loc. 2746).

Some, however, argue that the visible expression of the universal church is not essential, arguing that the New Testament allows for a "one body, two communities" model of church with "two distinct categories for the body of Christ," Jewish and Gentile (Jameson and Scalevich 2000, 35). Although one body in Christ, Jews and Gentiles opted to be one "in Spirit" rather than in practice, remaining separate "in almost all aspects of everyday life" (ibid., citing 1 Cor 9:19–20). As the Jews continued to follow the law, so many contemporary Muslims are finding it necessary to maintain their distance from the traditional Christian community in order to stay within their Muslim context. Christian dietary practices, dress, and worship styles make it difficult for Muslim believers to freely fellowship with them. To do so would destroy their credibility in their own community, as it would have for first-century Jewish believers (ibid.)

Like Jewish believers, who were free to continue following the law and keep unclean Gentiles at arm's length, so Muslim followers of Jesus are free to continue following their traditions and remain separate from Christians, whom some Muslims consider "unclean"—for the sake of maintaining their witness to the Muslim community. While the universal body of Christ is affirmed as a spiritual reality, its visible expression through tangible fellowship is set aside for the higher priority of maintaining solidarity and connectedness to one's birth community for the purpose of witness.[102]

Several insider advocates, however, push back against this "one body, two communities" theology of the universal church, viewing separation as a temporary,

---

[102] Such a view appears to be found in a particular group studied and reported by Woodberry. A series of questions was to understand their attitudes toward traditional Christians, and a diversity of responses were found. Woodberry lists the following five responses:
"They are brothers of the same faith."
"If we follow their traditions, we can't work with our own people."
"They eat forbidden (haram) food."
"We don't like them because of their behavior, dress, and food."
"We must love them 100 percent, but in our culture we must stay separate." (2005, 21–22)
  At best, unity with traditional Christians is expressed in terms of being members of the "same faith" and giving/receiving love; however, cultural and physical separation is maintained.
  Another example is the case study cited by Duerkson and Dyrness from the southern Philippines, in which an indigeneous church movement has sought to intentionally reject and distance itself from practices associated with the Christian church, due to the historic oppression of Muslims by the Christian Filipino majority (2019, 102–3).

pragmatic reality at best that should eventually move towards tangibly expressed unity with the wider body of Christ, which is the biblical norm (Dutch 2000, 22; Higgins 2009, 80). Insider communities, while adopting Islamic forms, ought to eventually adjust their community life so as to express their solidarity and connection with the universal body of Christ (Woodberry 2015b, Loc. 5978–96).

Insider advocates report some examples of insiders expressing fellowship with the universal church in low-key and security-sensitive ways, including through friendships, interactions at mission staff conferences, regular consultation in sharing ideas and strategies in Bible correspondence schools, insiders sent to represent the insider church to the national church in other countries, and an "annual gathering that includes insiders from various countries and outsiders from multiple denominational backgrounds, meeting together for a week of bible study and discussion" (Dutch 2000, 22; Higgins 2009, 80).

Another example is an insider movement with "low key but formal links with an international Christian denomination" with a "mutual recognition of each others' ministry and ethos, ... the denominational leadership recognizes the ministry and 'ordinations' of the insiders" (ibid.). Such links are seen as "a fruitful way forward, and a viable expression of a more faithful ecclesiology of the 'glocal' church, a church that is at once and in essence both local and global, both particular and catholic" (ibid., 80–81). Although expressing the universal church is a challenge, some insider proponents advocate for insider communities moving toward appropriate, low-profile ways to forge connections with the wider body of Christ.

The universal church is an important issue in the insider model of church. The insider paradigm affirms the universal church as a spiritual reality that transcends religious affiliation, encompassing all who have been incorporated into Christ's body through faith, whether Muslim, Christian, or other. While most insiders see themselves as part of a larger community of faith, the nature of insider movements is such that visibly expressing their connection to the global church is superseded by the priority of maintaining connection to the Muslim family and community. While some insider advocates see this as a biblically legitimate option, others see it as a temporary necessity, with the ideal of insiders moving toward limited, low-profile ways of connecting with the wider body of Christ.

The challenge of visibly expressing the universal church relates directly to the next key topic, which is how the insider vision of the church relates to the visible and invisible church.

Insider Church: Visible or Invisible?

One way to frame the insider debate is with the question: "Can someone say 'yes' to Jesus and 'no' to the visible church?" (Tennent 2006, 101). This raises the question of how the visible and invisible church shapes insider ecclesiology. Insider advocates reflect diverse perspectives on the concepts of the visible and invisible church that reflect different denominational backgrounds. However, the paradigm as a whole reveals a particular expression of visibility and invisibility in insider ekklēsia.

Herbert Hoefer, from a Lutheran perspective, utilizes the visible/invisible church concepts in expressing an ecclesiology for Hindu insiders who refuse baptism and membership in the church in India. Initially referring to them as an example of "churchless Christianity," Hoefer later reported that these believers had rejected the "churchless" moniker and affirmed that they *are* part of the church, even if they understand and practice it differently (Hoefer 2007; 2015, Loc. 6687–6705).

Hoefer believes that the visible/invisible church concept creates space for such believers who are not baptized or church members: "not everyone who is on the church rolls (the visible Church) is actually in the body of Christ through faith (the invisible church, known only to God). Likewise, there are people unknown to us in the visible Church, but known to God as His own" (ibid., Loc. 6705).

The visible church, for Hoefer, is especially connected with church membership, and this is the primary problem for these insiders (ibid., Loc. 6758–77). The reason they reject church membership is because it carries the cultural meaning of their abandoning family and community, with significant legal and social implications. In order to remain inside their family and culture as a witness, church membership is avoided. This does not mean that these insider groups (called *Jesu bhaktas*) have a problem with fellowship with other believers, which they seek in a variety of forms, as there are

> new forms of faith communities evolving. The *Jesu bhaktas* do not despise fellowship with fellow believers; indeed, they desire it and are developing various ways to achieve it. They are doing this separate from the established church bodies: through pilgrimages, Christian *sanyasis*, mass rallies, Christian friends, standing outside the church on Sundays, joining in Christian worship, Holy Communion, Bible correspondence courses, Christian ashrams and internet discussions. These are forms of spiritual fellowship and accountability that are familiar and comfortable to them from their Hindu cultural background. (ibid., Loc. 6758)

These insiders pursue fellowship with other believers, but they do so outside the bounds of membership in a Christian church and in forms shaped by their cultural background.

For Hoefer, fellowship with believers is essential, but membership in the established Christian church is not. Luther's *adiaphora* principle states that "any church practice or policy that does not compromise the gospel of salvation by grace through faith is a matter of adiaphora, a matter of indifference and freedom" (ibid., Loc. 6706). Since church membership is not essential to salvation, it should be considered *adiaphora*, says Hoefer (ibid., Loc. 6759). On the other hand, "Some form of fellowship is highly helpful for sanctification; however, the form that this faith community takes may differ from culture to culture" (ibid.).

However, despite not being in visible communion with the Christian church, these Hindu insiders are united with them spiritually in the invisible church, sharing a common faith and life in the Spirit (ibid., Loc. 6863). This may not express itself in organizational membership, but it should express itself in relational openness to the other and mutual edification and growth into Christian maturity.

However, other insider advocates are less comfortable with using "invisible ecclesiology" in the context of insider movements. Duerkson, from an Anabaptist believers church perspective, pushes back on Hoefer's use of the visible/invisible church, affirming that the New Testament understanding of the church includes visible community as essential. While affirming the reality of "a wider and unseen Church," Duerkson emphasizes that the New Testament "seems to primarily understand church as *gathered groups of disciples* that are visible to the wider community" (2012, 162; emphasis in original). Therefore, "While it is possible to be a follower of Christ and not a member of a local church, Christ's ideal is for people to be committed to a local group of believers who together represent Christ to their context" (ibid.). The reality of the invisible church, says Duerkson, should not eclipse the necessity of visible community in a New Testament church.

Duerkson is not the only one who wants to preserve visibility in insider ekklēsia. Kevin Higgins affirms, in response to critics:

> I believe in the visible church, that is, in a church made up of believers who meet and can be seen, touched, and heard. My definition refers to these as communities. The whole focus of the work I do and the training I have developed over the years is to see the extension and establishment of such communities of disciples, such churches. My view of insider movements is not inconsistent with the development of forms of church community and forms of church leadership that are biblical, and also fit the context of the culture. ... Thus, the visible church and its visible forms are biblical concepts. Insider proponents believe in the visible church. (2009b, 70–71)

Higgins fully ascribes to the visible church, understanding it to refer to tangible, observable gathered communities of disciples, affirming it to be completely consistent with insider ekklēsia.

In the end, the emphases of Hoefer and of Higgins and Duerkson can be generally reconciled in the insider paradigm. While insider ekklēsia generally affirms the importance and necessity of visible community, understood as committed participation in local ekklēsia (the emphasis of Duerkson and Higgins), it also generally avoids official membership in the *existing, established* visible church (the emphasis of Hoefer). Furthermore, the existing "visible" church is encouraged to welcome insiders as members of the body of Christ even if they are not officially identifying with the existing visible church.

Thus, insider ekklēsia seems to be shaped by both the visible and invisible nature of the church in different ways. As regards the visible nature of the church, the insider paradigm envisions insiders not as secret believers (C6), but believers who openly live out their faith as Muslim followers of Jesus. We have already seen the concept of local ekklēsia includes visible, tangible communities of faith in Muslim social networks. Some are "underground" churches that meet discreetly with a lower profile, while others can be more open and public, depending on the context and social skills of the insiders (e.g., the case of "Jesus mosques"; Travis and Woodberry 2015; cf. Massey 1996, 151). At the very least, the ideal seems to be for gatherings that are at least visible enough to family members and friends to facilitate the spread of the gospel within the social network, leading to a potential movement.

Along with an affirmation and pursuit of the visible church, insider ekklēsia is also shaped by aspects of the invisible church. In response to what is perceived as an overly institutional ecclesiology, the insider paradigm affirms the unseen, spiritual nature of the church, such that the church is a spiritual creation of God, and all who are saved are united to the body of Christ by the Spirit. Therefore, insiders *are* part of the church, the body of Christ, prior to and regardless of any participation in any church structure or institution.

Another aspect of invisibility in insider ekklēsia is in the expression of the universal church. While visibility is strongly affirmed by some insider advocates, this is focused primarily at the local church level, whereas the universal church is allowed to be, by and large, a spiritual, invisible reality, as discussed previously. Insiders' spiritual bond with the wider visible Christian community typically is not visibly expressed, instead remaining mostly a hidden spiritual reality of the heart and mind. While some insiders have found ways to engage in fellowship with the wider body of Christ, such ties are not overly visible—not only for security reasons, but also to maintain an insider identity. If the goal is for the insider movement to retain its Muslim identity, then any ties to the visible Christian community must remain under the radar at best, if not functionally invisible.

In summary, insider ekklēsia is both visible and invisible. With respect to local gatherings of insiders in Muslim communities, insider ekklēsia is visible, if low profile. With respect to the universal Christian church, insider ekklēsia is functionally invisible. The next chapter examines the ways that a robust understanding of the visible and invisible church affirms and challenges this understanding.[103] Before doing so, however, it is also important to understand how the attributes and marks of the church are expressed in insider ekklēsia.

Attributes, Marks, and Insider Church

The question of the attributes and marks of the true church provides another vantage point to illumine the unique ecclesiological vision of the insider paradigm. Overall, the insider ekklēsia engages more with the Protestant marks than the classical attributes, but ultimately emphasizes its own particular marks to guide the evaluation of churches and movements.

Some insider advocates argue that the classical attributes, as well as the Protestant marks, are historically and contextually shaped, responding to particular temporal concerns that are far removed from contemporary insider movements (Dyrness 2016,

---

[103] The insider paradigm has at times highlighted the nature of the church as a "mixed community", which recalls the basis of Augustine's original distinction between the visible (mixed) and invisible (pure) church. However, this concept is applied differently in the insider paradigm; rather than an argument for retaining fellowship with the institutional church, despite the presence of unbelievers (the point of Augustine and the Reformers), the concept is applied to support a church that emerges within Muslim community networks and exists as an open community that does not draw hard, visible lines between believers and not-yet-believers (Parsons 2006; Higgins 2015, Loc. 5421).

Loc. 2678; Duerkson and Dyrness 2019, 34, 36). Thus, it is not surprising that insider ekklēsia, by and large, is not significantly influenced by the classical attributes of the church (one, holy, catholic, and apostolic). Some exceptions exist, such as a lone mention of "catholicity" in the context of encouraging fellowship with the universal church (Higgins 2018, 27), and a reinterpretation of "unity" as a key marker of the biblical church (Duerkson and Dyrness 2019, 165).

More significant in the insider paradigm are the Protestant marks of the Word, baptism, and communion. Although not considered universal criteria for recognizing the true church, they are broadly considered important ecclesial practices, as previous discussion has made clear related to local ekklēsia.

Each of these practices, however, may be expressed and understood differently in insider contexts. In some insider fellowships, the study of the Word does not exclude a role for the Qur'an and the hadith as respected texts. The Qur'an and the prophethood of Muhammad may be "revalued" without being rejected; teachings in line with Scripture are affirmed, while Jesus and the Scriptures gradually supersede and relativize the Qur'an and the prophet (ibid. 2019, 141). Such a process has been compared to the way God revealed his truth in Scripture "against the backdrop of religious traditions and practices of local cultures" that "helped to illuminate" aspects of God's truth (ibid., 141–42). All of this provides an insider "twist" to the ministry of the Word.

It has already been noted that many insider movements among Muslims are reported as practicing a form of water baptism. A priority, however, is to express baptism in a way that is not "a ritual of social disruption" or of changing religious communities but rather as an identification with Christ and one's new life in him (Travis and Woodberry 2015, Loc. 1516; Duerkson and Dyrness 2019, 135). The practice of communion appears to be less frequent, though it has been described as "remember[ing] the sacrifice of Jesus for the forgiveness of sins during a meal shared together" (Travis and Woodberry 2015, Loc. 1516).

Some insider advocates have argued that it is the theological meaning only and not the form of baptism and communion that is normative. Baptism and communion were adapted from existing Jewish cultural rituals (a purification ritual and the Passover, respectively), and insiders (and others) are free to utilize existing cultural or religious rituals in their context that can be adapted to communicate the meaning of baptism and communion (Duerkson and Dyrness 2019, 137–38). In some contexts, such corresponding rituals can be found, but in other contexts, it is more difficult, which leads some insiders to de-emphasize these practices.[104]

---

[104] Duerkson and Dyrness note two contrasting examples in the southern Philippines. In the case of the Manobo people in Davao del Norte, there is an ancient ritual in which "the spirit priest drinks the blood of sacrifices on behalf of good spirits that offer protection against *busow*," who are malevolent spirits that "search for blood to satisfy their cravings." This caused great confusion in understanding communion, causing people to wonder if God was a *busow*, and whether they would be possessed by an evil spirit if they drank Christ's blood. Therefore, the churches in that area rarely practiced communion. On the other hand, in Bangsamoro, an ancient Moro ritual called *sandugo* involved people winding themselves and drinking one another's blood, "creating a new community of blood," and some believers in Christ have appropriated it in their communities as a ritual of Christ's love (2019, 138).

In summary, the insider paradigm affirms, in various ways, the importance of the practices associated with the Protestant marks, and yet allows some flexibility as to the particular cultural form that these practices take so as to avoid "Christian" meaning which would signal a change in religious community. However, of these practices, only the ministry of the Word appears to be treated as a universal "mark of the true church," while baptism and communion are simply important "ecclesial practices" through which God's presence is manifested in a particular community.

Rather than focusing on the classic attributes or Protestant marks, insider advocates offer their own set of criteria that mark out true churches, marks which they affirm can be and are increasingly present in emerging "insider" communities. One example is the six "devoteds" of the early church in Acts, taken as indicators of a healthy movement: (1) prayer, (2) the apostles' teaching and fellowship, (3) breaking of bread and prayer, (4) meeting in the temple and house-to-house, (5) leaders devoted to the Word and prayer, and (6) relational discipleship (Higgins 2015b, Loc. 5507–634).[105] These marks of healthy movements are presented as fully compatible with fellowships that maintain a "socio-religious" insider identity, in line with the pattern of the early Jewish church.

Another set of marks that have been proposed to identify the "emergent reality of the church" among insiders include: (1) hearing and obeying the story of Christ, (2) the formation of a community around the story, (3) response of the community to this story in prayer and praise, (4) living at peace with one another and with the wider community, and (5) witness of the community to Christ and the transformation of the Spirit. The first mark is an intentional revision of the Protestant mark of proclamation of the Word, while the fourth is an expansion of the classical mark of unity that affirms the church is not distinct from its community, but rather "yeast in the dough" seeking to bless its community in shalom (Duerkson and Dyrness 2019, 155–71).

In the following chapter, we will look at the strengths and weaknesses of how the insider paradigm "marks out" the true church. Here we note that the insider paradigm offers a distinctive approach to the marks of the church. Largely bypassing the classical attributes, insider advocates affirm a modified "insider-friendly" version of the practices of the Word and sacraments, not as universal marks of the true church, but as ecclesial practices of varying importance. Furthermore, insider advocates have proposed their own set of marks of emerging churches that are understood to be fully compatible with insider churches.

Besides the marks of the church, the insider paradigm also offers a distinct approach to the question of the relationship between salvation and the church.

---

105 Another version of this list broadens beyond the "devoteds" to other aspects of the early church community, indicating a "primary marks of a mature expression of the church": apostolic teaching, fellowship, breaking bread (both as real meals, and the Lord's Supper), prayer/worship, the miraculous work of the Holy Spirit, radical generosity in community life, intentional gathering together (publicly in the "Temple," and as believers house to house), and the ongoing addition of new believers (Higgins 2006, 119; cf. 2015c, Loc. 12748).

Salvation and the Insider Church

One critique of the insider paradigm is that it reflects a contemporary evangelical tendency to bifurcate the doctrine of salvation and the doctrine of the church (Tennent 2007, 215). This raises the question, however, of how the insider paradigm actually does characterize the relationship between salvation and the church. A closer look at the writings of insider advocates reveals that they affirm salvation to be both *outside* and *inside* the church in different respects.

Insider advocates clearly affirm that salvation can be found *outside* the existing institutional Christian church, a point which by now is eminently clear. Significantly, this fact reflects a distinctively Protestant theological conviction, as insider advocates affirm unequivocally that salvation is by faith alone, not through membership in any church or religious community. Hoefer includes the Reformational principle of *sola fide* (faith alone) as one of his principles for developing an ecclesiology for Hindu insiders, asserting that church membership in the visible "Christian" church is not a requirement for salvation, and therefore *adiaphora,* or a matter of "indifference" and Christian freedom (2007).

However, insider advocates take a step further in their application of the *sola fide* principle. Not only can salvation be found *outside* the institutional Christian church; salvation can flourish *inside* a *non-Christian* "socio-religious" community. The Travises argue that *sola fide* is a basis for the possibility of being "saved" and yet remaining part of one's "original non-Christian religious community of birth" (Travis and Travis 2005, 403). Joining the "right" religious community is not necessary for salvation, and those who insist upon it are in danger of adding an additional requirement or "work" for salvation (Hoefer 2007). For this reason, insider advocates sometimes claim that the gospel itself is at stake in the "right" of insiders to remain in their religious birth community (Lewis 2015a, Loc. 6479–533).

While the insider paradigm clearly affirms salvation outside the church in terms of the institutional Christian community, it affirms salvation to be *inside* the church in certain ways. The insider paradigm does not promote an individualistic view of salvation in which people come to faith individually without ever entering or expressing the body of Christ. In fact, the household/oikos model of insider churches envisions salvation and church formation as happening simultaneously; when a family comes to faith together, they experience salvation and immediately become an expression of church (Lewis 2007, 76; cf. Lewis 2015b, Loc. 12528–47).

Kevin Higgins likewise depicts salvation as closely linked to the insider church. Higgins affirms that salvation by grace through faith results in immediate spiritual incorporation into God's church. As insiders come to faith, they are "added" by the Holy Spirit to the church, in a spiritual sense (2006, 119). In this sense, no one can "join" the church or apply for membership— it is an act of God that takes place at conversion (ibid., 118–19). Once this happens, "membership" in the body of Christ becomes a part of insiders' identity which should be lived out "as a full time lifestyle in every venue of life," both in community life with other Jesus followers and in ongoing participation in Muslim religious life (ibid.; cf. Higgins 2015c, Loc. 12730). While salvation does not require connection with the institutional Christian church, salvation inevitably results in being incorporated into the church spiritually, which ideally will take shape in ecclesial insider communities or churches.

Salvation includes not only forgiveness and justification, but also spiritual formation/sanctification. Insider advocates acknowledge a role for the church in sanctification, though with varying levels of emphasis. Hoefer acknowledges that "some form of fellowship" is "highly helpful" for spiritual development of believers, which he understands broadly to include Bible correspondence courses, mass rallies, Christian friends, and Internet discussions (2015, Loc. 6758).

Insider advocate Bernard Dutch uses stronger language, urgently arguing the necessity of biblical churches for the spiritual endurance and maturity of believers. After posing the question, "Can believers flourish and grow without a distinct identity and community?" Dutch's answer is worth quoting at length:

> When a community of believers is small and weak, it is difficult to meet together regularly and meaningfully. Individual believers then have difficulty retaining their passion for Christ. I have seen many believers fall out of fellowship and then lose all signs of spiritual life…. Where I live the spiritual battle is not so much for Muslims coming to faith in Jesus; it is for Muslim background believers forming themselves into local fellowships. I have heard similar comments from colleagues working with Muslims elsewhere in the world. Believers in the church have a collective strength for spiritual victory that individuals do not (Matt 16:18). I believe Satan knows this and opposes the formation of the church at every opportunity. This spiritual opposition confirms to me that forming local fellowships of Muslim background believers is the right strategy…. We must persist in prayer for breakthroughs in establishing the church among believers of Muslim backgrounds. We must continually encourage and teach them about the crucial role of the local church in God's plan for His Kingdom…. To reach significant numbers of Muslims, we need growing numbers of vibrant, Biblically based churches that remain in and relevant to Muslim society. The Muslim world will only be reached through indigenous church planting movements that explode far beyond what outsiders can direct or fund. (2000, 22–23)

Dutch's impassioned plea for biblical churches highlights the necessity of the church in the spiritual formation and perseverance of Muslim-background believers. Without the spiritual strength of a local church, new believers are in danger of succumbing to Satanic influence and backsliding into unbelief. In general, then, the insider paradigm affirms the importance of the church in the sanctification of believers, with various insider advocates falling somewhere on the spectrum between the church being "highly helpful" and "necessary" for sanctification.

The insider paradigm has a unique approach to the question of the relationship between salvation and the church. Salvation can indeed be found outside the institutional church and inside other (non-Christian) religious communities. On the other hand, salvation is closely related to the church, in that it results in immediate incorporation by God into the body of Christ and often immediate formation of a church if a whole family is saved together; furthermore, the development of church forms plays an important role in the spiritual formation of insider believers.

Before evaluating this perspective, along with those discussed in the other topics, I will look at one final topic which has great relevance to the question of insider movements: the relationship between the church and the world.

Insider Church in the World

The insider paradigm expresses the church-world relationship in distinctive ways which are critical for understanding the shape of its vision. One aspect of the church-world relationship is the relationship between the church and culture, which brings us back to the issue of contextualization.

Insider advocates have reflected a variety of understandings and postures towards contextualization and its relationship to insider movements. Some of the earliest, most prominent insider advocates have defended insider movements and C5 fellowships as a natural outgrowth and logical outcome of biblical contextualization, based on the way that religion and culture are intertwined in Muslim societies. Hence, Travis has described insider movements and C5 as an example of high-spectrum contextualization (1998a), and Higgins has defined insider movements partly as movements that are "expressed within as much of the culture as possible, including religious culture" (2004, 156). Furthermore, Travis acknowledges the danger of syncretism, giving several recommendations to avoid it in C5 movements (1998b, 414). Abdul Asad likewise distinguishes between "syncretistic C5" and "appropriate C5" (2009, 155–56).

Some insider advocates, however, have sought to separate contextualization from insider movements. Rebecca Lewis distinguishes contextualization (along with the "C-spectrum") from "insider movements," since insider movements focus upon the relationship between believers and their preexisting family/social network, not the language and cultural forms of the believers' worship (2007, 76). Duerkson and Dyrness argue that contextualization is not the best model for capturing the way the church is emerging in insider situations, proposing a new model of "reverse hermeneutic" and "emergence theory" (Duerkson and Dyrness 2019, 27–28; cf. Duerkson 2016, Loc.108).

Those insider advocates who emphasize the contextualization paradigm include an evaluative element that is aware of the possibility of syncretism, arguing that insider movements avoid it. Duerkson and Dyrness' model, on the other hand, is more descriptive, emphasizing pragmatic evaluative criteria, related to practical positive and negative relational results. Rebecca Lewis avoids the issue of contextualizing altogether, at least explicitly, though even she herself is involved in contextualizing a form of church which is more relevant to communal societies—the household church model. Despite these different frameworks, the insider paradigm generally sees religion and culture as a unified whole that cannot be separated, affirming that a significant amount of religious culture and identity can be legitimately retained and expressed in the biblical church.

A closer look at the insider paradigm shows that, despite the varying postures towards contextualization, the insider paradigm offers a particular way of characterizing the identity of the church in relationship to the world—and especially the world's cultures, social structures, and religious communities. As I show below, the insider vision emphasizes the positive value of cultures and religious structures as spheres in which God and his kingdom are at work, and which therefore should be retained and preserved rather than rejected or overturned by the church. The church-world relationship is envisioned in terms of the church as a change agent embedded within the world's social, cultural, and religious structures, best expressed in the biblical metaphor of "yeast in the dough."

The insider paradigm affirms a largely positive view of the social structures and institutions of the world as having God-given value. Family, government, courts, and other societal institutions and norms are divinely ordained to counter evil and sustain human society, and therefore should be preserved: "Especially in view of the power of sin in our fallen world, these structures must be guarded and secured or sin will run rampant and the world will self-destruct" (Hoefer 2007; 2015, Loc. 6744). The family structure in particular is viewed as having a special role in God's salvific plan, based on God's promise to Abraham to bless all "families" of the earth (Lewis 2010, 34; 2015, Loc. 6340). This framework undergirds the insider paradigm's vision of a church which aims to avoid disrupting families, communities, and social institutions in its relationship to the world.

In addition to a positive view of social structures, the insider paradigm emphasizes the positive value of cultural and religious structures of the world as venues in which God is at work in bringing his kingdom. Human "religions" in particular are often included under the umbrella of God's kingdom:

> The Kingdom of God includes the Church, but is bigger than the Church. The Kingdom refers to the whole range of God's exercise of His reign and rule in the universe. This includes religions. The Kingdom paradigm acknowledges there is another kingdom as well, and takes seriously the battle for the allegiance and hearts and minds of people. (Higgins 2009a, 87)

In comments reflective of the insider paradigm as a whole, Higgins emphasizes the universal scope of the kingdom of God, rejecting the idea that the kingdom is limited to the church.[106] Higgins does not expound upon how exactly God's kingdom reign relates to human religions, but he is intent on including them in the scope of the kingdom, which creates the space for God's presence and work in them.

The presence of God within the cultural and religious values and narratives of the world becomes a strong basis for preserving and affirming cultural and religious identities, rather than rejecting them. While acknowledging that God is present in the church in a special way, "God is present throughout creation, and even in other religions" (Duerkson and Dyrness 2019, 71), which motivates us to find God in non-Christian cultural and religious traditions:

> We have argued throughout this book that the particular shape a community of Jesus-followers takes always reflects a reverse hermeneutic, a situated reading of Scripture and the story of Jesus in terms this group can understand and embody. This process prompts us to be attentive to *the way in which God is in the midst of cultural and religious values, practices, and identities, seeking to affirm and not replace these.* (ibid., 172, emphasis mine)

Not only does the church read Scripture from its cultural and religious context, but God himself is understood to be present and at work within these structures in a way which preserves these structures and identities. While an element of transformation is acknowledged, the overall preservation of cultural and religious structures is emphasized:

> This creates an emergent process whereby God enhances and transforms, but does not overturn, the community's social customs and identities. Ecclesial practices like these are uniquely able to locate the community's own cultural narrative within that of the gospel and in turn to identify *the presence of the gospel within the community's historical and ongoing cultural narrative.* This dual movement—people locating themselves in the ongoing biblical story and recognizing *God's presence and work within their own community's narrative*—allows the emergence of new church communities that will be both in continuity with and distinct from their social context. (ibid., 146; emphasis added)

Duerkson and Dyrness's model clearly assumes that both God and his gospel are already present in cultural narratives, a reality which can be recognized when churches develop worship practices shaped by their own cultural and religious milieu. The church's relationship to the world, while acknowledging ways in which the church challenges cultures and religions, is shaped by an overall positive view of cultures and religions as spheres in which God is present and at work.

---

106 Another example is that of Herbert Hoefer, who supports his ecclesiology for insiders with a similarly expansive view of the kingdom: The rule of God extends to more than the Church. God's love, concern and will are extended to all people, whether they acknowledge and serve him or not. John 3:16 says, 'God so loved the world.' God's prophets spoke not only to his people, but to the nations.... His kingdom comes wherever and whenever his will is done" (2007; 2015, Loc. 6744–58).

With such an emphasis on the positive value of cultural, social, and religious structures, the insider paradigm characterizes the church-world relationship primarily in terms of embedment: i.e., the church is a change agent *embedded* in the world, spreading through its cultural and religious structures. At times this is connected with an understanding that churches, like all human communities, are necessarily and inescapably embedded in culture (Duerkson and Dyrness 2019, 28).

However, this is most clearly highlighted by the insider paradigm's favored image for depicting insider movements—the yeast in the dough. As mentioned previously, insider advocates widely utilize this kingdom parable as a lens through which to understand insider movements and churches, the yeast being the insider church/movement, and the dough being the Muslim social, cultural, and religious structures in which the insider church is embedded and through which it spreads (Travis and Travis 2005, 404; Travis and Woodberry 2015, Loc. 1353). Higgins explicitly applies this to the nature of the church and its role in the world, combining the yeast-in-dough image with that of seed-in-soil in another kingdom parable, depicting the world as the environment within which the seed or yeast of the kingdom—the church—exists, grows, and spreads (2015a, Loc. 5397). This results in a vision of church as embedded in the social and religious structures of the world with all its messiness of "weeds, rocks, and dough," facilitating the growth and spread of the kingdom throughout these structures.

The embedment of the church within the cultural and religious structures of the world does not leave the "world" unchanged, however. The insider paradigm affirms the church as a change agent within these structures, which can be described in terms of kingdom "transformation" and "new creation." While God intends to preserve and enhance local cultures and identities, he does not stop there:

> We must be clear that God's purposes in the kingdom are not satisfied by simply making believers into better Americans and Kenyans or Japanese. Rather, God is always making things new (Rev 21:5). These emergent markers then represent ways that the gospel, the story of Jesus, by the work of the Spirit will create something new in and through the cultural values of any people group. ... all these offer ways for us to push back against our cultural situation—both affirming and transcending that culture. (Duerkson and Dyrness 2019, 172)

While their book mostly emphasizes the positive value of existing cultural and religious structures and identities, Duerkson and Dyrness here acknowledge that the kingdom also involves God's "new creation" taking place "in and through" the culture.

In the end, the insider paradigm affirms the church as "in, but not of" the world, even if in modified fashion. When insider churches remain embedded in their Muslim religious communities, they are fulfilling their calling to remain in the world (Anna Travis 2015, Loc. 11904). However, insiders are born again spiritually through faith in Christ, they live according to the Bible as the Word of God, and God's kingdom reign is manifested in their lives (Higgins 2006, 118). Insiders will, over time, reject some Muslim beliefs and practices that are contrary to Scripture, while retaining and modifying others (Travis 2015a, Loc. 832–47), creating some degree of difference with the wider Muslim community (for example, in regard to the authority and purity of the Bible, the death and resurrection of Jesus, and salvation by grace rather than works (Travis and Travis 2005, 406–7; Travis and Woodberry 2015, Loc. 1426).

Higgins describes this process as highlighting the way the church is "in" but not "of" the world:

> Kingdom sowing is incarnational, adopting the religious and cultural forms of our Muslim friends. A community of believers will remain in their world, though not of it. Many behaviors, customs, and values will be retained by a believing community, and will need to be adopted by the cross-cultural missionary. But unbiblical values will also be challenged and changed from within, by believers under the guidance of the Holy Spirit (Jn. 16:13). (2015a, Loc. 5438)

Insiders do not simply absorb their cultural and religious context wholesale; Scripture will also challenge and change aspects of the context as well.

Another way the insider church is "in, but not of" the world is through its engagement with the kingdom of Satan which attempts to subjugate God's purposes in the world (Higgins 2009a, 87; Anna Travis 2015, Loc. 11918–32). The church's relationship to the world is characterized by spiritual warfare, not giving any place to the devil, and releasing people in the world from spiritual bondage and oppression, a special emphasis in places dominated by folk Islam (Anna Travis 2015, Loc. 11932).

However, the "otherworldliness" of the church is not seen as hindering the church from remaining embedded "in the world," including its social and religious structures. Although the insider church indeed will reject and modify certain unbiblical beliefs and practices, it will also need to retain enough of the Muslim worldview and way of life to maintain membership in the Muslim community. Practically, this may mean that while certain beliefs will not be rejected outright, they will be reinterpreted or minimized (cf. Travis and Woodberry 2015, Loc. 1426). Similarly, the church's spiritual origin is not taken to contradict with its status of being embedded within the religious communities of the world:

> On one side, I do see church as a closed set, for only those who are born from above and incorporated by the Spirit into His Body are members of the church! But as such, they are not thereby excluded from living in and among other social and religious structures as yeast in the dough. (Higgins 2006, 118; 2015a, Loc. 12738)

Anna Travis applies a similar line of reasoning with respect to the dominion of Satan and the call of the church to remain in the world:

Praying for his followers, Jesus said, "I am not asking you to take them out of the world, but I ask you to protect them from the evil one" (John 17:15). In the parable of the wheat and tares, Jesus describes the people of the evil one and the people of the kingdom as mixed together in the world; God's plan in this age is not to separate the two, since it could harm the people of the kingdom to do so (Matt 13:24–30, 37–43). Paul expects that Jesus' followers will continue to relate with people in the world (1 Cor 5:9, 10). John tells us that the whole world lies under the power of the evil one, but that Jesus protects those who are born of God (1 John 5:18, 19). (2015, Loc. 11932)

Citing a variety of texts, Anna Travis argues that the otherworldly identity of the church is not cause to disengage from the spiritual battle in the world.

But she takes this one step further, arguing that insiders do not necessarily need to immediately and publicly "renounce what we consider idolatrous practices associated with the religious community of their people" (Anna Travis 2015, Loc. 11948–64), since idolatry is "a matter of the heart" and "what is inside a person." What is most important, Travis says, is to claim in the mind and heart that "the evil one has no place—no claim or power over us" and "renounce and get rid of whatever the evil one has in us in order to live in victory over him in this world—in this evil age where he is still the ruler" (ibid., Loc. 11948–64). Being "not of" the world does not mean insiders cannot remain embedded within the religious structures of the world, even in spiritual warfare. In a variety of ways, insider advocates affirm that the church is "not of" the world, bringing about transformation and new creation within the world, and yet this fact does not preclude the church from remaining embedded in the social and religious structures of the world as yeast in dough.

The relationship between the church and the world is a critical facet of the insider model of the church. While acknowledging the presence of the kingdom of darkness in the world and the need for God's transforming work, the insider paradigm emphasizes the positive value of social and cultural structures and religious structures as either established by God or as spheres within which God is present and at work. The insider church is envisioned as a community embedded within the social, cultural, and religious structures as yeast in the dough, a change agent which spreads the transformation of the kingdom and God's new creation within these structures without rejecting them or separating from them.

Conclusion

The insider paradigm presents a particular vision of the church for insiders, a vision shaped by a variety of assumptions, themes, and perspectives on the nature of the church. Insider advocates appeal to an array of **biblical themes and paradigms** in Old and New Testaments, and especially in the Gospels and Acts, to argue that Scripture fully supports, and at times encourages, a church for religious insiders.

Standing on this framework, the insider paradigm affirms that insider churches express the ***core essence of the church***, which is not to be found in affiliation with an institution, a particular cultural form, or a given religious identity, but rather in the presence and work of God in regenerating believers and uniting them to the body of Christ, something which can and does happen among insiders.

The insider paradigm envisions the ***local church*** taking shape as believing families and social groups come to faith together, becoming expressions of the local church while retaining their family ties and their Muslim identity. While insiders may continue to gather with Muslims at the mosque, they also gather together with other insiders for Bible study, prayer, and fellowship, hopefully growing into more mature expressions of the biblical church under the guidance of the Spirit.

The insider paradigm affirms the ***universal church*** as a spiritual reality that transcends religious communities, including both born-again Christians and born-again Muslim followers of Jesus in one body. Due to the commitment of insiders to protect solidarity with their Muslim community, the universal church is largely a spiritual reality for insiders that seldom finds visible expression, with some exceptions.

Despite diverse uses of terminology, the ***visible and invisible church*** shapes the insider vision in various ways. The insider paradigm affirms the necessity of visible community at the local church level, but rejects the necessity of officially joining the existing institutional church. The insider paradigm, furthermore, emphasizes the invisible, spiritual nature of the church as having theological priority over any human structures or institutions.

In terms of the ***marks of the church,*** the insider paradigm offers its own criteria for discerning the work of the Spirit in forming emerging, healthy insider churches. In addition, the insider paradigm affirms a modified version of the teaching of the Word, baptism, and communion, not as marks of the true church, but as important ecclesial practices which are fully compatible with insider movements.

The insider paradigm affirms that ***salvation*** can certainly be found outside the existing institutional church by those who remain in their non-Christian "socio-religious" community. Salvation leads to an immediate incorporation into the body of Christ spiritually, and this can also lead to an immediate visible expression of the church when whole families and social groups come to faith together, which facilitates spiritual formation.

The insider paradigm envisions the church as embedded within the ***world***. The structures of the world are affirmed as worthy of preservation: cultural and social structures are God-given, and religious structures and identities are spheres within which God and his kingdom are present and working. The church is envisioned as neither separate from nor undermining these structures, but embedded within them as yeast in dough, spreading the transforming work of the kingdom from within.

The contours of insider ekklēsia are now clear. But how should we assess this vision? To what extent does it reflect a viable model for multiplying robust, biblical churches in Muslim communities? In what areas does it push us in helpful directions, and in what areas does it leave us desiring better solutions? To these questions, we now turn.

CHAPTER FIVE

Evaluating Insider "Ekklēsia"

I sat before a national Christian pastor from a majority-Muslim country. He had faced imprisonment and threats against his family on account of his ministry. When many Christians fled his nation because of violent turmoil and persecution, this pastor stayed. He was deeply committed to reaching his nation for Christ, desiring to see the next generation of the church come from Muslim backgrounds.

After he shared his vision for reaching Muslims in his country, we began asking him about his approach. We discussed some challenging questions. When Muslims come to faith, how should they do church? Should we encourage them to join the national church and disciple them there—despite the cultural differences and misunderstandings they may encounter in the Christian community—or should we encourage them to keep their distance from the church and seek to plant a new house church in their family and community? Is it possible to do both?

These are difficult questions, and we had an invigorating exchange of ideas, knowing that our decisions in these areas not only have practical implications in BMBs' lives but that our choices also express and promote certain beliefs and ideas regarding the nature and role of the biblical church.

Mission practitioners among Muslims have varying ideas about what the biblical church is, what it should be, and how it interfaces with Muslim culture. Although our overarching goals are the same—multiplication of believers and vibrant, biblical churches in Muslim communities—there are a variety of approaches to pursuing these goals. The insider paradigm represents one such approach, and a controversial one. The previous chapter demonstrated the particular understanding of the nature of the church which undergirds and motivates insider ministry. The task now is to evaluate and respond to insider ekklēsia, assessing its strengths and weaknesses for facilitating biblical churches among Muslims.

In what follows, I bring together the various strands of this book and offer a holistic, interdisciplinary evaluation of insider ekklēsia in light of Scripture, theology, and the nature of contextualization, showing how the insider paradigm both stimulates fresh understandings of the biblical church and falls short of reflecting the fullness of the biblical church. If we learn from both the strengths and weaknesses of insider ekklēsia, our vision and practice of multiplying biblical churches among Muslims will be strengthened and sharpened.

The assessment of this chapter addresses the strengths and weaknesses of insider ekklēsia in the framework of the biblical narrative, the six dimensions of the nature of the church, and biblical contextualization:

- Biblical theology of the church
- Essential identity of the church
- Local and Universal Church
- Visible and Invisible Church
- Marks of the Church
- Salvation and the Church
- The Church, the World, and Contextualization

Insider church, when viewed from the perspective of a robust, biblical vision of the nature of the church, reflects both assets and liabilities in each of these seven areas.

Biblical Theology: Evaluating Insider Themes and Paradigms

If Scripture is our final authority, then an evaluation of the biblical framework undergirding the insider church is of foundational importance. The insider paradigm's selection, interpretation, and application of biblical themes reflects both fresh insights and problematic elements.

Old Testament Believers Outside Israel

The insider paradigm's emphasis on Old Testament worshippers of God outside the covenant community is helpful in a number of ways. First, it helps us to rejoice in the fact that God's self-revelation was not restricted to the covenant community of Israel, but also "spilled over" to those outside. While Scripture does not provide much explicit teaching on such believers outside the covenant community, it does clearly teach God's saving activity was not just for Israel's sake, but that all nations might hear and know *Yahweh*. Second, the mention of such people indicates the possibility of the existence of other such individuals among the nations who become worshipers of *Yahweh*. For instance, if Rahab heard of *Yahweh's* fame and mighty deeds, it is certainly plausible there were others like her in Egypt and Canaan who heard of *Yahweh* and came to believe and worship him, yet without joining the covenant community. From what we know of God's character and intentions in the New Testament to send his Son to save all nations, we cannot rule out the possibility that there were more "Namaans" and "Rahabs" and "Jethros" among the ANE peoples than are mentioned in Scripture.

However, there are at least two reasons for caution is applying such themes to contemporary insider movements. One reason is the lack of detail provided by Scripture, both in terms of these particular individuals, as well as in terms of the existence of others like them. The biblical silence here means we are not on strong grounds to assume and build solid conclusions on these individuals. We should not rule out the existence of other "non-proselyte" believers, but the lack of clear biblical revelation of such possibilities means we should not build any clear doctrinal conclusions on such things.

A second concern which should give us pause in applying this theme to contemporary insider movements is the need to balance these examples with clear and explicit teaching in Scripture elsewhere that prevents us from going too far in our conclusions. While it is apparent that Elisha does indeed grant Namaan's request for a pardon for continuing to participate in the religious ritual of his master, the rest of the Old Testament clearly warns Israel against the fatal dangers of mixing divinely prescribed worship of Yahweh with the worship practices of the nations. Furthermore, while such figures exist on the fringes of biblical faith, both the Old Testament and the New Testament clearly emphasize the covenant community of the people of God as the primary locus of God's Spirit and revelation in the world. Cornelius, a New Testament counterpart to Namaan, while not required to become a Jew, was incorporated into the new covenant people of God (Acts 10:44-48). Ultimately, these wonderful examples of biblical faith outside the covenant community are cause for rejoicing and wonder, but we should be careful not to draw too many conclusions either direction.

The Kingdom of God

Another area of the biblical framework for insider church which challenges us in good ways while also falling short of the biblical vision is the theme of the kingdom of God. The insider paradigm helpfully challenges us to view the church in light of the teaching and imagery of the kingdom, shaking us out of an overly institutional view of the church and returning us to the origin (and ongoing mission) of the church in the inbreaking reign of God. Furthermore, the insider emphasis on the kingdom helpfully emphasizes all human efforts of church planting as secondary to God's work in manifesting his kingdom. This kingdom vision relativizes all human efforts, structures, institutions, and denominations, helping orient our understanding of the church around God and his work, which transcends and animates all our human efforts and structures.

Less helpful, however, is the tendency to portray the kingdom and the church in a kind of competition for biblical importance, based on the number of times the word is mentioned in the Gospels. As chapter 1 makes clear, this line of thinking obscures the way Jesus' concern for the church is not limited to the word *ekklēsia*, but is expressed in the full array of themes and teachings in the Gospels related to Jesus' priority of creating a community of disciples, as well as Jesus' trained and commissioned apostles, who continued the mission of Jesus in the power of the Spirit. While the insider paradigm often does affirm the importance of the church, the rhetorical tendency to exalt "kingdom" above "church" is misleading and fails to capture the integral, dynamic relationship between the kingdom and the church in the vision of Jesus and his apostles.

Another questionable use of the kingdom theme in the insider paradigm is the way the kingdom is said to include and transcend "religions" or religious communities. Besides the confusion created by an ambiguous use of "religions," such claims obscure the full reality of the way God's kingdom unfolds in Scripture and in the world. The theology of the kingdom includes at least four different dimensions:
(1) the universal sovereignty of God,
(2) the climactic arrival of God's reign in the ministry of Christ (in his life, death, and resurrection),
(3) the effective manifestation and extension of the reign of Christ in and through the ekklēsia of Jesus, and
(4) the full, final realization of Christ's reign in the new creation.

All creation, including the religious communities of the world, fall under the universal sovereignty of God (#1), as well as the universal reign of the risen Christ (#2)—whether they acknowledge God's rule or not—and they will one day be held accountable to King Jesus. However, the reign of Christ does not "break in" and effectively manifest until Jesus' disciples "go" to the nations of the world—which remain "under the power of the evil one"—and implement Jesus' reign in the power of the Spirit by announcing the arrival of the kingdom and discipling people into communities that live under the reign of King Jesus (#3), as a sign and foretaste of the future fullness of the kingdom (#4). This not only highlights the fact that the church is central to the effective manifestation of the kingdom, but also that as the kingdom breaks in, there is an inevitable transformation that takes place which will not leave "religions" or "religious communities" unchanged, not by foreign culture, but by the kingdom of God. The insider paradigm's claims along the lines of the kingdom being "bigger than the church" and including "religions" leaves something to be desired in terms of capturing the full dynamics of the kingdom of God.

Oikos, the Jesus-Family, and the Household of God
Another example of the way in which insider ekklēsia helpfully challenges our biblical theology of church while also falling short of it is in the theme of the church as oikos/household/family. The insider paradigm highlights a neglected biblical theme of the household conversions in the book of Acts, pushing us in helpful ways to move beyond individualistically-oriented church formation common in Western societies to pursue a model which is more ideal for community-oriented Muslim societies. Even those who do not agree with the retaining of "socio-religious" Muslim identity can and do benefit from focusing more on household/family structures and working towards whole families coming to Christ together.

While this insight should be received with gratitude, it should also be balanced with other aspects of the biblical vision which are lacking in the insider vision. For example, the household conversions in Acts should be held in tension with Jesus' theology of the church as a new, spiritual family which trumps loyalty to the natural family, a counter-cultural notion exemplified by Jesus himself (Matt 12:49–50/Mark 3:31–35) and expected of his followers (Matt 8:21–22; 19:25; Luke 9:59–62). The presence of the household conversions in Acts remind us that a dramatic rupture with the family is not always necessary; however, the teaching of Jesus also chastens the insider paradigm's value of seeking to preserve the natural family at all costs, avoiding the creation of any alien social structure which could be perceived as "stealing" family members (Lewis 2015b, Loc. 12587). While pursuing household conversions is a valid, biblical goal that is especially relevant to communal societies, this must also be tempered by Jesus' clear teaching that the church is a new spiritual family, in some ways, "over against" the natural family (Luke 12:51–53; 14:25–27).[107]

Another element missing from the oikos/household theme is the full understanding of the church as *household of God*. While emphasizing household/oikos churches, the insider paradigm has not adequately fleshed out the relationship of households to the larger "household of God" (Higgins 2017, 50). As the PCA Study Committee on Insider Movements observed, "Scripture insists that those who profess faith form a household (*oikos*) broader than the familial household (Gal 6:10; Eph 2:19; 1 Tim 3:15; Heb 10:21; 1 Pet 4:17)" (2014, 2123). Thus, an "oikos" which comes to faith and becomes an household church *also* becomes a part of the larger "household of God" (cf. Eph 2:19)—the believing family is adopted into a new (and larger) Jesus family. Therefore, the insider

---
107 Furthermore, the coming to Christ of whole households should also be balanced with instances of people leaving their families to follow Jesus and join his community (Matt 4:18–22; Luke 18:28–30), both of which took place in the communal, collectivist society in the first-century Middle East.

paradigm's vision of social networks *becoming* the church does not yet fully express the nature of the church until it reflects the reality that these believing households become a part of *a new, larger social network* of the household of God that includes people outside the natural family, and even outside the nation.

Two Paradigms: Early Jewish and Gentile Churches

The insider paradigm's appeal to the early Jewish and Gentile church movements is helpful at a number of levels. It helps us to envision the church in the context of a movement that is multiplying throughout a people group and beyond, providing inspiring models with a plethora of insights and principles for those praying for church planting movements among Muslims today. Furthermore, the early church movement took place in the context of severe persecution and thus has a great deal of relevance to contemporary Muslim contexts. The insider paradigm shows us that the early church movements in the book of Acts may provide much richer and more relevant resources for church multiplication than our own personal experiences of church.

However, there are problems with the way the insider framework uses the early Jewish and Gentile movements as paradigms that support contemporary insider movements and churches. The insider paradigm applies both of them to insider movements, and each has its own set of problems, which I deal with in turn.

The early Jewish church in Jerusalem certainly exhibits a number of striking parallels with contemporary insider movements. They initially remained within the framework of the Jewish community, following the lead of Jesus, whose first mission was to lead a renewal movement among the "lost sheep of the house of Israel." When the church in Jerusalem emerged after Pentecost, they did not separate themselves from Israel like the Essenes did (e.g., the Qumran community), but continued to participate in key Jewish institutions such as temple worship and the religious festivals, being known as a faction within Israel, the "sect (*airesis*) of the Nazarenes" (Acts 24:5; cf. 24:14; 28:22; Blue 1994, 120; Gehring 2004, 84, n. 130).

Furthermore, many parallels exist between Jewish and Muslim communities, including monotheism, detailed ethical rules, cultural values, and common biblical figures and teachings. Both Jewish and Muslim communities include official teaching that rejects Jesus as the crucified and risen Lord. It is certainly understandable why some see the early Jewish community as a model for contemporary Muslim insiders remaining in Muslim community identity and rituals.

Despite the striking parallels, several factors indicate that the way the first believers related to their Jewish religious identity and rituals reflect a unique, unrepeatable state of affairs which should not be taken as paradigmatic or precedent-setting for believers in non-Jewish religious communities. The Jewish community is unique among all religious communities of the world as the recipient of God's covenantal promises and special revelation, all of which were fulfilled in Jesus the Messiah of Israel: "To them belong the adoption, the glory, the covenants, the giving of the law, the worship, and the promises. To them belong the patriarchs, and from their race, according to the flesh, is the Christ" (Rom 9:4–5).

These facts are true of no other religious community—God called and chose Israel to be the one community on earth in whom his presence would dwell, to whom he would give biblical revelation, and through whom he would send his Messiah. The early church consistently pointed to these facts when defending their faith and message as *not* anti-Jewish or contrary to the law of Moses (Acts 2:14–36; 3:11–26; 7:2–53; 13:16–41), showing that their relationship with their Jewish heritage was based precisely upon the unique relationship between the gospel and the story of Israel.

Therefore, the unbelief of the Jewish people and the official rejection of Jesus by the temple leadership did not hinder the early church from continuing to maintain their Jewish identity, since their Jewish identity did not rest upon the beliefs of the people *but upon the covenants and promises of God to Israel that were fulfilled in Christ* (cf. Rom 10:21–11:2). This unique foundation of Jewish identity highlights that the relationship between the early church and its Jewish heritage is truly in a unique category all its own rather than a paradigm or precedent for non-Jewish cultures or religious communities.[108]

Another factor bids us caution in seeing the Jerusalem church as paradigmatic for how the church relates to other religious communities. A close reading of the biblical narrative shows that *the biblical authors themselves* did not present the Jerusalem church's relationship to the Jewish community as paradigmatic for non-Jewish contexts. Not all descriptions in narrative are intended to be paradigmatic and abiding beyond their original context, and thus responsible application must look for clear patterns that are repeated by a biblical author and which are not unique to a particular cultural context (Ott and Wilson 2011, Loc. 961–76). The narrative of Acts does provide us with *some* elements of the Jerusalem church's relationship to the Jewish community which are repeated in non-Jewish contexts, and therefore are applicable beyond the Jewish context, such as bold testimony about Jesus in the heart of the community (Acts 3:1–26; 17:16–34), utilization of religious texts and ideas as a communicatory bridge for the gospel (Acts 2:17–28; 17:28), and confronting religious ideas contrary to the gospel (Acts 2:29–36; 17:24–25).

---

108 This same issue is pointed out by Coleman in his critique of the insider paradigm, who maintains that the "vital, organic theological link between Israel and the church means that the church has a unique relationship to Judaism, unparalleled among other religions" (2011, 222). Waterman concurs:

> Unlike Messianic Jews, "Messianic Muslims" don't share an inerrant Scripture with their non-Messianic counterparts or offer the fulfillment of a promise to which their scriptures point. God has established only one "tree" of salvation, having Jewish roots and Christ-following branches. True branches are not grown from the roots of any other religion, though they are to be grafted in from every culture.... We can't afford to pretend that Islam equals the Jewish religion of the first century as a soil in which the gospel (via a "messianic" version) can grow effectively. The roots affect the fruits. The family of true faith in God consists of multiethnic branches grafted into the Judeo-Christian tree. Maintaining any other set of religious roots will not bring forth the fruit pleasing to the Lord of the harvest. (2007, 58, 62)

However, the Jerusalem church's ongoing participation in temple prayers finds no biblical counterpart among Gentile believers. Unlike their Jewish brothers and sisters, Gentiles are clearly expected to separate themselves from their former worship practices. While not required to join the Jewish community or adopt its worship practices based upon the Jewish law (Acts 15:19), there remains an unambiguous call to separate from Greco-Roman religious practices (Acts 15:20–21; Acts 19:18–29; 1 Thess 1:9) and from practices so intertwined with false worship that they involve an unacceptable participation in things which compromise loyalty to Christ (1 Cor 10:19–22). We do not see the church in Antioch participating in prayers in pagan temples to remain within their Greco-Roman religious community, nor do we see the Jerusalem church burning copies of the Torah (as the Gentiles burnt their pagan magic books, cf. Acts 19:18–29). The clear contrast between how Jews and Gentiles were expected to relate to the worship practices of their communities is a clear indication that the biblical authors do not view the Jerusalem church as a paradigm or precedent for how non-Jewish churches relate to their religious contexts.

Some point to 1 Corinthians 8:10 as a possible counter-example to the general New Testament expectation that Gentiles separate from their pagan idolatrous worship practices (Higgins 2006, 37; 2014, 31). While some interpret this verse as implying tacit permission to eat in an idol's temple, there are several reasons why such an interpretation is unlikely.[109] (1) Nowhere in the larger unit (ch 8–10) does Paul explicitly permit eating in idol temples,[110] and the question in 1 Corinthians 8:10 is making a limited, specific point regarding the danger of destroying our brothers with our theological "knowledge" or "rights," not rendering a judgment either way

---

109 This passage provides a notoriously complex and subtle argument on the issue of food offered to idols, and scholars are divided over how to interpret it. It is clear that Paul permits eating idol-offered food in some situations (when bought in the market or served in private homes) and forbids eating it in other situations (when it wounds the conscience of someone present or when it amounts to idolatry). What is unclear is how Paul's warning in 1 Corinthians 10:14–22 against partaking of the table of demons relates to the issue of dining in an idol's temple in 1 Corinthians 8:10. Some scholars, such as Gordon Fee, argue that Paul forbids eating in an idol's temple (first for reasons of Christian charity, then for reasons of idolatry), but allows eating meat sold in the marketplace or served in private homes in certain situations. Others, such as David Garland, argue that it is not about location but about whether or not idol-offered meat is *known* or *mentioned* to be offered to idols, whether in the market, home, or temple (which obviously rules out the temple). Others, such as Bruce Fisk, argue that Paul permits certain kinds of meals in the temple in 8:10, but forbids participating in cultic meals where the idol is present in 10:14–22. While people will continue to interpret this passage differently, we should note that even those New Testament scholars who see 1 Corinthians 8:10 as permitting Gentiles, in principle, to participate in temple meals (as long as it did not offend a weaker conscience) usually limit this to "social" meals in the "temple restaurants." These scholars usually argue that "cultic" temple meals, accompanied by the sacrifice or the presence of the idol, are forbidden by Paul in 1 Corinthians 10:14–22 (e.g., Fisk 1989, Kim 2003).

110 It is notable that in the concluding section of 1 Corinthians 10:23–30 Paul does not mention temple meals at all, but rather addresses the eating of idol-offered food that is bought in the marketplace or that is served in a private home (which is allowed if not *named* as "idol-offered" food).

on whether idol-temple dining is inherently idolatrous.[111] (2) The overall tone and context of 1 Corinthians 8:7–13 is to *discourage* the Corinthians from eating in an idol temple, rebuking them for using their theological "knowledge" (which later is revealed to be incomplete; cf. 1 Corinthians 10:20) to justify their actions. (3) The full argument of 1 Corinthians 8–10, which culminates in ch. 10, makes it highly unlikely that Paul permits dining in idol temples, since 10:14–22 states that sharing in the sacrifices of the pagan altar is equivalent to dining with demons.[112] Paul concludes by permitting meat bought in the market or served in a private home as long as the food is not declared or known to be idol-offered (1 Cor 10:23–30).[113]

The best way to reconcile all of these statements is to recognize them as part of a multi-stage argument in 1 Corinthians 8–10, in which Paul first discourages eating in idol temples for reasons of Christian love and charity (chapters 8–9), then discourages eating in idol temples for reasons of idolatry (10:1–22), and finally permits eating idol-offered food bought in the market or served in homes only if not declared to be idol-offered (10:23–30). The fuller context of 1 Corinthians 8–10, therefore, does not seem to support the idea that Christian Gentiles could continue eating in idol temples without compromising their Christian faith. It would not seem prudent, then, to consider this passage as offering any clear exception to the overall New Testament expectation of Gentile believers separating from the religious rituals of their Greco-Roman heritage.

The New Testament shows that the early Jewish believers remained in their Jewish identity and religious rituals, but it does not clearly put this forward as paradigmatic for believers in other religious communities, as seen in the clear contrast between Jewish believers and Gentile believers as noted above, as well as the unique status and identity of the Jewish people in God's plan. These factors caution us against seeing the early Jewish movement as a precedent for contemporary insiders retaining "socio-religious" identity and continuing in Muslim religious rituals.

Paradoxically, the insider paradigm also finds paradigmatic significance in the early Gentile movement, in view of the Jerusalem Council. However, this too is of questionable validity. First, it should be recognized that the Jerusalem Council

---

111 Regardless of whether the statement is hypothetical (as Garland says) or referring to an actual practice common at the time (as Fee says), 1 Cor 8:10 falls short of a definitive statement on whether or not eating in idol temples is inherently idolatrous. Though Garland thinks it is hypothetical and Fee thinks it is descriptive, both agree that the context clearly rules out any condoning of the practice as theologically neutral.

112 Cf. Garland 2003. Higgins suggests that the warning of 1 Corinthians 10:14–22 is intended to warn against a personal, subjective evaluation of the believer's mind or heart with the idol or demon (2014). Therefore, a believer could dine in an idol's temple as long as he or she is not intentionally engaging with the idol or demon in his mind and heart. However, there is nothing in the passage that supports seeing the warning as one of the mind and heart only. Rather, the problem is of the objective reality—which is true even if not recognized by participants—that what is sacrificed at the altar is sacrificed to demons, and partakers of the altar are partakers with demons. The problem is *not* that the participants may engage with the demons in their mind and heart; the problem is that they are *unaware* of the presence of demons and *unknowingly* become participants with these demons when they partake of the sacrifices of the altar.

113 It is notable that Paul does not mention temple meals anywhere in 10:23–30.

decision focused on whether Gentiles should follow the law and become Jews, not whether Gentiles could continue participating in their pagan religious practices. Two of the four stipulations given to the Gentiles actually indicate a separation from pagan religious practices—food polluted by idols and sexual immorality (Acts 15:20). Gentiles were not expected to completely withdraw from their society (1 Cor 5:9–10; 10:27–30), but they were expected to abstain from false religious elements that might pollute their worship of Jesus (1 Cor 10:14–22), a calling which would risk social alienation in a society in which pagan religiosity was interwoven into the fabric of everyday life and culture (cf. 1 Pet 4:3–4; Acts 17:6–7; 19:23–31).[114]

Second, the decision of the Jerusalem elders to allow Gentiles to follow Jesus "as Gentiles" is *not* equivalent to "retaining their former (socio)religious identity." "Gentile" is not a religious identity with positive content; rather, it has negative meaning, simply meaning "not Jewish." Following Jesus "as Gentiles" is not equivalent to following Jesus as Zeus-worshippers, imperial cult devotees, or Greco-Roman mystery religionsists.

Third, while the Gentiles were not required to join the "Jewish community," they were considered as full members in the new, believing Jew-Gentile church. This in many ways is the point of the Jerusalem Council, not only concerned with issues of salvation of the Gentiles, but whether or not they should be considered full, equal members in the people of God (Acts 15:14–17). Far from encouraging a "bilateral" or "multilateral" ecclesiology (Talman 2015, Loc. 6093–109), the Jerusalem Council provides *a single, expanded ecclesiology* that makes room for Jews and Gentiles in the one people of God. It is incorrect to understand the Jerusalem Council as condoning a separation of "Jewish" and "Gentile" churches. While the predominantly Jewish and predominantly Gentile congregations would certainly reflect different cultural practices, both were expected to make adjustments in order to maintain solidarity in the one body of Christ. The last two stipulations in Acts 15:20–21, as well as Paul's instructions in Rom 14:1–15:9, reflect ways that Gentiles were to make accommodations for their Jewish brothers and sisters, while Jews were

---

114 Garland's comments on Paul's instructions in 1 Corinthians 10 for the Corinthians to avoid food known to be sacrificed to an idol are instructive for the social implications of such actions:

> Avoiding all overt associations with idolatry would invite hostility, especially when one was a guest at the home of a religiously minded host who offered food that had been sanctified by an idol. If the host was a patron, one's refusal to eat idol food could be taken as a grave insult to the god and the host, and such an affront could lead to financial retribution. If the host was a family member or a neighbor, the refusal could result in being cast into the outer darkness of social banishment. After her conversion and renunciation of idols and idol food, Aseneth laments being hated by her family and her people (Jos. As. 11:3–9). In the face of such pressure, Christians would be tempted to compromise and rationalize their decisions (Cheung 1999:38). The social problems created for Christians who abandoned idolatry are described in 1 Pet 4:3–4: former friends are surprised at the Christians' new temperance, and in their irritation they malign them and blaspheme God. Withdrawing from all idolatrous functions would scuttle any ambitions for social advancement, impair patron/client relations, fuel ostracism, and damage economic partnerships. (Garland 2003, Loc. 10796)

expected to risk offending their countrymen through the controversial act of eating with "unclean" Gentiles (Gal 2:11–16).

These factors indicate a significant gap between the situation of the Gentiles and that of contemporary insider movements. This does not mean that the Jerusalem Council has no relevance for emerging churches in Muslim cultures. The Jerusalem Council is not merely descriptive and historical, but a salvation-historical turning point with abiding implications for the church in every age. Unlike in Islam, the church does not have a single divinely authoritative culture that it must conform to; rather, it can take root in any and every culture (Ott and Wilson 2011, Loc. 1364). This means that emerging churches in Muslim cultures are not required to adopt any one specific cultural identity, whether American Christian culture, Arab Christian culture, or any other culture. Established Christian churches should take care not to become new "Judaizers" who add unbiblical, cultural requirements to emerging churches. However, the Jerusalem Council provides no clear, unambiguous license to retain religious identity and continue to participate in former religious practices. Both the early Jewish movement and the early Gentile movement in the book of Acts provide invaluable resources for the nature of the biblical church in the Muslim world, but they do not provide any strong grounds for an insider church that "retains "socio-religious" identity," as this phrase is understood in the insider paradigm.

Some Missing Pieces

As seen above, the insider paradigm seeks to root its vision of the church in a variety of biblical themes and teachings, at times challenging our biblical vision in positive ways, and at other times obscuring the fullness of those biblical themes. In addition, it should be noted that there are certain key biblical themes of the church that are overlooked in the insider paradigm which would balance out and qualify certain claims, goals, or emphases in the insider vision.

One theme whose implications are neglected in the insider paradigm is the church as a "holy, set-apart people" (e.g., Ex 19:5–6; 1 Pet 2:9–12). The theme of the church as a "holy people" highlights the church's "other-ness" with respect to society, qualifying other images of the church emphasized in insider ekklēsia, such as "yeast in dough" or "seed in soil." While such imagery should certainly shape our understanding of the church, it has at times been overemphasized in the insider paradigm at the expense of other biblical themes and images of the church, such as the church as a holy, set-apart nation. Holiness certainly includes "restored and restructured relationships" (Duerkson and Dyrness 2019, 117–20), but it also involves an element of "set-apartness" from practices or relationships which would compromise or "defile" the presence of God among his people (2 Cor 6:14–7:1; Eph 5:7). The insider model of the church as deeply embedded in Muslim community as "yeast in dough" needs to be qualified and balanced by the "other-ness" of the church as a holy, set-apart nation, a point to which we will return later regarding the church-world relationship.

Another important theme whose implications are overlooked in the insider paradigm is the church as *the new humanity*. Insider biblical theology tends to emphasize the retention and preservation of social, religious, and cultural identity and solidarity. However, the insider paradigm does not adequately attend to the way this emphasis should be qualified and nuanced by the church's identity as a "new humanity" in Jesus, the "second Adam" who inaugurates a new ancestry—a diverse, Jew-Gentile community reconciled to God and each another in Christ (Eph 2:11–22; 1 Cor 15:21–23, 45–49; Rom 5:12–21; cf. Gal 3:28–28). This provides believers a new heritage and destiny that relativizes and supersedes social and cultural ancestries and inheritances, impacting "old" solidarities and creating new ones in which there is "neither Jew nor Greek." Insider advocates should reflect further how this biblical theme should chasten and further nuance the emphasis on preserving existing solidarities and identities.

Finally, the insider paradigm overlooks key aspects of the theme of the church as *the people of God*, the full understanding of which seems to question certain assumptions in the insider paradigm. Specifically, this theme highlights the fact that the identity of the church is constituted by the biblical narrative, and thus all who are in Christ are grafted into a new story and community defined by the biblical drama. The insider paradigm envisions, however, the insider church "remaining" in and "retaining" of Muslim identity, and Muslims have their own narratives and history which shape how they express their identity in the Muslim *umma*—a narrative which, for many, revolves significantly around the life of the prophet Muhammad, his reception of the Qur'an, and his mission to (re)establish Islam on earth. There are multiple expressions of Muslim identity, and different defining narratives play a key role in this. My Shi'ite Muslim friends share with Sunni Muslims the narrative of Muhammad's life and message, but their Muslim identity is defined by an alternate narrative *post*-Muhammad that revolves around the revered "imams," whom the Shi'a consider the legitimate successors of the prophet that were persecuted and martyred by the Sunni caliphs (Pinault 2016, 624–28). Whatever the expression of Muslim identity, it is largely constituted by a particular defining narrative within which that community identifies.

However, regardless of what kind of Muslim background people come from, when they are united with Christ, they are grafted in to a different history—the story of Abraham, Isaac, Israel, Jesus, and the Spirit-filled church. This "adoptive past" becomes a new overarching narrative which defines believers' identity as part of the people of God (Walls 1982, 99), superseding, relativizing, and correcting all other narratives, whether cultural, tribal, political, or religious.[115] The insider narrative often expresses and defends insider identity in terms of a

---

[115] This not only relates to how believers read and interpret Scripture, but also in terms of the ritual practices which are participated in or adopted, since rituals rehearse and reinforce these identity-shaping narratives.

simple binary of retaining "Muslim identity" versus adopting "Christian identity." However, such a simple binary lacks the sufficient clarity and nuance in regards to how the biblical narrative of the people of God expands, relativizes, and transforms Muslim narratives and identities, as well as how this narrative unites believers in Christ with a single, common "people of God" identity with people from other cultures and narratives. [116] The insider paradigm should allow the full scope and implications of the "people of God" theme to shape the way it affirms and articulates the notion of retaining Muslim identity.

It is now clear that the insider vision of the church is rooted in a variety of biblical themes and paradigms. The biblical underpinnings for the insider church alerts us to some significant themes which have been neglected in a theology of the church and traditional models of church planting. At the same time, there are several important aspects of the biblical theology of the church which are either missing or misapplied in insider biblical theology of the church which, if grasped, temper or modify certain aspects of the insider model of the church. Scripture is foundational for our theology, and thus the strengths and liabilities in the biblical foundation of the insider church affect the insider vision of the church as a whole, as will be made clear in the remaining categories, the next of which is the core essence of the church.

Core Essence: Evaluating Insider Ekklēsia

The essential nature of the church speaks to what essentially makes the church *the church*—what gives it identity and distinguishes it from all other communities. The insider paradigm offers a particular account of the core essence of the church that is compatible with the church remaining in a "socio-religious" Muslim insider context. This account challenges our vision of the church in important ways, but it also falls short in key respects.

The clear distinction between the biblical essence of the church and Western cultural experiences and institutions of the church is an important distinction that forces the issue of distinguishing between what is biblical and what is cultural. The insider paradigm rightly emphasizes the importance of not importing Western cultural expressions of the church into Muslim contexts, which may make it more difficult for the church to spread indigenously and organically in Muslim cultures.

Another strength of the insider vision is the way it focuses our attention on what is at the heart of the core essence of the church: the saving presence and work of

---

116 One place this weakness can be seen is in *Insider Jesus*, in which Dyrness advocates for a type of mission in which indigenous people understand and reframe the gospel in the framework of their own religious narratives (2016, Loc. 1953). His case study of a Muslim insider movement in the Philippines involves an insider group studying the concept of prophecy, but studying it in the context of Muhammad's ascension to heaven and an affirmation of his role as a prophet. Within this context, they would examine the centrality of Jesus in the Islamic tradition of the prophets (ibid., Loc. 1797). This kind of activity, and the model based upon it, undermines the authority of the biblical narrative—which transcends, challenges, and relativizes every cultural and religious narrative.

God in bringing people into his kingdom and uniting them to the body of Christ. Drawing upon a variety of biblical themes, the insider paradigm rightly highlights the spiritual and theological nature of the church as a creation of God and a Christ-centered, kingdom community. In so doing, the insider paradigm challenges us to place all our human efforts and institutions in proper perspective, remembering that it is ultimately God, not people, who creates the church.

While helpfully emphasizing the spiritual identity of the church, the insider paradigm falls short in fleshing out the full social implications of the church's spiritual identity—the way that the ecclesial identity of the church can and should eventually restructure and transform social identity in a variety of ways. The insider paradigm offers a largely accurate and biblical view of the core essence of the church; however it also contends that such a reality is perfectly consistent with, and does not contradict, the notion of believers retaining their "social" or "socio-religious" identity as Muslims (or Buddhists, or Hindus). The insider paradigm often distinguishes between "ecclesial identity" and "social/socio-religious identity," affirming that the former does not require one to change the latter (cf. Duerkson 2015, Loc. 3999; Lewis 2015, Loc. 12547). These two identities are described as "overlapping" and as a "dual identity," not mutually exclusive of the other.

However, such ways of relating "ecclesial identity" and "social/socio-religious identity" are problematic, since they do not fully recognize the way that "ecclesial identity" of the church can and should impact one's social identity. The church itself is a social—even a "socio-religious"—reality, and its spiritual, theological identity reconfigures one's social relations in profound, complex ways. In its efforts to keep social disruption to a minimum, however, the insider paradigm misses out on the ways that the essence of the church represents a powerful transformation of one's social identity, both inside and outside the community of faith. The insider paradigm does not address how one's membership in the body of Christ should change how a Muslim-background believer relates to his or her Muslim heritage, nor does it address how this theological identity transforms old solidarities while creating new ones. The insider paradigm rightly rejects a paradigm which requires a complete break with one's Muslim culture, heritage, and community; however, it has replaced it with a paradigm which lacks a nuanced understanding of the varied ways in which the body of Christ challenges and reconfigures one's social relationships, whether in the family, in society, or in the body of Christ.

Part of the problem here is the unfortunate tendency in the insider paradigm to portray "social/socio-religious" identity in terms of a binary choice: either you keep it or you change it. However, as some have pointed out, social identity is much more complex than this, and there are many layers and aspects to social identity (Barnett 2013, 26; Green 2013a). One can retain some aspects of identity while changing others. Furthermore, one can be less or more public about certain changes; for example, a person who decides they are no longer a

Muslim can choose to announce that fact, or they can keep it to themselves. The insider paradigm, however, through its language of "retaining" or "not changing" "social/socio-religious identity," glosses over these different nuances, portraying this complex reality as an all-or-nothing choice.

A more nuanced understanding is important for recognizing the complex way in which the core essence of the church interfaces with social and religious identity. The core essence of the church does not necessarily demand a complete break with all aspects of one's social and religious identity, nor does it leave social and religious identity unchanged. Rather, the biblical essence of the church can and should, over time, transform and reconfigure social relations and identity in a variety of different ways. The church's unique salvific relationship with God results in new social relationships which will transform one's social identity in complex ways.

One of the ways in which the core essence of the church impacts social identity is creating a certain distinctiveness of identity. The people of God in the Old Testament, and the church in the New Testament, were set apart as a people chosen by God and given a unique and distinctive identity which distinguished them from their surrounding society (Ex 19:4–6, Lev 20:24–26, 1 Pet 2:9–10). The insider paradigm, however, has not always fully captured the social distinctiveness of the biblical church in its community:

> Coming to Christ requires an identity-shift, and a transfer of allegiances. It is not enough to just purge unbiblical behavior while maintaining an Islamic identity. Of course, those who accepted Christ and joined his body, the Church, did not somehow instantly lose their culture. But a key difference between the early church and Insider models is that new believers belonged to a distinct new group, in the context of which they could sort out their new lives, aided by the Holy Spirit. Even for those who were able to remain in their families, they now had a new family. Now, "Whoever does God's will" had become their "brother and sister and mother." (Houssney 2011, 6)

> The Church is always other, separate and distinct. Its witness depends on its being different. It stands out like a light on a hill. In the Old Testament God calls it "my people," "my treasured possession." … Jesus calls it "my flock," "my body," "my disciples," "my bride." Muslims are invited to join a new community of the saints. (ibid., 14)

Houssney clearly affirms the theological distinctiveness of the church's identity as a new and unique community, expressed in the panoply of biblical themes and metaphors for the church. The church is set apart, a special and distinctive community by nature. The insider paradigm's model of the church, while affirming many aspects of the church's theological identity, soft-pedals the distinctive uniqueness of the biblical church.

Does this mean that emerging churches must completely reject their Muslim cultural identity and adopt a foreign "Christian" cultural identity? Not necessarily.

INSIDER CHURCH

The distinctiveness of the church does not require distinctiveness in *every* possible way; it certainly does not require a total rejection of one's ethnic and cultural identity. It also does not require conformity to the cultural distinctives associated with the culturally Christian community. For churches that seek to remain and flourish in Muslim societies, the distinctive identity of the church may need to be expressed with a great deal of wisdom and care so as to avoid bringing unnecessary suspicion or threatening the honor of the community. Emerging churches may choose, for pragmatic reasons, to express the distinctiveness of their ecclesial identity in ways which employ vocabulary and cultural forms that are familiar in the context which are not overtly associated with cultural Christianity in that community. Regardless of the forms that are employed, the core essence of the church should make emerging churches, to some degree, "strangers and aliens" in their community.

Therefore, the insider paradigm's emphasis on language of "retaining" or "preserving," or "not changing" "social/socio-religious identity" is less than adequate for expressing the full essence of the church. The church can co-exist with certain aspects of "social/socio-religious identity," but it should also express biblical distinctiveness.

The insider paradigm is to be commended for distinguishing between biblical church and Western culture, as well as for affirming the redemptive, Christological, and spiritual nature of the church. At the same time, the insider paradigm's stated strong commitment to ongoing identification with the Muslim community often prevents it from fully fleshing out the social implications and the theological distinctiveness of the church's essential identity as the special people of God.

The core essence of the church is no mere ephemeral, metaphysical reality, but rather takes shape concretely in the local churches and the universal body of Christ. These topics provide yet further insight into the strengths and weaknesses of the insider church.

Evaluating Local Ekklēsia in the Insider Paradigm

The insider paradigm is not content with a "church-less" movement to Christ—it envisions local communities of insiders that express biblical ekklēsia. To this end, the insider paradigm sets forth a particular vision of local ekklēsia for insiders, a vision which captures some elements of the biblical vision while missing other elements.

Insider ekklēsia challenges us to recover aspects of the biblical local church, directing us away from the cultural "trappings" of the local church and refocusing our attention on its essential features. The insider vision of the church as a "Christ-centered community" calls us back to the heart of what Jesus always intended his church to be—a community of disciples following their Master. The insider paradigm also affirms salvation through faith in Christ as integral to the nature of the local church.

Furthermore, the insider paradigm affirms many of the essential functions of the church, such as prayer, fellowship, Bible study, and commitment to one another.

Many insider advocates envision a process whereby an emerging church develops into a more mature church that includes elements such as praise/worship, regular patterns of meeting together, baptism, communion, and elders (e.g., Jameson and Scalevich 2000, 38; Travis and Travis 2005, 409; Brown 2006, 131; Corwin 2007a, 10; Higgins 2015c, Loc. 12752; Travis and Woodberry 2015, Loc. 1494).

Another strength of the insider vision of the local church is its vision for a church that spreads through existing social/familial networks. In its development of the oikos/household church model, the insider paradigm helps to highlight the ways that Western individualistic culture has affected our understanding of the nature of the local church and church planting. The insider paradigm helps show us that there are alternative models to expressing the nature of the church in a communal society, models which may minimize the social scandal of people coming to faith and which may increase the possibility that new churches are able to remain in their context and have social and familial support in their new faith, increasing their ability to witness for Christ throughout their networks.

Notwithstanding these strengths, the insider model of the local church also falls short in certain areas. Some definitions of local ekklēsia leave out one or more of its essential elements. At times, the local church is portrayed as not much more than a group of believers in Jesus (Hayes 2011, 4). Other times, a believing family which is living out the "one another" care of the church is considered a "local expression" of the church, without reference to any regular pattern of gathering or the other biblical functions of the local church (Lewis 2007, 76).[117] Some definitions include elements of the local church like baptized believers, along with some concept of organized community, and yet they lack many of the specific elements that are essential to the nature of a local church, such as regular gatherings, the unique purpose of these gatherings, and the presence of biblical elders (Talman 2004b, 9).[118] All of the above examples affirm aspects of the biblical local church, yet they each leave out one or more of the essential elements of New Testament local church communities.

It has been claimed that the insider paradigm operates with a "simple church" or "two-or-three-gathered" ecclesiology (Bartlotti 2013, 139), and my analysis suggests that this is an accurate assessment of some insider advocates' definitions of the local church. This is not to deny that such communities could be a beginning, the first steps of the local church being formed in those contexts. A "simple church" approach is helpful in many ways, especially if its main goal is to strip away all unnecessary add-ons that distract from the essence of the church and keep the church from being easily reproducible. However, we must not leave out any *essential elements* of the church, lest we make the church more "simple" than the New Testament church itself.

---

117 House churches in the New Testament clearly had patterns of regular, intentional gatherings (Acts 2:46; 12:12; 20:7; Rom 16:5; 1 Cor 11:17; 14:26; 16:19), and when some neglected this habit, this earned explicit rebuke (Heb 10:25–26).

118 By Talman's definition, any Christian organization which requires baptism of its members would be defined as a local church. Such a definition effectively does away with the distinction between "church" and "parachurch."

INSIDER CHURCH

Some of the more robust insider definitions of the local church include baptism, communion, and mutual commitment, while leaving out other essential elements such as a regular pattern of gathering or biblical elders (Duerkson 2012, 162; Duerkson and Dyrness 2019, 151).[119]

Duerkson and Dyrness' suggestion that the offices of the churches (including elders) are functions of the whole community before being delegated to specific individuals is helpful in envisioning how new, emerging churches might function before biblically qualified elders are available. However, this should be combined with the clear biblical pattern in which Paul regularly appointed elders in every church he planted; he did not simply leave it up to each church to remain indefinitely without elders until they felt the need for them. Thus, the appointment of biblical elders should be included as an essential component and a significant milestone in the establishment of a biblical church.

Some insider advocates acknowledge that the emerging insider fellowships do not always reflect the full biblical teaching on the church (Higgins 2006, 119; Dyrness 2016, Loc. 2678). The fact that these local communities are often referred to as "fellowships," "communities," and "expressions of the church/ekklēsia" may indicate the awareness that such communities are not full local churches in the New Testament sense. Kevin Higgins affirms much of what is included in my definition of the local church, including the presence of biblical elders, as marks of a "mature church." However, Higgins still seeks to affirm the groups which are not yet fully expressing all of these components as an "expression of the Church body."

It is important, however, to distinguish between a definition of the local church, and a vision of an *ideal, healthy, and spiritually mature church*. The latter includes many elements which may or may not be present in local churches; the Corinthian church was still considered a church despite significant deficiencies in maturity and church health. The definition of the local church, however, deals with elements which are necessary for a group to be even *considered* a church in the first place.

If a group does not yet contain all of the elements of the local church, this does not mean that it does not express *any* aspects of ekklēsia. Informal groups of believers, as well as parachurch groups, reflect aspects of the body of Christ in their fellowship. However, such groups are not *churches*. Unless new elements are added to their community structure, they do not reflect the particular kinds of communities that we see in the New Testament which regularly gather together for particular functions under the leadership and authority of biblical elders.

Rather than softening the meaning of church to fit groups of believers that fall short of the full biblical picture of the church, a better way forward is to understand

---

[119] This is not to say that Duerkson and Dyrness envision a community that never gathers; it is quite difficult to have a community committed to one another in familial ways that never sees each other. However, it is possible to have a committed community that does not have a regular pattern of meeting together, and such a regular pattern of gathering seems to be an important part of the New Testament picture of the local church.

simple gatherings of believers as incomplete, potential, or "embryonic" churches, which are not yet a church but are potentially on the way to becoming a church (Waterman 2011). Dyrness' suggestion is not far from this idea, when he suggests that insider movements have a status analogous to Protestant churches in Roman Catholic ecclesiology—as communities with "elements of sanctification and truth" which are still incomplete and not yet in communion with the full, biblical church of Christ (2016, Loc. 2678).[120]

The notion of churches as "emerging" through the social interactions between people and God in a particular context may prove helpful here (Duerkson and Dyrness 2019, 27–28). However, an emphasis on the "emerging," in-process nature of the church should be combined with a clear, robust definition of the local church which reflects all of the key elements in the New Testament understanding of local ekklēsia. Local groups do not "emerge" into local churches by accident—a clear understanding of what a local church *is*, biblically speaking, is critical to guide incomplete, emerging fellowships to develop into local churches.[121]

We ought to acknowledge that "elements of sanctification and truth" seem to be present in many insider fellowships, and that many of them do express aspects of the body of Christ, even if incompletely, for which we should rejoice and glorify God. However, we should not stop there, but should continue to pray and labor for such groups to become full local churches, and our prayers and labors should be guided and fueled by a clear, robust definition of the local church.

Finally, all of the deficiencies related to the core essence of the church also affect the vision of the local church, since one of the essential elements of the local church is having an identity *as an ekklēsia*. Insider definitions of the local church do not include an emphasis on local groups becoming aware of and consciously embracing their common inheritance as the people of God, the body of Christ, and temple of the Spirit, *as a new corporate theological identity as a believing community.*

---

120 Dyrness' proposal is to be commended for acknowledging that insider "churches" can fall short of fully expressing the biblical church (even as he advocates for affirming them as potentially possessing the core of church). However, his analogy is not without its problems, at least two of which deserve note, from both Protestant and Catholic vantage points, respectively. From the Roman Catholic perspective, Protestant communities *should change* and rejoin the Catholic Church. By analogy, this implies that insider communities *should also change* and become full, biblical churches. However, this runs counter to Dyrness' argument, which is that evangelicals should *not* impose any particular concept of church upon insider communities, but allow them to "emerge" on their own (2016, Loc. 2664). Dyrness tries to avoid this by switching to a Protestant perspective (ibid., Loc. 2694), but this raises another problem. For Protestants, the Roman Catholic assessment of Protestant churches is itself problematic, in that it ties the nature of the true church to formal, institutional fellowship with a particular institution, namely the Roman church—thus failing to recognize that Protestant churches can and do reflect the full, biblical nature of the church. Yet this, too, undermines Dyrness' argument, which is that insider communities, while they may contain "an incipient ecclesial form" (ibid., Loc. 2731), do *not yet* reflect the full biblical church (as other Christian communities presumably do).

121 In *The Bare Essentials for Helping Groups Become Churches: Four Helps for Church Planting Movements*, Steve Smith (2012) advises movement-practitioners to have a clear definition of the church which is biblical and reproducible; to have a specific lesson (or lessons) about the church early in discipleship; and to use "church health mapping" to track the development of all aspects of church life.

As shown previously, the insider paradigm has not captured the way this group identity interacts with and transforms various aspects of social, familial, and religious identity that cannot be accounted for by the "retaining socio-religious identity" language.

The insider vision of the local church stimulates us to recover several aspects of the local church as a Christ-centered community committed to following Jesus together and living in fellowship characterized by Bible study and prayer. It helps provide us a different model for reaching communal societies by planting the church in households that remain within existing social networks. Along with these strengths, the insider vision falls short by offering incomplete definitions of the local church that contain some, but not all, elements of the New Testament church, and particularly struggle to account for the way the local church should embrace and express its identity as the church in its context.

The strengths and weaknesses of the insider paradigm are evident not only in its vision of the local church, but also in its vision of the universal church.

Evaluating the Universal Church in the Insider Paradigm

The insider paradigm reflects several key aspects of the biblical vision of the universal church. While describing Muslim insiders as outside "Christianity" and "the (institutional) Christian Church," insider advocates affirm the universal body of Christ (sometimes in terms of the "Kingdom of God"), and affirm that Muslim insiders are part of it (Travis and Travis 2005, 402; Travis et al. 2006, 124; Travis and Woodberry 2015, Loc. 1477–86; Higgins 2009a, 76). It is encouraging to know that many insider believers are aware of this larger kingdom community of which they are members, even if they are not in significant tangible fellowship with that community (Travis and Woodberry 2015); also encouraging is hearing of some cases in which insiders are finding ways to express this unity in specific, controlled settings (2009a, 80–81).

However, the insider paradigm also has some clear problems in regard to expressing the universal church. One problem is that even if insiders are aware of the larger body of Christ, there still remains de facto separation from real, meaningful fellowship with the wider church. Insider advocates acknowledge this reality, and yet they disagree on whether or not this is problematic biblically. Some in the insider camp see this separatism as not only permissible but as having biblical precedent in the early Jewish and Gentile churches, resulting in a "one body, two communities" ecclesiology (Jameson and Scalevich 2000).

A growing number of insider advocates, however, see the separation between insiders and the wider church as a less than ideal situation which falls short of the biblical vision. Woodberry, Dutch, and Higgins have all expressed a hope that insider fellowships would eventually find ways to express their connection with the larger body of Christ, even if such expressions are low-profile and limited (Woodberry 2007, 28; Dutch 2000, 22; Higgins 2009a, 80–81).

I concur with this latter group of insider advocates that the de facto separation between insiders and the larger body of Christ falls short of the biblical vision of the church. A "one body, two communities" paradigm is antithetical to Pauline ecclesiology; it is clear from Paul's letters that churches were not segregated but included both Jews and Gentiles (i.e., the letter to the Romans). While Paul and Timothy adopted a bi-cultural flexibility in identifying with Jews and Gentiles for the sake of the gospel, it does not follow from this that they supported or advocated a principled separation between Jewish and Gentile communities. Paul strongly rebuked Peter for separatist behavior when he stopped eating with Gentiles after the arrival of the Jewish delegation from James (Gal 2:11–14), and Paul passionately affirmed the counter-cultural truth that Christ had demolished the dividing wall between Jews and Gentiles, making them one people, one new humanity (Eph 2:11–22). One body means one community, one family, one people (Eph 4:1–6). While pragmatic and geographical factors are unavoidable, we must never be content with any church being cut off from the wider body of Christ.

However, we cannot adequately address the problem without asking whether the insider paradigm itself contributes to this separation. By default, the insider paradigm prioritizes "socio-religious" solidarity with the Muslim community over solidarity with historical Christianity and churches identifying as "Christian." While this has certain practical advantages of further safeguarding "insider" status with Muslim family and friends, it also creates an inherent barrier to meaningful participation and fellowship in the global church, which, for the most part, identifies as "Christian." The apostle Paul encouraged flexibility and mutual submission on the part of both Jews and Gentiles in order to express the unity of the two groups in the one body of Christ (Rom 14:13–15:3; 1 Cor 8:7–13). Furthermore, all of this was grounded in a larger and more foundational single-community identity as the church, the body of Christ, shared by both Jews and Gentiles (Eph 2:11–22). Christ has demolished all barriers—ethnic, cultural, gender, social status—making all believers one in Christ (Gal 3:28–29). The convictions of the insider paradigm, however, at times seem to erect a barrier from the start that hinders the development of universal church identity.

Another way the insider paradigm hinders the full expression of the universal church is the principled distancing of "insiders" from non-Muslim "outsiders" (e.g., Dutch 2000, 22). For security reasons, and for pragmatic reasons, the insider paradigm aims to keep potential movements free from "contamination" from outside forces. Substantial contact by outsiders is limited to select cross-cultural "alongsiders" who serve as behind-the-scenes coaches or mentors to the leaders (cf. Travis 2013b), while Christians and traditional churches are kept at a distance in order to keep from compromising either the security or the rigorously insider nature of the movement. In certain contexts, protecting emerging movements from being publicly associated with foreigners may be prudent and even necessary.

However, when such purposeful separation is taken too far, it creates yet another barrier between emerging churches and the wider body of Christ.

For the above reasons, I humbly suggest that the insider paradigm is in danger of promoting a sectarian model of the church. Insider advocates have responded to such criticisms by pointing to rampant sectarianism in American denominations and churches, asking why critics should hold insiders to a standard to which our own churches have miserably failed to attain (Duerkson 2012, 165). This is an excellent point, and we should certainly remove the log from our eyes. However, sectarian ecclesiology at home should not be an excuse to export sectarian ecclesiology abroad.

Furthermore, we must recognize the difference between *denominationalism* and *sectarianism*, the former being a more or less acceptable state of affairs and the latter being an unbiblical division within the universal church (Williams 2007, 64–65). To be clear, I am not here advocating for denominationalism, but rather pointing out the difference between denominationalism and separatism. For example, a Baptist church that is open to and embraces meaningful fellowship with other evangelical churches in its city is different from a Baptist church that rejects fellowship with churches that differ in small points of doctrine. The latter church is sectarian, but not the former. It is possible for churches that are denominational (or nondenominational) in nature to still remain open to meaningful fellowship and partnership with churches outside its specific tribe. On the other hand, some denominations and churches focus so much energy upon their distinctive beliefs/practices that, functionally, they are sects (ibid.). Woodberry describes one particular insider-fellowship network as a potential "denomination in the making" (2005, 21). However, I ask whether the insider paradigm makes it just as likely for a given movement to become a separatistic "sect in the making."

While there are a growing number of voices calling for a more substantial connection with the universal church, the insider paradigm as currently defined seems to place barriers in the DNA of the church to fully expressing the universal church. Bartlotti notes,

> Granted, insider proponents argue that insider believers do, in fact, identify with the larger body of Christ. But this identity would appear to be largely in their hearts, in the meeting room, and with select individuals who, in effect, mediate that relationship. For *security* reasons, for *social* reasons, and now for *theological* reasons, Christian identity is not assumed or marked in public, or in the now globalized public square. (2013, 145; emphasis in original)

Identifying with the universal church is, for various reasons, internalized, limited, and privatized in the insider paradigm. This falls short of expressing the biblical richness of the church as the new humanity which reconciles enemies into one global family in anticipation of that great eschatological, multiethnic, multinational, multilingual company of the redeemed. No individual local church can fully express this ideal, but the local church should teach and fully embrace that they are part of this global community—which in turn shapes their own self-understanding and identity as the local body of Christ as they express and anticipate this global, eschatological gathering of the church triumphant. Clearly, high-persecution, underground church contexts will not be able to express the universal church in a fully public, legal form, but neither did the churches in the New Testament, whose house-church movements did not prevent churches from meaningful, tangible, and personal fellowship and partnership with the universal church— including across Jewish-Gentile lines (2 Cor 8:15; Acts 21:17–20; Rom 16:1–16). While the insider paradigm affirms the universal church in many commendable respects, its vision of an insider church sets up some roadblocks to developing and expressing the fullness of the biblical vision of the universal church.

This discussion of the universal church relates directly to the visible and invisible nature of the church, which presents yet another opportunity to gain a fresh look at the strengths and shortcomings of the insider paradigm.

Evaluating Visible and Invisible Elements in Insider Church

In chapter two, I offered a biblical perspective on the visible and invisible nature of the church, and the insider model reflects many elements of this biblical vision. Multiple insider advocates rightly affirm the church as a "visible," observable community at the local level, as is clear from its local church vision. While the visibility of insider fellowships may need to remain low-profile for security reasons, there remains a clear affirmation of a real, physical expression of a community of insiders that is visible to Muslim family and friends within the larger Muslim family/social network (e.g., Travis and Travis 2005; Higgins 2009b, 70; Duerksen 2012, 162).

Additionally, even if not all are comfortable with the terminology, insider advocates rightly affirm legitimate aspects of the invisible church. The insider paradigm affirms the biblical teaching of the church as a "mixed community," and it emphasizes the spiritual, invisible nature of the church, into which all believers are incorporated before they physically participate in a visible community. Furthermore, the insider paradigm strongly advocates for insider believers, and insider fellowships, to be considered part of and "expressions of" the body of Christ, even if their communities do not completely live up to the fullness of the biblical picture of the church. While this at times leads to confusion regarding the definition of the local church, it is consistent with the invisible nature of the church, which is that the church ultimately belongs to God and not to us, that he alone knows its full membership, and that our imperfect attempts to visibly express the church do not detract from its true, glorious reality.

However, the insider paradigm, also falls short of the visible/invisible nature of the church in certain ways. One way is the tendency at times to be content with important aspects of the church remaining "invisible"—that is, affirmed as spiritual realities but not visibly expressed. One example would be Hoefer's perspective of insiders reflecting "some form of fellowship" ranging from Christian friends to Internet discussions, which falls short of the visible, gathered community of the local church. Another example of this tendency would be with respect to ecclesial identity; even among many who strongly affirm visible, local congregations, ecclesial identity is often affirmed, but it is primarily described as a theological, spiritual reality, not something which visibly and concretely impinges on social and religious identity.

Another way the insider paradigm allows the church to remain "invisible" is with regard to the universal church, as just discussed. Although the universal church is affirmed as a spiritual reality, it is largely hidden and invisible, disconnected from the global church. While there is visible fellowship among insiders, their fellowship with believers outside the Muslim community remains invisible, which hinders their ability to provide a glimpse and foretaste of the eschatological church.

Another weakness of the insider paradigm is a failure to capture the biblical integration of the invisible and visible dimensions of the church. This can be seen in this previously cited statement from Higgins on living out one's membership in the church:

> No human being can "make" a church or join the Church and as such, is called to live out their membership in the Body of Christ, the Church, as a full time lifestyle in every venue of life…. *One's identity as a born again member of the Body can and does overlap with one's identity in other spheres of life, including one's religious life.* (2006, 118–19; emphasis in original)

Higgins rightly highlights that membership in the body of Christ is first and foremost an act of God—an aspect of the invisible dimension of the church. However, he then curiously explains the visible expression, or "living out" of that identity as a whole-life activity that "overlaps" with other social and religious communities. While our identity as followers of Christ is certainly a full-time lifestyle, our identity as the church is something more specific and limited in scope. The New Testament calls believers to live out their membership in the body of Christ—a spiritual, invisible reality—in very specific ways, i.e., in the context of *visible Christian community*—bearing with one another in love, preserving the unity of the Spirit in the bond of peace, engaging in the mutual upbuilding in a local congregation, giving and receiving grace in the context of a loving community, etc. (e.g., Eph 4:1–6; 1 Cor 12:12–30).

Higgins clearly affirms the importance of visible and tangible local expressions of church community (2009b, 70–71); however, the language he uses here is incomplete. It is only half true that no one can join the church; although God joins believers to the body of Christ, believers are to live out this identity by also *actively participating in the body of Christ, which is the visible church*. The body of Christ image in 1 Corinthians 12, Rom 12, and Ephesians 4 is vividly physical and *bodily* in its outworking in tangible Christian community. Higgins' commitment to advocate for a "dual identity" for insider churches results in a statements which do not fully capture the way the Scriptures portray the invisible nature of the church as specifically and integrally connected to the visible body of Christ.

Another way in which the insider paradigm falls short of a full biblical understanding of the visible/invisible church is in its principled rejection of the terms "Christianity," "Christian," and "the (institutional) Christian church." There are clear pragmatic benefits to separating insiders from such terms and entities, as it helps insiders to more rigorously avoid the charge of apostasy in their communities. However, the insider paradigm's posture towards these words and entities is problematic with regard to the visible/invisible nature of the church. The reality is that the visible church includes churches and institutions that have identified as "Christian." Unless they are wholly corrupted, these Christian churches and institutions—past and present—express the visible church. Therefore, the insider paradigm's principled separation of insider communities from these terms and entities creates a barrier to fellowship with a large part of the visible church. Granted, Christian churches, communities, and institutions can at times be a mixed bag of true believers and nominal, cultural Christians. However, the doctrine of the visible church, as advocated by Augustine and the Reformers, has always emphasized that the presence of imperfection in Christian communities should not keep us from seeking fellowship with the visible church—the doctrine of the "mixed community" cuts both ways.

This is not to say that Muslim-background churches must adopt a "Christian" culture, should legally change their religion to "Christian," or begin calling themselves "Christians." Nor does it mean that Muslim-background churches must become organizationally affiliated with existing Christian churches. It is one thing to avoid using certain terms and cultural forms to minimize negative baggage; it is another thing to explicitly and strongly reject terms of "Christianity" and "Christian churches/institutions." Our goal, at least in principle, should be a Muslim-background church which is in tangible fellowship and unity with the visible Christian church, locally and around the world. I have suggested some ways that Scripture provides guidance on how to visibly express such unity and fellowship, not as an organizational unity, but as a familial unity. My point here is that the insider paradigm's explicit, strong rejection of terms and entities such as "Christianity" and "the (institutional) Christian church" places an obstacle that undermines the possibility of such fellowship and identification with the visible Christian church.

The insider paradigm reflects many aspects of the visible-invisible church in its vision of a church for insiders, though only in part. Certain aspects of the nature of the church find visible expression in the insider paradigm, while other aspects are affirmed as spiritual realities that do not find visible expression, and thus remain functionally "invisible," diminishing the luster of the church's present glimpse of the full, future glory of the people of God.

As we discussed, the visible-invisible church discussion relates directly to the question of the marks of the church by which the true, "invisible" church becomes visible in the world, a topic which provides yet further insight into the assets and liabilities in the insider paradigm.

Evaluating the Attributes and Marks of the Insider Church

In chapter two, I argued that the four classical attributes of the church (one, holy, catholic, apostolic) are biblically supported, not as marks or criteria for being considered a true church, but as indicative realities that are true of the spiritual, invisible church as well as imperatives the church is called to live out in its visible community. A robust vision of the church should encourage emerging churches to come to understand these realities as part of their inheritance as the church as well as encourage them to progressively learn to "be what you are in Christ."

In certain respects, the insider vision of the church would seem to help facilitate churches coming to understand, embrace, and live out aspects of the church's one, holy, catholic, and apostolic nature. By encouraging church planting within existing social and family networks, there is already a certain natural *unity* and solidarity in existing social ties, which may facilitate living out unity in that particular believing community. With regard to *holiness*, the insider paradigm affirms the importance of ethical transformation, as well as the fact that insider communities evaluate beliefs and practices based upon Scripture, which involves rejecting and modifying certain beliefs and practices contrary to Scripture. With regard to *catholicity*, the insider paradigm affirms the universality of the church (or "the Kingdom") as a spiritual reality of which many insiders recognize. The essential commonality of the church is expressed in terms of the church as a Christ-centered, kingdom community of Jesus-followers. With regard to *apostolicity*, the insider vision of the church involves the centrality of Bible study in ecclesial communities, as well as the urgency of the apostolic task of proclaiming the gospel to one's birth family and community.

However, there are also several respects in which the insider vision of the church appears to neglect or undermine the development of aspects of the classical attributes. While *oneness* of the church is strengthened at the level of a familial/social network, oneness with the larger "household of God" is weakened, as an overriding emphasis on "socio-religious" solidarity with the Muslim birth community comes at the expense of solidarity with the church outside of the Muslim community. This means that the insider vision of the church may affirm the "gift" of oneness with the larger church as a spiritual reality, but it does not appear to facilitate concrete ways of helping churches live into the "task" of visibly expressing this oneness.

Not surprisingly, this will also impact the development of *catholicity*. I have argued that catholicity refers not only to universality, but also to the essential commonality or "sameness" of the church in all places at all times (Van Engen 2000, 119), a reality which counterbalances the contextual and local nature of the church. In nonessentials, the church varies from culture to culture (contextual and local); yet in essential matters, there is a transcultural unity—a core unity and identity across all the contextual variations (catholicity). The attribute of catholicity, therefore, is key to protecting us from the error of provincialism and sectarianism.

The insider vision of the church, however, contains elements which would appear to hinder insider churches from understanding and recognizing their essential commonality with the universal church. One barrier pertains to language; as discussed above, through a strong rejection of the language of "church" and "Christianity" (and its equivalents in the local language) and conceptualizing the church as "socio-religiously" "Muslim," the insider paradigm locates the insider "church" in a fundamentally different set of religious categories than the broader Christian church. Furthermore, a radical commitment to "socio-religious" Muslim "insider-ness" becomes a higher priority than developing and nurturing a common identity and heritage with the larger church of Christ. Catholicity also involves being open to learning from and dialoguing with the broader Christian community, past and present, regarding interpreting and obeying the Bible (Vanhoozer 2006, 118). The insider paradigm, however, with its radical commitment to working within the Muslim religious heritage and *outside* the historic Christian heritage, for all of its pragmatic benefits, will also inevitably prevent insider believers from the privilege of full participation in the historic, global Christian conversation about God, his Word, and what it means to follow Jesus.

The insider paradigm is also somewhat problematic for the *holiness* and *apostolicity* of the church, specifically in its support of insiders that continue indefinitely in some level of reverence for the Qur'an, modified participation in Islamic prayers, confessing the prophethood of Muhammad (to some degree), and embracing a "religious" aspect of Muslim identity. While such things may be present in the beginning of the faith journey of new believers, they are problematic for a church that seeks to visibly express its nature as "holy" and "apostolic." While "holiness" should be balanced with the "priestly," missional nature of the church, "holiness" means "set-apartness," not only from unethical behavior, but also from partnerships, commonalities, and agreements that compromise the holy presence of Christ in his church (cf. 2 Cor 6:14–18). The specifics of how this works out calls for wisdom in each particular context, and it is often not necessary nor prudent for an obvious and immediate rejection or public repudiation of the above practices; a church which aims to remain as salt and light in its Muslim community will likely need to seek ways to respect and avoid bringing shame upon their community's religious practices. However, the insider paradigm's tendency to defend and support some level of ongoing participation in the above practices raises questions for how the church is to fully express and live out its nature as the holy, set-apart temple of the Holy Spirit.

But these matters also are problematic for expressing the apostolic nature of the church. A rigorous, theological assessment of the teaching of the Qur'an, the implicit theology of the Islamic prayer ritual, the narrative of Muhammad's prophetic career, and the implications of solidarity with the Muslim *umma* are beyond the scope of this book. However, it is widely agreed that all of the above contain at least some elements which undermine the worldview and values of the Scriptures. Furthermore, these compromising elements are embedded in the "sacred canopy" of the Muslim community, a "canopy" which is shaped and reinforced by ritual community practices by which Muslims collectively reinforce their theology to one another through formative social rituals.[122] It follows, therefore, that an ongoing, indefinite participation in these community rituals opens up insiders to an ongoing, powerful, formative influence alongside the influence of the apostolic Scriptures. In addition, such ongoing participation potentially compromises apostolic witness to their community, since even if insiders privately worship God in their own hearts, they are, by their act of joining their community in these practices, actively participating in the collective reinforcement of the publicly embraced Islamic meaning and theology implicit in the community ritual.[123]

The four classical attributes are not qualifications for being a true church, and the absence of any of them do not disqualify a group from being a church. However, a robust vision of the church should encourage, and not hinder, the church from first grasping these truths about its identity as the church, and second, aspiring to live them out in its visible community. The insider paradigm, therefore, both helps and hinders the expression of the one, holy, catholic, and apostolic nature of the church.

The strengths and shortcomings of insider ekklēsia are also evident with respect to the traditional Protestant marks of the Word and the sacraments/ordinances. With regard to the preaching of the Word, the insider paradigm is, in one sense, quite strong in its emphasis of the inductive, corporate study of Scripture as a central focus of insider fellowships. The proposed recasting of this mark from "preaching/proclamation" to "hearing and obeying" is eminently helpful in distinguishing the biblical essentials from a particular cultural form of "preaching," as well as in emphasizing the all-important receptivity to the Word (Duerskon and Dyrness 2019, 155).[124]

On the other hand, all of the concerns related to apostolicity are also concerns with respect to the mark of the Word. The allowance for ongoing reverence of the Qur'an and participation in Islamic community rituals exposes the church to multiple, powerful sources of theological, spiritual input which, at times, project narratives, values, and beliefs which are odds with those taught in Scripture. This fact threatens one important aspect of the original meaning of this mark,

---

122 The term "sacred canopy" refers to the all-encompassing, religiously-integrated social reality in pre-secular societies. The term comes from Peter Berger, *The Sacred Canopy: Elements of a Sociological Theory of a Religion* (Anchor, 1990).

123 By analogy, if an American church began to consider and treat the US Constitution or Declaration of Independence as included in God's holy documents, that would pose a danger of undermining biblical apostolicity.

124 In actuality, the concept of receptivity is not excluded from Calvin's original understanding of the mark of the Word: the marks of the true church were considered marks because they would always bear fruit in the community that practiced and received them (Calvin 1959, Book IV, Chapter 2, Section 10, 1024).

which is unfortunately obscured by a shift to "hearing and obeying" the Word, and that is the *right* or *pure* teaching of the Word. As I clarified previously, this is not a requirement for theological perfection or precision, but rather for sufficient true content to consistently present the real Jesus and not a false one; the Holy Spirit, and not another spirit. Insider advocates consistently argue that insiders reject beliefs in Islam which are contrary to Scripture. However, they have not fully addressed how ongoing reverence of the Qur'an, confession of Muhammad's prophethood, and Islamic ritual prayers encourage insiders to grow in a robust understanding of the Christ of the Scriptures.

In addition to the Word, I have argued that baptism and communion are important biblical practices which express and cultivate the ecclesial identity of the church, and many insider advocates, with varying degrees of emphasis, recognize them as commands of the Lord and key practices in the New Testament church which insider churches should ideally practice in some form. Insider advocates affirm important aspects of the theological meaning of these practices, and some helpfully suggest and encourage the utilization of alternative cultural forms for these rituals in order to minimize unnecessary social and cultural disruption, such as celebrating the Lord's Supper through a community meal.

However, the insider paradigm, at times, allows cultural and contextual considerations to eclipse aspects of the full biblical understanding and importance of baptism and communion. Additionally, insider advocates are concerned that baptism not be interpreted as leaving or abandoning one religious community and joining another; instead, it should be understood as identifying with Jesus and receiving new life in him (Travis and Woodberry 2015). What is missing, however, is the social implication of baptism—identifying with Jesus results in incorporation into a new society—the body of Christ, the church. The insider paradigm's aversion to any hint of changing religious communities puts it at risk of missing out on this key aspect of the meaning of baptism.

Another aspect that is missing in some insider advocates' expression of the ordinances is the *catholicity* of baptism and communion—the fact that these are practices that, in principle, should unite the whole body of Christ.[125] At times, the cultural particularity and contextual freedom with regard to baptism and the Lord's Supper is so emphasized at the expense of the universal nature of the church (Duerkson and Dyrness 2019, 131). However, baptism and communion are not only local practices, but also "catholic" practices, shared with the universal church—amidst the various contextual expressions, there is ultimately "one baptism" and "one loaf" (1 Cor 10:17; Eph 4:5). This puts some constraints on how much such practices should be contextualized, lest the practice is so transformed that *any* meaningful continuity with the universal church is lost.

---

125 I first heard the concept of the "catholicity" of baptism from Derek Rishmawy in the "Mere Fidelity" podcast ("For and Against: Infant Baptism," April 7, 2020).

A final concern is that some insider advocates reflect an incomplete view of the importance and centrality of these practices to the nature of the church. Some express little concern if insider chuches spiritualize baptism or if they de-emphasize baptism or communion because of a lack of a positive, contextual counterpart. Even those who emphasize these practices the most do so in the context of either obeying the commands of Jesus or reflecting the practices of the vibrant church of Acts. However, I have argued that baptism and communion are not only commands of Jesus, but crucial formative practices which express, rehearse, and cultivate the biblical identity and core essence of the church as the body of Christ. Therefore, the degree to which baptism and the Lord's Supper are practiced and biblically understood directly impacts the degree to which the church expresses and grows into its identity and nature as the church. While the insider paradigm at times affirms these ordinances in important ways, it also falls short at times in failing to emphasize and express them in ways which fully capture and cultivate the identity of the church as the local and universal body of Christ.

Insider advocates offer their own lists of attributes that mark out the true church. Marks of the church taken from the book of Acts are helpful and simple, and contain many valid, beneficial criteria for guiding and evaluating the health of biblical churches, which even include several aspects of the classical attributes and Protestant marks of the church. However, such insider marks also problematically include ongoing participation in religious rituals and identity as fully compatible with a healthy church and movement, based on the faulty assumption, as previously discussed, that the early Jewish church is paradigmatic for contemporary insider ekklēsia.

The five "markers of the transformative church" proposed by Duerkson and Dyrness are helpful in many respects, containing many valid aspects of the nature of the church (Duerkson and Dyrness 2019, 155–71). The picture of the church as a community that forms around "the story of Jesus," responding in obedience, prayer, praise, shalom, and witness, captures a great deal of the biblical nature of the church. I agree that the presence of such markers may indicate that the church is in the process of "emerging" in that context. However, I would argue that a local church has not yet fully "emerged" until it also includes baptized believers, a clear identity as a biblical church, regular gathering, and (eventually) biblical elders, which do not seem to be included in their definition of the church.

Additionally, I would question whether the fourth item in their list, "living at peace with one another and the wider community," should be properly considered a mark of the church. Peace in the church is a biblical mandate and a fruit of the Spirit, but as we learned from the classical attributes, it is not a marker of the true church (case in point, the Corinthians!), but rather an invisible, spiritual attribute which the church is called to visibly express. Peace with the "wider community" is even more questionable as a mark of the church; while it is certainly an element of the mission of the church to be ambassadors of Christ's peace, the nature of this peace needs to be more robustly defined so as to include the fuller biblical teaching on bold witness for Christ and the expectation of hostility and opposition to Christ's followers.

The attributes and marks of the church provide a unique vantage point on the strengths and weaknesses of the insider vision of the church. The insider church supports and encourages aspects of unity, holiness, catholicity, and apostolicity, while at the same time including obstacles that hinder the full expression of the same. The Protestant marks of Word and sacraments/ordinances are likewise partially affirmed, with some deficiencies. The lists of marks put forward by insider advocates are helpful and valid in certain respects, though they are also incomplete as well as naive regarding the potential problems with ongoing, indefinite participation in existing religious practices and "socio-religious" identity.

The relationship between salvation and the church in the insider paradigm likewise exhibits strong and weak points, as outlined next.

Evaluating Salvation and the Insider Church

The claim that the insider paradigm separates "Christian conversion from visible Christian community" is not fully accurate (Tennent 2005, 174). In many respects, the insider paradigm affirms a strong relationship between the church and salvation. As is clear by now, insider advocates affirm and encourage participation in fellowships of insiders that express biblical ekklēsia. In the household/oikos model in particular, churches develop naturally as insiders come to faith together as a family, which transforms the family into a "church" without leaving the family network (Higgins 2006, 118–19; Lewis 2007, 76).

In this household/oikos model, salvation and the church are linked together even closer than in the traditional Western church model which emphasizes conversion as an individual experience distinct from the voluntary decision to join a church. In addition, some insider advocates affirm a strong theological relationship between salvation and the church, affirming that salvation results in people being immediately spiritually joined by God to the church, the body of Christ, whether they know it or not (Higgins 2006, 119). Furthermore, insider advocates rightly affirm *sola fide*, affirming that church membership/participation is not necessary for salvation, which is by faith alone (Travis and Travis 2005, 403; Hoefer 2007).

Along with these strong points, there are also important aspects of the church-salvation relationship which are missing from the insider vision. One of these is reflected in the tendency among some insider advocates to make statements which fail to capture the necessity of robust biblical churches for a key aspect of salvation—sanctification and spiritual formation. Thus, statements that the church is not necessary for salvation are only partially correct, for salvation includes both justification and sanctification (Tennent 2007, 213). While some insider advocates emphasize the necessity of biblical churches for growth in spiritual maturity of BMBs (Dutch 2000, 23), some only claim that some "form of fellowship" and accountability are "beneficial" to sanctification and spiritual growth (Hoefer 2007).

The latter statement falls short of the essential, irreplaceable role that the biblical church plays in the spiritual formation of disciples.

This relates to another weakness in the insider vision. While many insider advocates fully affirm the importance of biblical churches, some insider definitions of the church either lack essential elements of the church or allow additional elements in the church (e.g., participation in formative religious rituals), both of which may have a negative impact on the spiritual formation of disciples. All the aspects of the biblical church discussed thus far—regular gathering, clear identity as the church, biblical patterns of community (worship, edification, fellowship, and witness), biblical elders, the teaching of the Word, baptism and communion—play an important role in the spiritual formation of believers (eg., 1 Cor 11:27–32; Eph 4:1–6; 4:11–16; 5:18–20; Heb 10:25; 1 Pet 2:4–5). The extent to which such elements are present or missing in a church will strengthen or hinder the spiritual growth of disciples, accordingly. Furthermore, the inclusion of other elements through long-term participation in certain religious rituals allows the ongoing influence of extra-biblical practices that could have detrimental impact on the long-term, spiritual formation of mature disciples.

Another deficiency with respect to the church-salvation relationship relates to the "common faith" of the whole church, "the faith once for all delivered to the saints" (Jude 3; Tennent 2007, 213). "The faith" refers especially to the truth in Christ as something which has been handed down and entrusted to the church, "the pillar and foundation of the truth" (1 Tim 3:14), which is to guard, steward, and pass down "the faith" to future generations. This common faith is part of the foundation for the church's unity as a body, as seen in Ephesians 4:4–6: "There is one body ... one hope ... one Lord, *one faith*, one baptism, one God ..." (emphasis mine).

In the insider paradigm, however, believers/fellowships are largely kept away from the teachings of the broader church, and cross-cultural "alongsiders" intentionally avoid any directive teaching (Travis 2014, 162), seeking to allow the insiders to interpret and read the Bible for themselves, so as not to contaminate their faith with foreign interpretations and theological frameworks. While this has the benefit of keeping the fledgling church free from foreign theology and interpretations, it raises the question of whether there is ever a point in the development of such churches in which the historic body of Christ should help guide them towards orthodox teachings and away from unorthodox ones. It would be a mistake to impose creeds and doctrinal formulas from other times and places upon the BMB church as infallible authorities; however, it is also a mistake to neglect the biblical imperative to faithfully pass on, and preserve, the biblical faith from one generation to the next. As Hiebert said, self-theologizing of the local church should not be divorced from the universal church, which functions as a larger multicultural, global hermeneutical community as a check and balance for all local churches' understanding of Scripture and biblical faith (1987, 110).

Another weakness related to the church-salvation relationship in the insider paradigm relates to an issue referenced in several previous sections—the way that salvation creates a new social identity. Many insider advocates separate salvation from social identity, seeing insider believers as experiencing salvation in Christ but retaining their social identity as Muslims (Duerkson, Lewis). However, as discussed previously, this misses the social implications of salvation, and the fact that salvation brings a new social identity:

> Following Christ, then, involves a *radical break* with the past; regeneration and sanctification through the sacrifice and Spirit of Christ inevitably "rescue[s] us from the domain of darkness" and bring us "into the kingdom of the Son he loves, in whom we have redemption, the forgiveness of sins" (Col 1:13–14). Importantly, this "rescue" has visible dramatic *social* consequences beyond an inner conversion of heart and worldview or an ethical change, viz. a *new social identity.* (Bartlotti 2013, 141; emphasis in original)

Bartlotti aptly highlights the fact that a new social identity is built into the dynamics of salvation itself. This does not necessarily imply "destroying" or "overturning" all aspects of one's previous social identity, but it does claim that regeneration and new life includes an unavoidable element of a radical break/discontinuity which changes how one identifies in relation to others. Lesslie Newbigin, in response to a version of insider ecclesiology in his time, likewise affirms this strong link between salvation and social identity:

> Presumably the acceptance of Jesus Christ as central and decisive creates *some* kind of solidarity among those who have this acceptance in common. If it did not do so, it would mean nothing. The question is, what is the nature of this solidarity? It has always been understood to include the practice of meeting together to celebrate with words, songs, and formal actions the common faith in Jesus… . It is almost inevitable that some common cultural forms and some common social bonds will develop among those who are united by a strong faith in Jesus. (1977, 121)

The confession of Jesus as Lord, says Newbigin, must inevitably result in a new, shared social (and, to some degree, cultural) identity and solidarity with all those who share that confession. Rebecca Lewis maintains that in the insider model the relational bonds already exist and are not new—what is new is allegiance to Christ. D. W. McKeon critiques this approach, saying,

> Such a statement depreciates the redemptive work of our Lord Jesus in making spiritually dead people alive in Him, being joined together as "members of one another" (Eph 4:25). It doesn't matter how close two or more people are naturally; once they find their new life in Christ in *His* redeemed community, there is a *qualitatively different relationship* that could not have existed before; the new relationship with God through Christ transforms the relationships among His people. (2014, 42; emphasis in original)

What is missing, then, in Lewis' analysis is the way that salvation radically transforms social identity vis-à-vis all others who have experienced salvation in Christ. As Tim Green helpfully explains, conversion results in a transformation at all layers of our identity—core, social, and collective:

> The overarching identity of all Christ's followers, whatever their background, is individually as children of God and corporately as members of Christ's body, his one global community with its wonderfully diverse local expressions. To be "in" Christ does not obliterate cultural differences, but it does relativize them. It is at times necessary to distinguish between different groups of Jesus-followers according to their background, but it should always be remembered that where we come "from" matters less than where we are heading "to." (2013c, 362–63; cf. also 2013a)

Salvation results not only in a transformed individual (or "core") identity, but also transformation of our social and collective identities; our new "in Christ" social identity relativizes (not destroys) other cultural identities. David Greenlee likewise captures the identity transformation that occurs in salvation:

> Through God's gracious call and our response in faith, a transformation takes place that brings us into his family. We are justified by grace; we are heirs, having the hope of eternal life (Titus 3:7). Because we believe and are "in Christ" we are no longer aliens but fellow citizens with God's people, members of God's household, part of that holy temple he is building (Eph 2:19–22), the body of Christ (1 Cor 12:27), with a mutual responsibility of service (Gal 5:13) and fellowship (Heb 10:25). (2013, 10–11)

Saving faith results in being incorporated into a new society, a new people, which results in a *new social identity* in the church. Salvation does not just result in a transformed heart or interior life, leaving one's larger social identity unaffected. Rather, it has strong social implications, which are integrally related to the nature of the church. The insider paradigm, does not fully capture this transformed social identity which characterizes the relationship between salvation and the church.

The rich, integral relationship between the church and salvation is partially present in the insider paradigm: salvation theologically results in being joined spiritually to the church, and believing families become churches immediately upon salvation. However, the insider paradigm does not yet fully reflect other important aspects of this relationship, such as the powerful impact of full, biblical churches in spiritual formation, the common faith of the church, and the transformed social identity of the church.

The final key area for evaluation is the relationship between the church and the world.

Embedded in the World:
Evaluating the Insider Church-World Relationship

The "mixed blessing" of insider church, evident throughout this whole analysis, certainly extends to the church-world relationship. There are a variety of ways that the insider vision challenges us in positive ways with regard to the church-world relationship. The insider paradigm's emphasis on the positive value of the social structures of the world, such as family, society, and government, captures elements of biblical teaching and cautions us against creating unnecessary division or disruption. Such an emphasis is an important corrective for those coming from "Western" cultures, which tend to value individuals challenging or reforming existing social structures, while many Muslim cultures highly value preserving unity and *tawhid* in family and society.[126]

The insider paradigm's emphasis on the positive value of the cultures and religions of the world as spheres within which God may be present and at work also has something to teach us. At times, in our zeal to win people for Christ, we are tempted toward overly negative postures towards cultures and religions, which cause us to miss aspects of common grace and the image of God reflected therein. Such an insight is important for emerging churches that seek to remain in their Muslim contexts, which will likely only be possible if such churches find ways to affirm, respect, and honor some aspects of the culture, and even religion, of their community.

Along with such emphases, the insider paradigm's vision of the church as "yeast in the dough" challenges us in a missional direction, asking whether the church can be more "embedded" in the world than we thought possible, further facilitating the spread of the kingdom. Such a vision is a corrective to a vision of church that is unnecessarily "extracted" from the world, pushing us to re-imagine a church which is even more accessible to Muslim families and societies in unreached, resistant Muslims in high-persecution contexts.

Along with these strengths are some deficiencies in the way the church-world relationship is envisioned in the insider paradigm. One weakness is an *overemphasis* on the positive value of social structures, cultures, and religions of the world that does not adequately capture the full scope and nuance of biblical teaching. The God-givenness of human social structures of family, society, and government does not imply an absolute commitment to affirming and preserving these structures at all costs; Scripture teaches us that people's reaction to the gospel and to the church will sometimes lead to disruption in the family structure (Luke 12:51–53), unrest in society (Acts 17:6), and government opposition (Matt 10:17–18). The church should not use the gospel as an excuse to unnecessarily divide or undermine such social structures (1 Pet 2:13–17), but the church should also realistically understand and accept that the gospel, in reality, is an implicit

---

126 Cf. Chapter 3, "Tawhid: Perfect Unity" in *Searching for Heaven in the Real World: A Sociological Discussion of Conversion in the Arab World* (Katheryn Kraft 2012).

challenge to parts of the social order—if Jesus is king, then Caesar is not (Acts 17:7). When people rebel against the gracious offer of Jesus' kingship, social disruption will sometimes occur, and the church should be ready for this and accept it.[127] In addition, there are times when God calls his people to speak out against sin and evil in social structures (2 Sam 12:1–15; Micah 3:1–4; Matt 14:4). These realities should balance out and qualify the insider paradigm's overemphasis on affirming and preserving social and family structures.

The insider paradigm's overly positive view of the world extends beyond social institutions to human cultures and religions as largely neutral and harmless environments in which the church can emerge and flourish. While there is a residue of grace and truth in the world's cultures and religions, this should be balanced by the full biblical understanding of the world being in hostile rebellion against God and under the power of the evil one. While cultures and religions reflect aspects of the image of God and common grace, they also reflect human sinful repression of the truth about God (Rom 1:18–20), the blinding influence of Satan (2 Cor 4:4), and the spirit of the antichrist undermining the gospel (1 John 2:18–24). The insider paradigm, however, primarily emphasizes the positive value of human cultures and religions, not sufficiently capturing the full complex of positive *and* negative influences in human cultures and religions.

God does not call the church to intentionally overthrow or destroy human institutions or cultures, but neither does God call the church to remain full participants and partakers in every institution and cultural structure, but rather to exercise wisdom regarding what to affirm and embrace and what to reject and separate from in the world. Without withdrawing from the world, the church is called to keep itself "unstained by the world" (James 1:27), refraining from partaking in the world's idolatry and sinful rebellion (1 John 2:15). This realistic and nuanced perspective about the nature of the world is lacking in the insider paradigm, which describes Muslim religious culture and communities as largely benign contexts within which the church can embed itself in an insider form.

Along with this one-sided picture of the world's structures, the insider paradigm presents a one-dimensional picture of the church's relationship to the world. As already mentioned, the insider paradigm over-emphasizes the "yeast in the dough" image without sufficiently balancing it with other images such as "city on a hill" and "holy nation." The insider paradigm's failure to capture the full implications of the biblical attribute of the holiness of the church results in a defective overall picture which does not fully account for the church's "other-ness," or "set-apartness," in the world. This image of the church as "embedded" in the world can only go so far—there is a limit to how embedded the church can be without "losing its saltiness."

---

127 Those in Acts 16:7 were not entirely off the mark when they charged the Christians with disobeying Caesar and "saying there is another king, Jesus."

The insider paradigm does acknowledge some ways in which the church is "other" and "not of" the world, as churches are said to reject, modify, and de-emphasize certain Islamic beliefs that are contrary to Scripture. However, at times this "other-ness" is understood in a largely interior, spiritualized way—idolatry is a "matter of the heart" and "what is inside a person" (Anna Travis 2015, Loc. 11948–64). Furthermore, as we discussed previously, the insider paradigm's trend of supporting the ongoing participation in key Islamic rituals such as ritual prayer, confession of Muhammad's prophethood, and Qur'an-revering practices poses questions for how the "other-ness" of the church is being expressed in these situations. Support for such practices reflects a defective vision for the church-world relationship, raising serious questions for how the church's "otherness" as a "holy nation" can truly be reflected when the church participates in rituals which positively communicate to society an ongoing allegiance to Muhammad, the Qur'an, and religious Islam (Ex 23:20–26; 1 Cor 3:16; 10:14–22; 2 Cor 6:14–18; Eph 2:21–22; cf. Parshall 1985, 184; Daniels 2014).[128] This does not mean that there should not be a gradual process by which new groups of Christ-followers learn to discern, and eventually remove themselves from, aspects of community which are incompatible with their holy identity. It does mean, however, that maturing believers and churches growing into their identity as the holy temple of God will eventually need to dispense with aspects of the world which taint their faith and confession of Christ.

In addition, the deficiencies of the insider paradigm's handling of the kingdom of God theme often lead to misconstrued relationships among the kingdom, the church, and the world. A sound understanding of these three realities recognizes the integral relationship between the kingdom and the church—that the kingdom advances in the world in and through the ekklēsia of Jesus, where the reign of Christ the King is acknowledged, celebrated, and visibly demonstrated among God's gathered people. The insider paradigm, however, envisions the relationship between the kingdom and the church as much looser, as two different spheres, with the kingdom being the larger sphere that includes the church but also extends beyond the church to include "wherever and whenever [God's] will is done" (Hoefer 2007; 2015 Loc. 6744–58)—or "the whole range of God's exercise of his reign and rule in the universe," including "religions" (Higgins 2009a, 87).

There is certainly truth to the fact that God's kingdom is at work outside the sphere of the gathered church, from the very inception of the seed of the gospel

---

128 Nabeel Jabbour, a sympathizer and sometimes defender of insider movements, has disavowed the practice of encouraging ongoing worship in the mosque by converts. "Some BMBs and Christian missionaries feel free to stand behind the imam in the mosque and to synchronize with the forms of Muslim prayer while praying over texts from the Scriptures. Standing behind the imam while he is praying implies endorsing his prayer. Such a practice shows communal solidarity in Islamic religious belief and practice, which a follower of Christ should not do. Encouragement to do this from a Western missionary often comes from the Westerner's individualistic approach to faith…. There is a need for caution lest the BMB find himself in fellowship with demons if he participates in worship inside the Islamic religious institutions" (Jabbour and Seelinger 2014, pgs. 2311, 2330).

being planted in the hearts and minds of people who are deeply entrenched in another religious community. However, the way that kingdom theology is applied in the insider paradigm obscures the integral, even necessary, role that the biblical church plays in advancing and revealing the kingdom in the world.

The church-world relationship also includes the issue of the contextualization of the church. In chapter 3, I defined authentic contextualization of the church as follows: *Following the biblical patterns of contextualization of Israel and the church, authentic contextualization avoids the twin dangers of cultural foreignness and syncretism by faithfully reflecting the biblical nature and purpose of the church in ways which are meaningful to the local context; which critically engage with and transform the beliefs, practices, and symbols within the culture; and which reflect the indigenous-pilgrim character of the people of God.*

With regard to the biblical principles of contextualization in the Old and New Testaments, the insider paradigm is strong in the principle of *cultural continuity*. It emphasizes continuity with Muslim culture—i.e., those ways in which Islam has shaped the culture of Muslim societies. By rejecting overly negative views of Islam, the insider paradigm challenges us to consider whether there are many more elements than we previously considered within Muslim religion, culture, and identity which are redeemable and can be appropriated by biblical churches. Furthermore, the insider paradigm strongly distances the biblical church from many aspects of cultural foreignness, including culturally foreign Christian institutions, vocabulary, church forms, individualistic models of conversion and church planting, and even the influence of other culturally foreign Christians (aside from "alongsiders" who quietly shepherd leaders).

On the other hand, the insider paradigm is weak in upholding the second biblical principle, which is *cultural discontinuity/divergence*. While important elements of discontinuity and divergence exist (such as salvation through faith in Jesus, acceptance of the spiritual authority of the Bible, etc.), I have highlighted ways that the insider paradigm is lacking in fully reflecting the distinctive, holy identity of the people of God, who are the temple of the Holy Spirit, a community of strangers and aliens whose citizenship is in heaven. The insider paradigm's often binary depiction of preserving/remaining in their religious cultural context (as opposed to "rejecting/overturning" it) does not fully capture the way that the gospel, and the biblical church, bring about a transformation that introduces elements of discontinuity and distinction from the culture.

Along these lines, the insider paradigm is very strong in the *indigenizing principle*, but weak in expressing the *pilgrim principle*. With regard to the indigenizing principle, the insider paradigm rightly affirms that God accepts Muslims who believe in Jesus "as they are," with all their Muslim cultural identity and social relations (Walls 1982, 97). Furthermore, the insider paradigm provides a vision of church which is, quite literally, "at home" in Muslim families and communities, with social networks intact and a great deal of Muslim culture and identity preserved. However, the insider vision does not fully capture the other side of the equation, which is that while God may save and accept Muslims followers of Christ "as they are," God does not intend them to fully stay that way, but rather he "takes them in order to transform them into what He wants them to be" (ibid., 98). As we have seen, the insider vision of the church so emphasizes the affirmation and preservation of Muslim social and religious identity that it becomes a place that is so much "at home" in Muslim society that "no one else can live there" (Walls 1982, 99). The insider vision does not fully account for the way that the indigenizing impulse is qualified by the pilgrim impulse, which brings an outside cultural frame of reference through the history of Israel and the people of God, the multicultural fellowship of the universal church, and the ways that Christ and his kingdom transform elements of the local culture.

Some insider advocates seem to be committed in principle to both indigeneity and the pilgrim character of the church, to cultural continuity as well as distinction; Walls' (2015) essay is, after all, reprinted in *Understanding Insider Movements*. However, my study suggests that the insider paradigm does not yet strike the right balance, being overly weighted toward indigeneity and cultural continuity at the expense of the pilgrim principle and cultural distinction. Thus, it is not surprising to see some insider advocates explicitly abandoning the pilgrim principle in favor of a primary focus on indigeneity (Duerkson and Dyrness 2019, 59–60).

Insider advocates themselves have acknowledged that the insider paradigm carries an inherent risk of unbiblical syncretism (Travis 1998b, 414; Asad 2009, 155–56). The preceding analysis confirms such an assessment and suggests that such a risk extends to the nature of the church. That is, the insider vision of church props the door open to certain elements which could potentially undermine the biblical nature of the church.

The church-world relationship in the insider paradigm, like the other aspects of the church, carries strengths and weaknesses. The insider paradigm advances a highly missional vision of the church which cautions us against an overly negative view of the world and its structures, challenging us to envision a church which is embedded as salt, light, and yeast. However, it also represents a one-dimensional view with an overly positive, naïve view of the world's structures, cultures, and religions—a view which lacks the full biblical teaching on the nature of the world as both an object of God's love and a system in enmity against God, the full biblical tension between the church as a "kingdom of priests" and "holy nation" and the integral, dynamic connection between the church and the kingdom. The result is a vision of the church which is strong on cultural continuity and the indigenizing principle, but weak on cultural discontinuity/distinction and the pilgrim principle.

INSIDER CHURCH

Summary

The insider paradigm has a unique set of beliefs, assumptions, and hopes regarding the nature and character of the church in an insider context, converging with the biblical vision at some points and departing from it at others. I have shown the ways in which the insider paradigm positively stimulates our vision of the church with fresh biblical insights while simultaneously undercutting the biblical nature of the church, summarized in the following table.

Table 3: Strengths and Weaknesses Summary

	Strengths of the Insider Church	Weaknesses of the Insider Church
Biblical Theology of the Church	• Fresh view of the church through the lens of the parables and theology of the kingdom • Fresh emphasis on the household (oikos) theme • Relevant focus on the church in Acts for emerging churches and movements	• Mischaracterization of the kingdom-church relationship • Problematic application of biblical paradigms to insider contexts (Namaan the Syrian, the early Jewish and Gentile movements) • Under-emphasis of themes and narratives that should balance/qualify insider convictions (household of God, the Jesus family over against natural family, holy nation, new humanity, people of God)
Core Essence of the Church	• Distinction between essence of the church and Western culture/institutions • Focus on the saving presence and work of God in bringing people into the kingdom and body of Christ • Emphasis on the role and work of God over human efforts and institutions	• Fails to capture the ways that the spiritual, theological identity of the church transforms the social and religious identity of the church in complex ways
Local Church	• Focuses on Christ-centered community of disciples rather than the cultural trappings of the church • Affirms several essential elements of the local church (prayer, Bible study, fellowship, commitment to one another), and varied affirmation of others (praise, gathering, baptism, communion, elders) • Relevant model of planting the church within existing social networks	• Some overly "simple" definitions of the local church leave out one or more essential elements • Affirmation of groups as "churches" which do not yet express all the essential elements of the New Testament church • Overall weakness in full, concrete expression of the full biblical identity as the church
Universal Church	• Affirms the universal church as a spiritual reality	• Functional separation from the wider body of Christ • Risk of sectarian model of church
Visible-Invisible Church	• Affirms the church as a visible, local community • Affirms the church as a "mixed community" • Affirms the priority of the spiritual (invisible) nature of the church	• Several aspects of the nature of the church are functionally invisible (universal church, social implications of the church's identity, fellowship with the wider visible Christian church)

INSIDER CHURCH

	Strengths of the Insider Church	Weaknesses of the Insider Church
Attributes and Marks	• Facilitates aspects of the classical attributes (unity in believing households, holiness and apostolicity in ethical transformation based on Scripture, catholic commonality in terms of discipleship and the kingdom) • Centrality of the Word in insider fellowships • Affirmation of baptism and communion as commanded by Jesus • Offers different sets of "marks" which express several aspects of the true church	• Obstacles to catholicity and oneness in principled separation from the broader Christian community • Obstacles to holiness and apostolicity in ongoing participation in Muslim rituals • Ongoing spiritual input from the Qur'an and Muslim rituals risks tainting the Word • Overlooks aspects of the full biblical significance of baptism and communion for cultivating the identity of the church
Church-Salvation Relationship	• Strong link between church and salvation in household/oikos model • Strong spiritual link between salvation and spiritual incorporation into the body of Christ • Affirmation of *sola fide*	• Underestimates the impact of the full biblical church on sanctification and spiritual formation • Neglects the role of the common faith of the whole church • Neglects the way regeneration creates a new social identity
Church-World Relationship	• Corrective of overly negative views of the world, culture, and religion, helping churches respect culture and community • Missional impulse of the church as salt, light, and yeast that transforms and structures and networks of the world • Strong cultural continuity and indigenizing principle	• Overly positive view of the world's structures, cultures, and religions that does not adequately account for the presence of sin, evil, and hostility to the gospel in these structures • Unbalanced view that does not fully reflect the "other-ness" of the church's relationship to the world • Lacks cultural discontinuity/distinction and the pilgrim principle

Our vision of the church is expanded and deepened by fully recognizing and learning from both the strengths and weaknesses of the insider paradigm of church. This assessment of the insider church has particular implications for how we assess and respond to the insider-movement paradigm and multiply biblical churches among Muslims.

CHAPTER SIX

Implications for the Insider Movements Conversation

My friend Muhammad is a young single man living in a highly conservative neighborhood.[129] While studying Islamic law in college, Muhammad discovered some things that disturbed him and left him wanting to search for alternate answers. His mother always had a positive view of Christians, and she had even visited a traditional, historic church once to light a candle for blessing. So Muhammad decided one day to visit one of these churches in hopes of finding someone to help him. He met with a priest, requesting to learn more about Christianity, but the priest told him it was too dangerous for him to do that in this city—he should go to another part of the country to inquire about these things, a place which was too far and impractical for Muhammad to visit.

---

129 The names in this story have been changed.

Luckily for Muhammad, one of his friends, Hussein, had emigrated to Europe and become a follower of Christ. Hussein shared his faith with Muhammad through social media, and when Hussein learned of his friend's desire to learn more, he connected him with a national evangelical Christian in the same city who could help him. Muhammad began meeting with this discipler regularly, and he grew in his knowledge and love for Jesus, occasionally attending an evangelical church and regularly attending a Bible study for BMBs.

Muhammad is the first believer in his family, and being from a conservative area, he rarely makes his faith directly known to others. His family knows that he attends church, but he also has experienced pressure and resistance related to his faith in Christ and his lack of desire to participate in certain Muslim faith rituals.

How should Muhammad live out his faith in front of his family? Is there a way for him to live faithfully as a follower of Jesus while continuing to honor and respect his family, his community, and their Islamic religion? Which aspects of his Muslim heritage and identity are incompatible with his new faith in Jesus? How does he distance himself from these things in a way which brings the least amount of shame to his family? What aspects of his Muslim culture and identity are extrabiblical, but not necessarily unbiblical, and thus can be retained without compromising his faith? What aspects of Muslim culture and identity are fully biblical and should be affirmed and embraced?

These are important, challenging questions for Muhammad, and the way he wrestles with them and answers them will determine a great deal about his relationship with his family, the health and viability of his faith long-term, and the vitality of his witness to his community. And one day, when some of Muhammad's friends and family members begin following Jesus, the way they wrestle with these questions will determine a great deal about the extent to which they can grow into a sustainable, multiplying, biblical church.

The insider paradigm provides a particular set of principles and guidelines for how disciple makers journey with people like Muhammad and his friends in such questions. This paradigm has stimulated some to take a more radical approach which embraces a great deal of Muslim culture and identity as compatible with faith in Christ, including wholehearted embrace of the label "Muslim" in a "socio-religious" sense, rejection of "Christian" labels, and modified ongoing participation in certain Muslim beliefs and practices such as the prophethood of Muhammad, revering of the Qur'an, and Islamic ritual prayer. Such proposals have also stirred great controversy, provoking vigorous opposition from many disciple makers, church leaders, and some BMBs.

My goal in this book is not to settle this intractable debate, but rather to increase understanding related to insider movements and planting biblical churches among Muslims. I have attempted this through a deep dive into one of the key issues at the heart of insider movements—the nature of the biblical church.

My starting point was a biblical and theological proposal for the identity of the church and how it takes shape in culture, which I laid out in three successive stages. The first step was to define the church biblically, situating the church in its identity-defining narrative of the people of God, which includes the family of Abraham, the nation of Israel and its faithful remnant, the community of Jesus, the apostolic church, the eschatological gathering of the redeemed—with the wondrous array of themes and images of the church. The next step was to further clarify the nature of the church in its many dimensions—essential identity, local and universal, visible and visible, distinguishing attributes and marks, relationship to salvation, and relationship to the world. Then, I proposed a framework for the way the biblical identity of the church—in its varied aspects—takes shape in culture in a way which is faithful, meaningful, and transformational.

With this framework in place, we looked directly at insider movements, and specifically the vision of the church that is affirmed, promoted, and assumed in the insider paradigm. I outlined the various commitments of the insider paradigm in the various dimensions of the nature of the church, showing that despite some diversity, the insider paradigm presents a distinctive overall perspective on multiple angles of the nature of the church. Then, in light of the biblical nature of the church defined in the first part of the book, I evaluated the insider vision of the church, showing the strengths and weaknesses of insider ekklēsia in each dimension of the nature of the church, positively stimulating new insights while also creating obstacles which may hinder the full flowering of the biblical church among Muslims.

My conclusion is that the insider paradigm indeed offers a model which unleashes the yeast of the kingdom among Muslim communities, while simultaneously leaving the door open to another yeast that risks "leavening" the pure, unleavened bread of the biblical nature of the church. The insider paradigm opens our eyes to neglected aspects of the church's identity, accurately capturing a significant portion of the biblical nature of the church, stimulating us toward creative ways of "implanting" the church in Muslim contexts. However, the insider paradigm also neglects certain biblical themes and aspects of the biblical identity of the church, and it includes certain claims, concepts, and principles which potentially hinder the expression of the church's full biblical nature.

It is important to qualify what has not been concluded by my study. It has focused exclusively on evaluating the ecclesiological vision of the insider paradigm, as advanced by its advocates and promoters, not the ecclesiology of actual insiders. The assumptions and vision of insider advocates does not necessarily imply anything about the ecclesiology of insiders. My study has been motivated by the fact that everyone brings to the table their own framework and assumptions regarding the nature of the church, and those frameworks and assumptions directly influence one's practice of evangelism, discipleship, and church planting.

Of course, it is quite possible, and even likely, that the vision and framework of disciple makers and church planters will exert an influence—for good or for ill—upon the vision of new Christ-followers as well. Even if disciple makers take a less direct role and work more as guides and coaches rather than prescriptive teachers, their vision and framework regarding a variety of issues—including the nature of the church—will impact the kind of guidance given to emerging disciples, as well as the overarching ministry strategy for disciple making and church planting.[130]

This study has also not demonstrated whether any particular insider fellowships or groups of believers *are* or *are not* legitimate biblical churches. Such an assessment can only be made on an individual basis, focused not on the literature of insider advocates, but rather focused through observation and research of actual insider fellowships and gatherings. I have provided some biblical and theological benchmarks that would be useful in shaping such a study. A key question of such a study would be to ask to what extent insider fellowships actually reflect the characteristics of the biblical church. It would be instructive to see how the strengths and weaknesses of actual insider fellowships relate to the strengths and weaknesses in the insider paradigm itself.

However, my study does suggest that, to the degree which insider advocates accurately describe insider fellowships, these fellowships are indeed "expressions" of ekklēsia and the body of Christ, places in which the church may be "emerging." Those insiders who possess genuine, persevering faith are indeed members of the body of Christ, brothers and sisters in the family of God, and members of the universal church—God knows those who are his. While they may not yet reflect all aspects of the local church, they do reflect significant parts of the essence of the biblical church, and therefore, we can safely say that the church may be in the process of "emerging" in these contexts, and that they possess elements of the body of Christ. For those longing to see the gospel penetrate Muslim communities, this is truly good news and reason for rejoicing.

On the other hand, my study also suggests that some insider fellowships (as described by insider advocates) may not yet be local churches, since such descriptions and definitions often lack one or more essential components of the communities that are described as "churches" in the New Testament. These fellowships may very well be moving towards eventually becoming local churches. However, it is important to make this distinction so that we are clear what we are dealing with, biblically speaking.

It is also important because not every group that "expresses" aspects of the church will necessarily fully "emerge" and become a full church. For example, there may be aspects of ekklēsia present in an informal, committed group of friends who study the Bible together regularly, or in a missionary team which meets regularly

---

130 According to Prenger's *Muslim Insider Christ Followers*, it can go both ways. Prenger shows how sometimes the theological frames of "alongsiders" exert influence on the theological frames of "insider" leaders with whom they are connected, and yet other times there seems to be very little significant theological influence (2017, Loc. 5541–53).

to pray and worship, or in a campus ministry group which has highly structured community for discipleship and accountability. While such groups have a place in the universal church, we should not consider such groups "churches" or "local churches," as they do not reflect all of the components of New Testament churches. Furthermore, such groups (with some exceptions) do not usually see themselves as churches, nor do they intend to become local churches. If they did, then they would seek to intentionally begin developing the form of their community and adding various elements that are necessary to being a local church.

A clear understanding of what is (and what is not) a local church, as well as *sustained, intentional movement in that direction*, is crucial for fellowships or believing groups to fully emerge into local churches. The question is, does the insider paradigm provide an ecclesial vision that will encourage and facilitate this to take place? This study suggests that the insider paradigm, as currently defined, includes commitments and principles which create functional obstacles to the development of key aspects of the biblical nature of the church.

My study relates in important ways to the broader insider movements conversation. First, it sheds further light on previous critiques of insider ecclesiology of Tennent (2007) and Coleman (2011). Tennent's evaluation of insider movements was framed by the issue of ecclesiology, yet it was a broader critique that considered a variety of aspects of the insider paradigm, not just ecclesiology. (Only two of his points related specifically to ecclesiology, focused mainly around the issue of the church-salvation relationship.) Likewise, Coleman devoted one chapter of his dissertation to analyzing the ecclesiology of the insider paradigm, and yet space limitations only allowed him to focus on a few specific issues. By contrast, the present study has provided a more comprehensive, multifaceted look at the biblical and theological nature of the church and the insider paradigm. It has provided a broader, more complex picture of the variety of ways in which the insider paradigm supports and yet undermines the biblical nature of the church.

Second, my study relates to developments from the Bridging the Divide consultations which have sought to bring greater understanding and clarity to both sides of the insider question. Ecclesiology has emerged as one key theme of the BtD discussions, as people on different sides of "the divide" have a commitment to biblical ecclesiology, while bringing to the table a multiplicity of ecclesiologies which influence how they evaluate the viability of insider movements. This study suggests that to make real progress in this discussion, we must engage more specifically at the level of our theological assumptions of the nature of the church and the way those assumptions are supported by the themes and narratives of Scripture. Furthermore, it suggests that the ecclesiology of the insider paradigm contains a mixture of both healthy and unhealthy elements; there are many elements which support the development of the biblical nature of the church in Muslim contexts, and these should be recognized and affirmed by both critics and advocates of insider movements as common ground that can be built upon. At the same time, the insider paradigm contains certain commitments and tendencies that create serious problems for expressing the full biblical nature of the church, which need to be recognized and addressed by all sides if we want our ministry strategy to be aligned with the fullness of Christ's vision for the building of his church in the Muslim world.

Third, my study provides an alternate perspective to that of Duerkson and Dyrness in *Seeking Church*. Their project differs from mine in several respects. They assume the validity of insider movements and communities, seeking to offer an account for such realities sociologically and theologically, while I have approached the validity of insider movements and communities as an open question, seeking to provide a biblical and theological basis for evaluating the ecclesiology of the insider paradigm. They emphasize the ways that our theology of the church is embedded, and in some ways determined, by our cultural location, while I emphasize the ways that our theology of the church can be more or less supported by, and faithful to, the biblical text. Their project is helpful in terms of describing, historically and sociologically, the way elements of "church" emerge in particular communities, including insider communities. My study suggests, however, that biblical ekklesia should be defined by the full range of themes and teachings on the nature of the church, which in the end ought to challenge and qualify our assumptions regarding the validity of insider identity.

When deciding upon any mission strategy, we must be careful to clarify the goal and vision that drives that strategy. One of the key goals which drives the "insider movement" paradigm is to keep believers inside their Muslim families and communities so that the gospel can spread more deeply and rapidly. While this is a worthy goal, we must also include in our vision a larger biblical goal of creating spiritually mature disciples. As Waterman says,

> It appears that much of the rationale for religious insider movements is predicated on answering the question "How can people be saved and still remain in their community?" and then turning that answer into a strategic goal. While it is valuable for believers to stay connected to their communities and remain appropriately a part of their culture, it is *imperative* that they move beyond initial conversion toward maturity in Christ. Texts such as Eph 4:13, Matt 28:19; Col 1:28 and Acts 20:27 all clearly express that our ministry should lead to spiritual maturity among those we impact, not just to large numbers of minimally mature believers. (2007, 59)

The larger goal is not simply remaining inside one's community of birth, but seeing believers grow and flourish to spiritual maturity. If growing as a mature disciple is the ultimate goal, then a key question for evaluating questions of contextualization will be "whether a particular teaching or pattern of behavior enables one to live as a disciple of Jesus Christ or hinders doing so" (McDermott and Netland 2014, 255). Miriam Adeney likewise brings this broader perspective to bear on the topic of Muslim contextualization, noting that the insider-movement debates are often more focused on the issue of evangelism and conversion while ignoring the larger question of discipleship and spiritual maturity. Acknowledging that aspects of Muslim belief can help lead people to faith in the gospel, ultimately Adeney concludes that "Islam is not a context that promotes long-term spiritual health and growth" (2001, 76). She summarizes her argument this way:

> Is Islam a nurturing context for discipling Muslim-background believers, the discipling that the gospel requires? No. In doctrine, in community, and in sacrament, it is difficult to grow as Christ's disciple while remaining within Islam. Positively, Islam does contain God-given patterns of wisdom, beauty, and caring. In these we take joy. Sadly, Islam also contains creedal and social structures that systematically turn people from Christ, that defraud people from a relationship with their Lord. (ibid., 82)

Adeney argues that remaining religiously connected to Islam is problematic for converts to grow into healthy, mature disciples. Thus, the goal of remaining within one's context and community, however worthy and preferable, must not override the biblical goal of growth to spiritual maturity.

But our goal should be to produce not only mature biblical disciples but also *mature biblical churches*. These two are inseparably connected: maturing disciples lead to maturing churches, since life in Christian community, the church, is an integral part of growing in spiritual maturity (ibid.). Therefore, we should not only be asking whether retaining significant connections to Muslim religious identity helps people grow as spiritually mature disciples of Christ, but also whether it helps groups of believers grow into a full, mature, and dynamic expression of the biblical church (Little 2015, 122–26). As Waterman says,

> Church planting and church planting movements must be clearly tethered to the biblical meaning of *ekklesia*, rather than to humanly determined criteria of success. John Travis's "C Scale" has played a very helpful role in describing various gatherings of followers of Jesus, but is less helpful as a descriptor of ministry *goals*. An "insider movement" is an inadequate ministry goal, because it elevates a church growth principle (remaining connected to one's culture) to the level of an essential standard, potentially overriding biblical priorities. The goal of remaining within a religious community (being viewed by that community as an "insider") must be secondary to embracing one's identity in Christ, and living out that primary identity, regardless of the consequences. The New Testament presents our new identity in Christ as essential, and the culture's response to it as secondary. (2007, 60)

Waterman rightly identifies the true biblical priorities that should guide contextualization in Muslim contexts. Helping BMBs live out their new identity in Christ—including their new social identity as the church, the body of Christ—is the essential biblical priority of our mission approach. All other goals and issues should be evaluated based on whether they contribute to the growth and maturation of believers into a biblical, Spirit-filled, church.

Mark Williams asks the question, "What legacy will we leave believers in these contextualized communities of faith?" (2007, 70). This key question should guide and continually test our disciple making and church planting missiology in Muslim contexts. Muslims are coming to faith in Christ in unprecedented ways, and it is crucial that the church responds with biblical wisdom and spiritual discernment as it seeks to disciple new believers and follow Jesus as he builds his church in the house of Islam.

EPILOGUE

Recommendations for Multiplying Biblical Churches among Muslims

Planting churches in the house of Islam is a humanly impossible, supernatural work that cannot happen apart from divine intervention. Yet the unique difficulties of the context can influence us to settle for a smaller vision of the church, the bare minimum. Why not dream bigger dreams? As Waterman says,

> While acknowledging the creativity needed for discipleship and spiritual growth in contexts with much persecution, it seems unwise to stretch a description of church to fit the challenges of special cases. Better to keep pleading with Jesus to do in those very challenging contexts what he has promised: "I will build my church, and the gates of hell shall not prevail against it." (2011, under subheading "Field Applications in Challenging Contexts")

Waterman rightly encourages us to preserve, rather than water down, the full biblical meaning of the church. Keeping this as a baseline for what the church *is*, we are better equipped to help other fellowships of believers grow into full, biblical churches.

> We can perhaps diminish some of the conflict between more traditional descriptions of church and attempts to deal realistically with the challenges of high persecution contexts by viewing church development as a dynamic process, rather than a static condition.... New Testament models and teaching leave room for great variety in the church. Yet without certain vital ingredients, a gathering (or non-gathering) cannot rightly be called a church. (Waterman 2011, under subheading "Church in Process")

One can maintain the full biblical definition of the church, holding fast to its essential biblical features, while recognizing that becoming a true church is not something which happens overnight. Waterman advocates for the notion of the "embryonic church" as a helpful category in this regard:

> George Patterson and Richard Scoggins propose the helpful concept of "embryonic church" (Patterson and Scoggins 2003, 24, 144). This describes a small fellowship of obedient disciples moving toward becoming a full-fledged multiplying church. It would not yet contain all the biblical characteristics of a "church," but would include the right "DNA" and be moving toward being "church." An oikos of believers is better seen as an embryonic church, rather than a full ekklēsia. (ibid.)

An "embryonic church" is not a full biblical church, but may be "on the way" to becoming one—that is, it is "a gathering with potential that is not (yet) a church" (Waterman 2011, under subheading "Why Discussion Is Needed"). Such a concept better preserves the biblical meaning of the New Testament ekklēsia, while also taking into account the fact that some groups or gatherings of believers can contain some elements—yet not all—of a full church. However, it is crucial that even from the beginning, the embryonic church has the right "DNA"; that is, it needs to include elements which will grow and flower into the full expression of the biblical church. If any key elements are missing from this DNA, or if other elements are mixed in which hinder the development of a fellowship into a full biblical church, then the result will be something less than the biblical vision of the body of Christ.

Therefore, to conclude my study, I recommend adopting the following eight goals and priorities to help guide our disciple making and church planting strategy, to help believers and fellowships grow and develop into the fullness of the biblical church.

1. To develop a healthy, biblical identity as the church, emerging churches should be immersed in and indwell the fullness of the biblical narrative of the people of God and the full scope of biblical images of the church in the Old and New Testaments. This is the first and most important recommendation, and under girds all the rest. When Muslims begin to believe in and follow Jesus as their Lord, they acquire a new narrative, which defines and transforms their community identity as part of the people of God, the church. This new narrative does not destroy other social and cultural narratives and identities; but it does transcend, transform, and challenge all other narratives—whether cultural, national, religious, tribal, or other. Following Christ does not mean rejecting one's own cultural and social narrative and community in order to adopt a new, foreign cultural and social narrative and community. Rather, it means gaining a new, larger, all-encompassing narrative—an "adoptive past" which explains, relativizes, and transforms all other identities and communities, putting them in their proper place and context.

This also means challenging and correcting all narratives which, in whole or in part, contradict, undermine, or replace the biblical narrative. One of these narratives is the traditional Islamic story (and its variations) that shapes the identity of the Muslim *umma*. While containing faint echoes of the biblical narrative, the Islamic narrative represents a fundamentally divergent narrative from the true narrative of God and his people in the Scriptures.[131] If Muslim-background believers and fellowships are to grow and develop into the biblical church, they need to be formed and shaped by the full biblical narrative, from Abraham to the New Jerusalem.

In addition to the biblical narrative, Scripture also provides a rich array of biblical images which shape and define the nature and identity of the church. The people of God, kingdom of priests and holy nation, the family of Jesus, the salt and light of the earth, the temple of the Holy Spirit, the body and bride of Christ, the city of God—these are just a sample of the many themes and metaphors Scripture uses to describe the rich identity that is the rightful heritage of all who are in Christ. As Muslim-background believers and fellowships seek to learn what it means to be in Christ and a part of his community, the biblical images of the church provide rich, powerful resources to the church—each one giving unique insight into different aspects of our privileged identity as Christ's body. We must be careful not to rely on a select number of images while ignoring others, but rather to allow the full kaleidoscope of biblical images and metaphors to nurture in believers the full, panoramic understanding of the mystery of the church. This is especially important as Muslims who come to faith are likely to face some degree of persecution or community shame (whether or not they adopt an "insider" identity). The rich array of biblical images of the church helps to root the church in its true identity, a community of great honor and privilege in the eyes of God.

The most crucial step to faithfully express the biblical nature of the church is by rooting it in the whole counsel of God—the full biblical narrative of the church and the full scope of biblical images of the church. If we get this wrong, then we handicap ourselves and risk falling short in all the areas recommended below.

---

131 Cf. Shenk 2014, chapter 9, for a concise and eloquent expression of this fundamental divergence.

If we get this right, then we lay a rock-solid foundation for Muslim-background believers and fellowships to learn, develop, and express the fullness of the biblical church.

2. To develop a healthy, biblical identity as the church, emerging churches should grow in their understanding of their salvation in Christ and the God who saved them. The core essence of the church consists in being the redeemed people of God, which bring the church and salvation into an integral relationship. Therefore, a healthy understanding of the identity of the church should be increasingly rooted in a growing grasp of "so great a salvation" as well as the God who reconciled us to himself. While a precise understanding of the intricacies of atonement and Trinitarian theology is not required for salvation, nor are they equally relevant in all contexts (though they are relevant in some), the New Testament authors took great pains to help churches come to a greater understanding of their salvation in Christ, as well as the Father, Son, and Spirit in whom salvation is found.

As emerging churches seek to develop their biblical identity as the church, they will be increasingly rooted in this identity if they continue to grow in understanding all that the Scriptures say about their salvation in Christ and the God of their salvation. The first and primary source of this growing understanding should be the ongoing study of the whole counsel of the Scriptures in the local church in its context as a hermeneutical guide to the church's dynamic experience and personal relationship with the triune God. Furthermore, the local church's growing understanding of their salvation and the God who saved them will be enhanced by the perspectives and insights of the global and historic church, which are not a replacement for, but a supplement to, local theologizing by emerging churches.

3. To develop a healthy, biblical identity as the church, emerging churches should find ways to corporately embrace, claim, and name their identity as the people of God in their context. This recommendation follows naturally from the first. As a fellowship of believers grows in their understanding of how the biblical narrative and biblical images shape and define who they are as a community, this should result in the development of a clear identity as the body and bride of Jesus.

Each emerging church has the responsibility and privilege of understanding and expressing the essence of the biblical church in a way that is meaningful in their own context. It does not in any way require claiming the terms "Christian" and "church" as their main identity labels; these are only two of the many terms and images in Scripture that express the identity of the biblical church. What is important is that as fellowships of Christ-followers grow in their understanding of the biblical narrative and images of the church, they begin to "own" and embrace this identity for themselves, as a community of disciples.

A church that aims to remain in its context will aim to discern wise ways to avoid unnecessarily shaming family and community, and thus believers may avoid terms and concepts which are negatively associated with Western civilization or colonialism. However, they will not avoid the fact that their redemptive relationship to Jesus Christ gives them a distinct biblical identity as a community that is not (yet) shared by those who do not yet share the same relationship with Jesus, an identity which brings with it incredible, eternal honor as the Bride and Body of Jesus. The emerging church thus will seek ways to express this glorious, wonderful identity as a community in bold, winsome ways that are meaningful in their context.

4. To develop a healthy, biblical identity as the church, emerging churches should have a clear understanding of the local church in all of its essential elements and engage in an intentional process of developing and expressing these elements in their context. The embryonic core of the church begins when two or three are gathered in the name and presence of Jesus; this itself is a marvelous victory for the kingdom of God. However, our prayers and efforts must not stop there, but should be fueled by the vision of seeing this fellowship grow and flower into a full expression of the local body of Christ as described in the New Testament.

This means that, eventually, faith in Jesus must be clearly professed and recognized through baptism. Second, this means that this community should commit to one another and begin to identify together as a biblical church, in line with the previous recommendations. Third, the community should develop a regular pattern of intentional gatherings as a community in Christ. Fourth, these gatherings should be shaped and guided by the purposes and functions of the local church in the New Testament—including, but not limited to, worshiping God, fellowship, mutual edification, and patterns of faithful communication and response to God's Word. Fifth, local spiritual shepherds should be appointed to lead, guide, and care for God's flock.[132]

Each local body of believers has the great responsibility and freedom to search the Scriptures and seek meaningful ways to express these essential components of the local church in their context. Unlike Islam, Scripture gives great freedom to express the biblical church in a variety of cultures, languages, and liturgies. This process of developing to fully express all the elements of the New Testament church does not happen overnight. What is important is that the vision and the goal should be clear from the very beginning, so that the key building blocks and "DNA" of the local church can be planted in local communities of believers, helping them to grow steadily toward expressing the full local church as taught in the Scriptures.

---

132 The apostle Paul did not consider his pioneer church planting work "finished" until local churches were organized and entrusted into the spiritual care of local elders, and we should not aim for anything less. Even then, he did not consider his responsibility to churches finished, as he continued to pray, visit, and write letters to the churches until they grew to full maturity in Christ (cf. Acts 14:21–23; 15:36; 20:1–6; Phil 1:9–11; 1 Thess 1:2).

5. **To develop a healthy, biblical identity as the church, emerging churches should understand their connection to the global family of God. They should find meaningful, healthy ways of identifying with, being supported by, contributing to, and cultivating commonality with the church universal.** As local fellowships of believers have the responsibility and privilege of expressing the local church in their context, they also need to learn that the body of Christ is larger than their own local fellowship. They are a part of a worldwide, multicultural, multinational body, from many times and many places, from different backgrounds, united in one body and Spirit.

The same identity—defined by the biblical narrative and images of the church—which binds believers together in a local body binds them together with *all* who are in Christ. This does not require formal, institutional participation in any particular church body, nor does it require adopting the same terminology or cultural expression of the church. Believers from Muslim backgrounds might refrain from joining a "traditional" Christian church, and they may express their faith in terms and cultural forms that are quite different from their elder brothers in the universal church.

However, biblical churches should find ways to express their fellowship and participation with other churches in the global body of Christ. Efforts to remain culturally rooted and locally relevant should be supplemented by efforts to cultivate commonality and "catholicity" with the broader church. This is a crucial aspect of the identity of the church for emerging Muslim-background churches, which are often small and significantly outnumbered in their Muslim community. The reality of the worldwide family of Jesus, which will one day gather as one before the throne of the Lamb, is absolutely essential to nurture and sustain the life and identity of the local church until the return of Christ.

6. **To develop a healthy, biblical identity as the church, emerging churches should learn to live out their identity and calling as the people of God in their context, giving tangible, visible glimpses of the full, spiritual ("invisible") glory of the church.** The essential nature and identity of the church is not just theory and theology; it is fundamentally practical. The essential nature and identity of the church not only shapes the self-understanding and corporate identity of the church—it is a calling to be lived out. The church's identity as the people of God, the body of Christ, the family of Jesus, the temple of the Spirit—these all imply a certain calling, a certain way of life, a certain kind of community. The classical attributes of the church—one, holy, catholic, and apostolic—are one way of expressing this dynamic. The church is one body, and it is called to be one. It is a holy nation, and it is called to holiness. It is a universal family, and it is called to brotherly love for all believers. It is the apostolic community, and it is called to preserve the apostolic gospel and mission for future generations.

As Muslim-background fellowships are growing into biblical churches, they must understand that their *identity* as the church shapes their *life* as the church;

their great privileges as the people of God also imply responsibilities to one another and to the world. This, of course, cannot happen apart from visible, face-to-face community. As believers in these fellowships grow in their understanding of their identity as the church, this should continually shape and transform their community life, how they relate to each other, and how they relate to the world. No church ever perfectly lives up to its nature and calling as the church, and no church ever stops aspiring and growing toward this calling. The important thing is that a church understands that its biblical nature has practical, real-world consequences, and it embraces this calling as a community, the calling to *be* the church.

But such efforts at visible community must be rooted in the full, glorious spiritual reality of the biblical identity of the church, a reality that is presently true in Christ and will be fully revealed on the last day. The full glory of the eschatological church is important for giving proper perspective to the emerging church in developing its biblical identity as the church. This picture shows emerging churches that their full identity and glory as the church is not dependent upon the perfection of their visible community, but on their glorious identity in the heavenly assembly in Christ, which will one day fully be revealed. As Muslim-background believers seek to express the church, they risk experiencing shame from the community for failing to fall in line with the societal line. Furthermore, church formation in such contexts is difficult, and there are likely to be roadblocks and disappointments along the way. The biblical vision of the future (and present) glory of the church is crucial to helping emerging churches remember and be sustained by the true reality of their unfathomable honor and glory as the people of God.

These wonderful realities help BMB churches see that their humble, ordinary gatherings to sing, study, fellowship, and encourage one another actually express and give a foretaste of the heavenly assembly in Christ. It also helps them to see that when they step out and build ties with believers from a *non*-Muslim background, or from another tribe or ethnic group, they are giving a glimpse of the great gathering of people from every tribe and tongue, redeemed and reconciled in the Lamb.

7. To develop healthy, biblical identity as the church, emerging churches should develop patterns of faithful communication and response to the Old and New Testament Scriptures, the practice of baptism, and the practice of the Lord's Supper. The Protestant marks of the Word, baptism, and communion are biblical practices that play a formative role in nurturing, shaping, and expressing the nature and identity of the church. We must be careful not to impose any particular cultural expression or liturgical practice upon another context, since each church has the freedom and responsibility to interpret and express the biblical teaching regarding the church in their context.

On the other hand, we must be sure that the church has all the possible tools to understand and apply the Word of God. These tools would include the full Scriptures made available, training and equipping to interpret and apply the Scriptures, guidance and assistance from experienced teachers and cross-cultural workers, as well as exposure to the insights from the historic and global church. Furthermore, the practices of baptism and the Lord's Supper, while they may be practiced differently at different times and places, are crucial practices for helping biblical churches to express, rehearse, and cultivate their biblical identity as the church.

By developing patterns of consistent immersion in the Word, baptism, and communion, churches nurture their biblical identity as the church, both locally and universally. By an increasing faithfulness to the truth of Scripture, churches grow in the "unity of the faith" with the church worldwide, even as they apply and express obedience to that faith in particular ways required in their context. By practicing baptism and communion, local churches not only declare their unity locally as one body, they also declare their unity with the body of Christ worldwide, participating in practices which, although they may have different variations in different contexts, are practices shared in and owned by the worldwide body of Christ.

8. To develop a healthy, biblical identity as the church, emerging churches should develop a holistic understanding of their missional role in the world as indigeneous and pilgrim, set apart from the world as holy and sent into the world as kings and priests to bring the nations under the reign of King Jesus and into his kingdom community. We should long to see Muslim-background fellowships remain in their Muslim communities, that they might be on mission as "priests" and emissaries of God's kingdom in that context. Yet at the same time our vision should be for these fellowships to be distinct and "set-apart" from their communities, not by a foreign culture but by the presence of Christ, the fruit of the Spirit, and the righteousness of the kingdom. The church's call to be a "set-apart" community is not an excuse for withdrawal from its calling to be a kingdom of priests on mission in the world, and its calling as a kingdom of priests must never be an excuse to compromise its calling to be a distinct, holy community in the world. This biblical tension should shape the way the church in Muslim contexts navigates its relationship with its Muslim environment, participating in God's mission in that context as the distinct, set-apart people of God. This means that the Muslim-background church should seek to avoid, when possible, prematurely leaving their context or *unnecessarily* provoking their family or community to expel them from their community. But the other extreme should also be avoided, which is becoming indistinguishable from the Muslim community and failing to express the uniqueness of Christ and his kingdom in ways that counter-culturally challenge the Muslim community. As it remains in the world, the church is a sign and foretaste of the kingdom of God to the world. The missional church in the Muslim world embraces the goal of seeing God's kingdom spread like yeast through Muslim communities and family networks. But part and parcel of this vision is biblical churches living as kingdom communities which reflect the distinctive reign and presence of the Messiah, providing their Muslim community a glimpse of the new heavens and the new earth.

These eight principles express goals and priorities that should shape our vision of the biblical church and our mission practice of disciple making and church planting among Muslims. We should not be content with the mass conversion of Muslims or the conversion of Muslim families. Our vision must include not only biblical discipleship, but biblical churches. The apostle Paul was not satisfied with conversions and fellowships of believers; his ultimate motivation and goal was to see churches become mature and complete in Christ, which Paul could present as a pleasing offering to the Lord on the last day (Rom 15:16; Phil 2:16; Col 1:28–29). We should follow this example by praying and working tirelessly toward the goal of presenting to the Lord an offering of mature, biblical churches from every corner of the Muslim world.

God is doing a new and unprecedented work in our days in bringing Muslims into the kingdom of his Son. As the global church participates in this great harvest, may our vision and ministry practice be aligned with the vision of Jesus, that we may be his faithful field laborers as he builds his church, his body, his bride.

Bibliography

Adeney, Miriam. 2002. "Rajah Sulayman was no water buffalo: Gospel, anthropology, and Islam." In *No other gods before me? Evangelicals and the challenge of world religions,* ed. John G. Stackhouse, Jr., 65–84. Grand Rapids, MI: Baker Academic.

Allison, Gregg. 2012. *Sojourners and strangers: The doctrine of the church.* Foundations of evangelical theology series. Wheaton, IL: Crossway.

Anderson, John D. C. 1976. "Missionary approach to Islam: Christian or 'cultic.'" *Missiology* 4: 285–300.

Anonymous ("A Missionary in the Near East"). 1941. "Dynamic converts." *The Moslem World* 31: 140–44.

Anonymous C-5 missionary. 1999. Letters to the editor. *Evangelical Missions Quarterly* 35, no. 3: 264–71.

Arrupe, Pedro. 1978. "Letter to the whole society on inculturation." In *Other apostolates today* (1981), ed. Jerome Aixala, 172–81. St. Louis: Institute of Jesuit Sources.

Asad, Abdul. 2009. "Rethinking the insider movement debate: Global historical insights toward an appropriate transitional model of c5." *St Francis Magazine* 5, no. 4 (August): 133–59.

Ascough, Richard. S. 2002. *Community formation in the early church and in the church today,* ed. Richard N. Longenecker, 3–18. Peabody, MA: Hendrickson.

Baeq, Daniel Shinjong. 2010. "Contextualizing religious form and meaning: A missiological interpretation of Naaman's petitions (2 Kings 5:15–19)." *International Journal of Frontier Missiology* 27, no. 4: 197–205.

Baker, Wayne. 2000. Letter to the editor. *Evangelical Missions Quarterly* 36, no. 2: 147–50.

Banks, Robert. 1980. *Paul's idea of community: The early house churches in their historical setting.* Grand Rapids, MI: Eerdmans.

Barnett, Jens. 2013. "Refusing to choose: Multiple belonging among Arab followers of Christ." In *Longing for community: Church,* ummah, *or somewhere in between?,* edited by David Greenlee et al., 19–28. Pasadena, CA: William Carey Library.

———. 2015. "Searching for models of individual identity." In *Understanding insider movements: disciples of Jesus within diverse religious communities,* ed. Harley Talman and John Jay Travis, Loc. 13093–13427. Pasadena, CA: William Carey Library. Kindle edition.

Barnett, Paul. 1997. *The second epistle to the Corinthians.* Grand Rapids, MI: Eerdmans.

Barney, Linwood. 1973. "The supracultural and the cultural: Implications for frontier missions." In *The gospel and frontier people,* ed. R. Pierce Beaver, 48–57. Pasadena, CA: William Carey Library.

Barth, Karl. 1956. *Church Dogmatics, Volume IV: The doctrine of reconciliation, Part 1.* Trans. G. W. Bromiley. Ed. G. W. Bromiley and T. F. Trrance. London: T&T Clark International.

Bartlotti, Leonard N. 2015. "Seeing inside insider missiology: Exploring our theological lenses and presuppositions." In *Understanding insider movements: disciples of Jesus within diverse religious communities,* ed. Harley Talman and John Jay Travis, Loc. 1902–2531. Pasadena, CA: William Carey Library. Kindle edition. (Orig. pub. 2013. *International Journal of Frontier Missiology* 30, no. 4: 137–53. http://www.ijfm.org/PDFs_IJFM/30_4_PDFs/IJFM_30_4-Bartlotti.pdf.)

Bate, Fr. Stuart. 1994. "Inculturation: The local church emerges." *Missionalia* 22, no. 2: 93–117.

Berding, Kenneth. 2006. *What are spiritual gifts? Rethinking the Conventional View.* Grand Rapids, MI: Kregel.

Black, Allen. 2012. "Called to be holy: Ecclesiology in the Petrine epistles." In *The New Testament Church: The challenge of developing ecclesiologies,* ed. John Harrison and James Dvorak, 226–42. Eugene, OR: Wipf and Stock.

Blomberg, Craig. 1992. *Matthew*. The new American commentary 22. Nashville: Broadman.

Blue, Bradley. 1994. "Acts and the house church." In *The book of Acts in its first century setting: Vol.2: The book of Acts in its Graeco-Roman setting*, ed. David W.J. Gill and Conrad Gempf, 119–222. Grand Rapids, MI: Eerdmans.

Bock, Darrell. 1994–96. *Luke*. 2 vols. Baker Exegetical Commentary on the New Testament. Grand Rapids, MI: Baker.

———. 2007. *Acts*. Baker Exegetical Commentary on the New Testament. Grand Rapids, MI: Baker.

Bonhoeffer, Dietrich. 1995. *The cost of discipleship*. New York: Simon & Schuster. Trans. by R. H. Fuller and Irmgard Booth. Orig. pub. 1959 by SCM Press. Trans. from orig. German edition *Nachfolge* first pub. 1937 by Chr. Kaiser Verlag Munchen.

———. 2009. *Life together: The classical exploration of Christian community*. Harperone.

Bosch, David J. 1991. "Transforming mission: Paradigm shifts in theology of mission." *American Society of Missiology series*, no. 16. Maryknoll, NY: Orbis.

Bridging the Divide. 2011. Bridging the Divide 2011 Consultation Report. Finalized June 23, 2011. http://btdnetwork.org/wp-content/uploads/2013/07/Bridging-the-Divide-2011-Summary-Report1.pdf.

———. 2012. Bridging the Divide 2012 Consultation Report. Finalized July 7, 2012. http://btdnetwork.org/wp-content/uploads/2013/07/Bridging-the-Divide-2012-Summary-Report1.pdf.

———. 2013. Bridging the Divide 2013 Consultation Report. Finalized June 7, 2013. http://btdnetwork.org/wp-content/uploads/2013/07/Bridging-the-Divide-2013-Summary-Report1.pdf.

———. 2014. Bridging the Divide 2014 Consultation Report. Finalized July 8, 2014. http://btdnetwork.org/wp-content/uploads/2013/07/Bridging-the-Divide-2014-Summary-Report.pdf.

———. 2015. Bridging the Divide 2015 Consultation Report. Finalized June 25, 2015. http://205.134.239.60/~btdnetwork/wp-content/uploads/2015/07/Bridging-the-Divide-2015-Summary-Report-1.pdf.

Brislin, Mike. 1996. "A Model for a Muslim-culture church." *Missiology* 24: 355–67.

Brown, Francis, S. R. Driver, and Charles. A. Briggs. 2001. *The Brown-Driver-Briggs Hebrew and English lexicon with an appendix containing biblical Aramaic*. Peabody, MA: Hendrickson. (Orig. pub. 1906.)

Brown, Rick. 2000. "What must one believe about Jesus for salvation?" *International Journal of Frontier Missiology* 17, no. 4. http://www.ijfm.org/PDFs_IJFM/17_4_PDFs/02_Brown_Beliefs_hw.pdf.

Brown, Rick. 2006. "Contextualization without syncretism." *International Journal of Frontier Missiology* 23, no. 3: 127–33. http://www.ijfm.org/PDFs_IJFM/23_3_PDFs/brown%20c45.pdf.

———. 2007a. "Brother Jacob and Master Isaac: How one insider movement began." *International Journal of Frontier Missiology* 24, no. 1: 41–42. http://www.ijfm.org/PDFs_IJFM/24_1_PDFs/Brown.pdf.

———. 2007b. "Biblical Muslims." *International Journal of Frontier Missiology* 24, no. 2: 65–74.

Bruce, F. F. 1958. "Eschatology." *London Quarterly & Holborn Review* 183: 99–103. http://www.theologicalstudies.org.uk/pdf/eschatology_bruce.pdf.

———. 1990. *The acts of the apostles: The Greek text with introduction and commentary*. 3rd rev. and enl. ed. Grand Rapids, MI: Eerdmans.

Calvin, John. 1959. *Institutes of the Christian religion*, vol. 2. Edited by John T. McNeill. Translated by Ford Lewis Battles. Louisville, KY: Westminster John Knox.

Carpenter, Eugene E. 2009. Deuteronomy. In *Zondervan illustrated Bible backgrounds commentary*, ed. John H. Walton, 418–547. Grand Rapids, MI: Zondervan.

Carson, D. A. 2006. Series preface, New studies in biblical theology. In Thompson, Mark, *A clear and present word: The clarity of scripture*, Downers Grove, IL: Intervarsity Press.

———. 2008. Biblical theology and interpretation. Class at Trinity Evangelical Divinity School, Deerfield, IL.

———. 2012. Jesus the Son of God: A Christological title often overlooked, sometimes misunderstood, and currently disputed. Wheaton: Crossway.

Carson, D. A., and Douglas J. Moo. 2005. *An introduction to the new testament.* 2nd ed. Grand Rapids, MI: Zondervan.

Chadwick, Henry. 1993. *The early church.* The Penguin history of the church, volume 1. Revised edition. London, England: Pelican Books. Kindle edition.

Chang, Eunhye J., J. Rupert Morgan, Timothy Nyasulu, and Robert J. Priest. 2009. "Paul G. Hiebert and critical contextualization." *Trinity Journal* 30NS: 199–207.

Christian Reformed Church. N.d. Belgic Confession. Christian Reformed Church website. http://www.crcna.org/welcome/beliefs/confessions/belgic-confession.

Clowney, Edmund. 1987. "The biblical theology of the church." In *The church in the Bible and the world: An international study,* ed. D. A. Carson, 13–87. Grand Rapids, MI: Baker.

———. 1995. *The church: Contours of Christian theology.* Downers Grove, IL: Intervarsity Press.

Coe, Shokie. 1976. "Contextualizing theology." In *Mission trends no.3: Third world theologies: Asian, African and Latin Americna contributions to a radical, theological realignment in the church,* ed. Gerald H. Anderson and Thomas F. Stransky, 19–24. (Orig. pub. 1973 in *Theological Education.*)

Coleman, Doug. 2011. *A theological analysis of the insider movement paradigm from four perspectives: Theology of religions, revelation, soteriology and ecclesiology.* Evangelical Missiological Society Dissertation Series. Pasadena, CA: WCIU Press.

Conn, Harvie M. 1979. "The Muslim convert and his culture." In *The Gospel and Islam: A 1978 compedium,* ed. Don M. McCurry, 97–112.

———. 2000. "Indigenization. Contextualization." In *Evangelical dictionary of world missions,* ed. Scott Moreau et al., 481–82. Grand Rapids, MI: Baker.

Corwin, Gary. 2007a. "A humble appeal to C5/insider movement Muslim ministry advocates to consider ten questions, with responses from Brother Yusuf, Rick Brown, Kevin Higgins, Rebecca Lewis, and John Travis." *International Journal of Frontier Missiology* 24, no. 1 (Spring): 5–20.

———. 2007b. "A response to my respondents." *International Journal of Frontier Missiology* 24, no. 2: 53–55.

Cullmann, Oscar. 1964. *Christ and time: The primitive Christian conception of time and history.* Rev. ed. Trans from German by Floyd V. Filson. Philadelphia: Westminster.

Cyprian. 1885a. *Treatise I: On the unity of the Catholic Church.* In Ante-Nicene Fathers 5: Hippolytus, Cyprian, Caius, Novation, Appendix, ed. Alexander Roberts and James Donaldson. Edinburgh: T&T Clark, 1885. http://www.ccel.org/ccel/schaff/anf05.iv.v.i.html.

Cyprian. 1885b. "Epistle LXXII: To Jubaianus, concerning the baptism of heretics." In Ante-Nicene Fathers 5: Hippolytus, Cyprian, Caius, Novation, Appendix, ed. Alexander Roberts and James Donaldson. Translated by Robert Ernest Wallis. Edinburgh: T&T Clark, 1885. http://www.ccel.org/ccel/schaff/anf05.iv.iv.lxxii.html.

Daniels, Gene. 2013. "Worshiping Jesus in the mosque." *Christianity Today* 57, no. 1: 22.

———. 2014. Saying the shahada: Matters of conscience, creed, and communication. *Evangelical Missions Quarterly* 50, no. 4: 304–11.

Daniels, Gene, and L. D. Waterman. 2013. "Bridging the 'socio-religious' divide: A conversation between two missiologists." *International Journal of Frontier Missiology* 30, no. 2: 59–66.

Decker, Frank. 2005. "When 'Christian' does not translate." *Mission Frontiers* 27, no. 5: 8.

Del Colle, Ralph. 2007. "The church." In *The Oxford handbook of systematic theology,* ed. John Webster, Kathryn Tanner, and Iain Torrance, 249–65.

Dillard, Raymond B., and Tremper Longman III. 1994. *An introduction to the Old Testament.* Grand Rapids, MI: Zondervan.

Duerkson, Darren. 2012. "Must insiders be churchless? Exploring insiders' models of 'church.'" *International Journal of Frontier Missiology* 29, no. 4: 161–67. http://www.ijfm.org/PDFs_IJFM/29_4_PDFs/IJFM_29_4-Duerksen.pdf.

———. 2015. "Ecclesial identities of "socio-religious" 'insiders.'" In *Understanding insider movements: disciples of Jesus within diverse religious communities,* ed. Harley Talman and John Jay Travis, Loc. 3977–4195. Pasadena, CA: William Carey Library. Kindle edition.

Dunn, James D. G. 2011. *Jesus, Paul, and the Gospels.* Grand Rapids, MI: Eerdmans.

Dutch, Bernard. 2000. "Should Muslims become 'Christians'?" *International Journal of Frontier Missiology* 17, no. 1: 15–24. http://www.ijfm.org/PDFs_IJFM/17_1_PDFs/Muslims_as_Christians.pdf.

Dyrness, William A. 2016. *Insider Jesus: Theological reflections on new Christian movements.* Downers Grove, IL: IVP

Dyrness, William, and Darren Duerkson. 2019. *Seeking church: Emerging witnesses to the kingdom.* Downers Grove, IL: IVP.

Eitel, Keith. 1998. "'To be or not to be?': The indigeneous church question." In *Missiology: An introduction to the foundations, history, and strategies of world missions,* ed. John Mark Terry, Ebbie Smith, and Justice Anderson, 301–17. Nashville: Broadman & Holman.

Elliott, Mark W. 2000. "Remnant." In *New dictionary of biblical theology: Exploring the unity and diversity of Scripture,* ed. T. Desmond Alexander, Brian S. Rosner, D. A. Carson, Graeme Goldsworthy, 723–26. Leicester, England: InterVarsity.

Erickson, Millard. 1998. *Christian theology.* 2nd ed. Grand Rapids, MI: Baker. *Evangelical Review of Theology* 37, no. 4.

Farah, Warrick. 2015. "The complexity of insiderness." *International Journal of Frontier Missiology* 32, no. 2: 85–91.

Farah, Warrick, and Kyle Meeker. 2015." The w-spectrum: Worker paradigms in Muslim contexts." *Evangelical Mission Quarterly* 51, no. 4: 365–74.

Ferreira, Johan. 1998. "Johannine ecclesiology." *Journal for the study of the New Testament supplement series* 160. Sheffield, England: Sheffield Academic.

Fisk, Bruce N. 1989. "Eating meat offered to idols: Corinthian behavior and pauline response in 1 Corinthians 8–10 (a response to Gordon Fee)." *Trinity Journal* 10 NS: 49–70.

France, R. T. 2007. *The gospel of Mathew.* The new international commentary on the New Testament. Grand Rapids, MI: Eerdmans.

Gallagher, Michael Paul. 1996. "Inculturation: Some theological perspectives." *International review of mission* 85, no. 337: 173–80.

Gallagher, Robert. 2005. "The Hebraic covenant as a model for contextualization." In *Appropriate Christianity,* ed. Charles R. Kraft, 135–54. Pasadena, CA: William Carey Library.

Garland, David. 2003. *1 Corinthians.* Baker exegetical commentary on the New Testament. Grand Rapids, MI: Baker Academic.

Garrison, David. 2004. "Church planting movements vs. Insider Movements: Missiological realities vs. mythiological speculation." *International Journal of Frontier Missiology* 21, no. 4: 151–54.

———. 2010. A handy guide to healthy churches: Part 2. Church planting movements: Best practices across the globe. http://www.churchplantingmovements.com/index.php?option=com_content&view=article&id=117:a-handy-guide-to-healthy-churches-part-2&catid=36:the-big-picture&Itemid=78.

———. 2014. *A wind in the house of Islam: How God is drawing Muslims around the world to faith in Jesus Christ.* Monument, CO: WIGTake Resources.

Gasque, W. Ward. 1979. "The church in the New Testament." In *In God's community: Essays on the church and its ministry*, ed. David J. Ellis and W. Ward Gasque, 1–13. Wheaton, IL: Harold Shaw.

Gehring, Roger W. 2004. *House church and mission: The importance of household structures in early Christianity.* Peabody, MA: Hendrikson.

Giles, Kevin. 1995. *What on earth is the church? An exploration in New Testament theology.* Downers Grove, IL: IVP.

Gilliland, Dean S. 2000. "Contextualization." In *Evangelical dictionary of world missions*, ed. Scott Moreau et al., 225–27. Grand Rapids, MI: Baker.

Glasser, Arthur. 1989. "Old Testament contextualization: Revelation and its environment." In *The word among us: Contextualizing theology for mission today,* ed. Dean S. Gilliland, 32–51. Dallas: Word.

Goldman, George III. 2012. "The church in Luke-Acts." In *The New Testament Church: The challenge of developing ecclesiologies*, ed. John Harrison and James Dvorak, 41–60. Eugene, OR: Wipf and Stock.

Goppelt, Leonhard. 1962. *Apostolische und nachapostolische Zeit.* Göttingen: Vandenhoeck & Ruprecht.

Green, Tim. 2013a. "Conversion in the light of identity theories." In *Longing for community: Church,* ummah, *or somewhere in between?,* edited by David Greenlee et al., 41–52. Pasadena, CA: William Carey Library.

———. 2013b. "Identity choices at the border zone." In *Longing for community: Church,* ummah, *or somewhere in between?,* edited by David Greenlee et al., 53–66. Pasadena, CA: William Carey Library.

———. 2013c. "Beyond the c-spectrum? A search for new models." *Evangelical Review of Theology* 37, no. 4: 361–80.

Greenlee, David. 2013. "Living out an 'in Christ' identity: Research and reflections related to Muslims who have come to faith in Jesus Christ." *International Journal for Frontier Missiology* 30, no. 1: 5–12.

Guder, Darrell L. 2005. "The church as missional community." In *The community of the Word: Toward an evangelical ecclesiology,* ed. Mark Husbands and Daniel J. Treier, 114–30. Downers Grove: InterVarsity.

Hagner, Donald. 2008. "Holiness and ecclesiology: The church in Matthew. 170–86." In *Built upon the rock: Studies in the gospel of Matthew,* ed. Daniel M. Gurtner and John Nolland, 170–86. Grand Rapids, MI: Eerdmans. (Orig. pub. in *Holiness and ecclesiology in the New Testament*, ed. Kent Brower and Andy Johnson, 40–56, Grand Rapids, MI: Eerdmans, 2007.)

Hamilton, Victor P. 1990. *The book of Genesis: Chapters 1-17.* International Commentary on the Old Testament. Grand Rapids, MI: Eerdmans.

Hansen, Collin and John Piper. 2012. "Piper responds to the insider movement." The Gospel Coalition website. Posted May 16. https://www.thegospelcoalition.org/video/piper-responds-to-the-insider-movement/.

Harland, Philip A. 2003. *Associations, synagogues, and congregations: Claiming a place in ancient Mediterranean society.* Minneapolis, MN: Fortress.

Harrington, Daniel J. 1980. *God's people in Christ: New Testament perspectives on the church and Judaism.* Overtures to biblical theology. Philadelphia: Fortress.

Harrison, John, and James Dvorak. 2012. *The New Testament Church: The challenge of developing ecclesiologies.* Eugene, OR: Wipf and Stock.

Hartley, J. E. 2003. "Holy and holiness, clean and unclean." In *Dictionary of the Old Testament: Pentateuch,* ed. T. Desmond Alexander and David W. Baker, 42031. Downers Grove, IL: IVP.

Hayes, Jeff. 2011. Written response to "Early gentile Christianity, conversion and culture-shift in the New Testament," by Terence Paige. BtD 2011 Pre-Readings and Presentations. http://btdnetwork.org/wp-content/uploads/2013/07/Houssney-Response-to-Terence-Paige-for-BtD.pdf.

Hayward, Douglas. 1995. "Measuring contextualization in church and missions." *International Journal of Frontier Missiology* vol. 12, no. 3: 135–38.

Heideman, Eugene S. 1997. "Syncretism, contextualization, orthodoxy, and heresy." *Missiology: An International Review* XXV, no. 1: 37–50.

Hellerman, Joe. 2009. *When the church was a family: Recapturing Jesus' vision for authentic Christian community.* Nashville: B&H Academic.

Hesselgrave, David, and Edward Rommen. 1989. *Contextualization: Meanings, methods, and models.* Grand Rapids, MI: Baker.

Hiebert, Paul, G. 1985. *Anthropological insights for missionaries.* Grand Rapids, MI: Baker.

———. 1987. Critical contextualization. *International Bulletin of Missionary Research* 11, no. 3: 104–12.

———. 2008. *Transforming worldviews: An anthropological understanding of how people change.* Grand Rapids, MI: Baker Academic.

Hiebert, Paul, and Eloise Hiebert Meneses. 1995. *Incarnational ministry: Band, Tribal, Peasant, and Urban Societies.* Grand Rapids, MI: Baker.

Higgins, Kevin. 2006. "Identity, integrity, and insider movements." *International Journal of Frontier Missiology* 23, no. 3: 117–23.

———. 2007. "Acts 15 and insider movements among Muslims: Questions, process, and conclusions." *International Journal of Frontier Missiology* 24, no. 1: 29–40. http://www.ijfm.org/PDFs_IJFM/24_1_PDFs/Higgins.pdf.

———. 2009a. "Inside what? Church, culture, religion and insider movements in biblical perspective." *St Francis Magazine* 5, no. 4: 74–91.

———. 2009b. " Speaking the truth about insider movements: Addressing the criticisms of Bill Nikides and 'Phil' relative to the article 'Inside what?'" *St. Francis Magazine* 5, no. 6: 61–86.

———. 2011. "Discipling the nations and the insider movement conversation." *Mission Frontiers* (January-February). http://www.missionfrontiers.org/issue/article/discipling-the-nations.

———. 2015a. "Jesus in Samaria: A paradigm for church planting among Muslims." In *Understanding insider movements: disciples of Jesus within diverse religious communities,* ed. Harley Talman and John Jay Travis, Loc. 5230–5437. Pasadena, CA: William Carey Library. Kindle edition. (Orig. pub. 2000. Under pseud. Caldwell, Stuart. *International Journal of Frontier Missiology* 17, no. 1: 25–31. http://www.ijfm.org/PDFs_IJFM/17_1_PDFs/Jesus_in_Samaria.pdf.

———. 2015b. "The key to insider movements: The 'devoted's' of Acts." (Orig. pub. 2004. *International Journal of Frontier Missiology* 21, no. 4: 155–65. In *Understanding insider movements: disciples of Jesus within diverse religious communities,* ed. Harley Talman and John Jay Travis, Loc. 5451–5822. Pasadena, CA: William Carey Library. Kindle edition.

———. 2015c. "Dual identity and the church in the book of Acts." In *Understanding insider movements: disciples of Jesus within diverse religious communities,* ed. Harley Talman and John Jay Travis, Loc. 12711–12778. Pasadena, CA: William Carey Library. Kindle edition.

———. 2017. "The household of God: Paul's missiology and the nature of the church." *International Journal of Frontier Missiology* 34, no.1–4: 47–51.

———. 2018. "Measuring insider movements? Shifting to a qualitative standard." *International Journal of Frontier Missiology* 35, no. 1: 21–27.

Higgins, Kevin, Richard Jameson, and Harley Talman. 2015. "Myths and misunderstandings about insider movements." In *Understanding insider movements: disciples of Jesus within diverse religious communities,* ed. Harley Talman and John Jay Travis, Loc. 1569–1896. Pasadena, CA: William Carey Library. Kindle edition.

Hodges, Melvin L. 1979. "Why indigenous church principles?" In *Readings in dynamic indigeneity,* ed. Charles H. Kraft and Tom N. Wisley, 6–14. Pasadena: William Carey Library.

Hoefer, Herbert. 2015. "Church in context." In *Understanding insider movements: disciples of Jesus within diverse religious communities,* ed. Harley Talman and John Jay Travis, Loc. 6687–6861. Pasadena, CA: William Carey Library. Kindle edition. (Orig. pub. 2007. *Evangelical Missions Quarterly.* http://www.emqonline.com/emq/issue-299/2040.)

Horton, Michael. 2011. *The Christian faith: A systematic theology for pilgrims on the way.* Grand Rapids, MI: Zondervan.

Houssney, Georges. 2011. Response to "Early gentile Christianity, conversion and culture-shift in the New Testament, by Terence Paige." Bridging the Divide Network. BtD 2011 Pre-Readings and Presentations. http://btdnetwork.org/wp-content/uploads/2013/07/Houssney-Response-to-Terence-Paige-for-BtD.pdf.

Ibrahim, Ayman S., and Ant Greenham. 2018. *Muslim conversions to Christ: A critique of insider movements in Islamic contexts.* New York: Peter Lang Publishing.

Jabbour, Nabeel, and Tom Seelinger. 2014. Minority Report 2014: Realities on the Ground. In *A call to faithful witness, part two: Theology, gospel missions, and insider movements: A eport (part two of two parts) of the ad interim study committee on insider movements to the forty-second general assembly of the Presbyterian Church of America, March 19, 2014,* by PCA Ad Interim Study Committee on Insider Movements, 2299–2332. http://www.pcahistory.org/pca/studies/scim02_2014.pdf.

Jameson, Richard, and Nick Scalevich. 2010. "First-century Jews and twentieth-century Muslims." *International Journal of Frontier Missiology* 17, no. 1: 33–39. http://www.ijfm.org/PDFs_IJFM/17_1_PDFs/Jews_and_Muslims.pdf.

Jenson, Matt, and David Wilhite. 2010. *The church: A guide for the perplexed.* London: T&T Clark.

Kang, S. Steve. 2007. "The Bible and the communion of saints." In *This side of heaven: Race, ethnicity, and Christian faith,* ed. Robert J. Priest and Alvaro L. Nieves, 223–42. New York: Oxford University Press.

Keener, Craig. 2012. *Acts: An exegetical commentary—Volume 1: Introduction and 1:1-2:47.* Grand Rapids, MI: Baker Academic.

Kelly, J. N. D. 1958. *Early Christian doctrines.* New York: Harper & Brothers.

Kerr, Hugh Thomson, ed. 1943. *A compend of Luther's theology.* Philadelphia: Westminster Press.

Kim, Seyoon. 2003. "Imitatio christi (1 Corinthians 11:1): How Paul imitates Jesus Christ in dealing with idol food (1 Corinthians 8–10)." *Bulletin for Biblical Research 13.2:* 193–226.

Kraft, Charles. 1973. "Dynamic equivalence churches: An ethnotheological approach to indigeneity." *Missiology* 1, no. 1: 39–57.

———. 1974a. "Distinctive religious barriers to outside penetration." In *Media in Islamic culture,* ed. C. Richard Shumaker, 65–76.

———. 1974b. "Pscyhological stress factors among Muslims." In *Media in Islamic culture,* ed. C. Richard Shumaker, 137–44. Marseille: International Christian Broadcasters and Evangelical Literature Overseas.

———. 1979a. "Dynamic equivalence churches in Muslim society." In *The gospel and Islam: A 1978 compendium,* edited by Don M. McCurry, 114–28. Monrovia, CA: MARC.

———. 1979b. "Dynamic equivalence churches: An ethnotheological approach to indigeneity." In *Readings in dynamic indigeneity,* ed. Charles H. Kraft and Tom N. Wisley, 87–114. Pasadena: William Carey Library.

Kraft, Charles (with Maruerite G. Kraft). 2005. Preface to the 25th anniversary edition, *Christianity in Culture: A study in biblical theologizing in cross-cultural perspective,* xix-xxix. Rev. 25th anniv. ed. Maryknoll, NY: Orbis. (Orig. pub. 1979.)

Kraft, Kathryn Ann. 2012. *Searching for heaven in the real world: A sociological discussion of conversion in the Arab world.* Oxford: Regnum Books International.

Ladd, George Elden. 1993. *A theology of the New Testament*. Edited by Donald A. Hagner. Rev. ed. Grand Rapids, MI: Eerdmans. (Orig. pub. 1974.)

Larson, Warren. 2011a. "Missionaries to Muslims agree to soften criticisms of each other." *Christianity Today,* October 13. http://www.christianitytoday.com/ct/2011/octoberweb-only/missions-muslims-criticisms.html.

———. 2011b. Review of *Chrislam: How missionaries are promoting an Islamized gospel*. Blog of Warren Larson. December 29. http://warrenlarson.wordpress.com/2011/12/29/review-of-chrislam-how-missionaries-are-promoting-an-islamized-gospel/.

Lausanne Committee for World Evangelization. 1978. Lausanne Occassional Papers: No. 2. The Willowbank report – Gospel and Culture. Wheaton, IL: Lausanne Committee for World Evangelization. http://www.lausanne.org/en/documents/lops/73-lop-2.html.

Leith, John H., ed. 1982. *Creeds of the churches: A reader in Christian doctrine from the Bible to the present*. 3rd ed. Atlanta: John Knox.

Lewis, Rebecca. 2007. "Promoting movements to Christ within natural communities." *International Journal of Frontier Missiology* 24, no. 2: 75–76. http://www.ijfm.org/PDFs_IJFM/24_2_PDFs/24_2_Lewis.pdf.

———. 2009. "Insider Movements: Honoring God-given identity and community." *International Journal for Frontier Missiology* 26, no. 1: 16–19.

———. 2010. "Running commentary in 'Inside out: Probing presuppositions among insider movements,' by Dick Brogden." *International Journal of Frontier Missiology* 27, no. 1: 33–40.

———. 2015a. "The integrity of the gospel and insider movements." In *Understanding insider movements: disciples of Jesus within diverse religious communities,* ed. Harley Talman and John Jay Travis, Loc. 6312–6546. Pasadena, CA: William Carey Library. Kindle edition. (Orig. pub. 2010. *International Journal for Frontier Missiology* 27, no. 1: 41–48.)

———. 2015b. "Honoring God-given identity and community." In *Understanding insider movements: disciples of Jesus within diverse religious communities,* ed. Harley Talman and John Jay Travis, Loc. 798–871. Pasadena, CA: William Carey Library. Kindle edition. (Orig. pub. 2009. *International Journal of Frontier Missiology* 26, no. 1: 16–19.)

Lingel, Joshua, Jeff Morton, and Bill Nikides. 2012. *Chrislam: How missionaries are promoting an islamized gospel*. Garden Grove, CA: i2 ministries.

Little, Don. 2015. *Effective discipling in muslim communities: Scripture, history, and seasoned practices*. IVP Academic. Kindle edition.

Longenecker, Richard N. 2002. "Paul's vision of the church and community formation." In *Community formation in the early church and in the church today,* ed. Richard Longenecker, 73–88. Peabody, MA: Hendrickson.

Lunde, Jonathan. 2006. Jesus' life and ministry. Class at Biola University, La Mirada, CA.

Marshall, I. Howard. 1992. "Church." In *Dictionary of Jesus and the Gospels,* ed. Joel B. Green, Scot McKnight, I. Howard Marshall, 122–25. Downers Grove, IL: Intervarsity.

Massey, Joshua. 1996. "Planting the church underground in muslim contexts." *International Journal for Frontier Missiology* 13, no. 3: 139–53.

———. 1999. "His Ways Are Not Our Ways." *Evangelical Missions Quarterly* 35, no. 2: 188–97.

———. 2000a. Editorial: Muslim contextualization I. *International Journal of Frontier Missiology* 17, no.1. http://www.ijfm.org/PDFs_IJFM/17_1_PDFs/Editorial.pdf.

———. 2000b. "God's amazing diversity in drawing Muslims to Christ." *International Journal of Frontier Missiology* 17, no. 1: 5–14.

———. 2004. "Misunderstanding C-5: His ways are not our orthodoxy." *Evangelical Missions Quarterly* 40, no. 3 (July): 296–304.

Matheny, Tim. 1981. *Reaching the Arabs: A felt need approach.* Pasadena, CA: William Carey Library.

Mathis, David. 2012. Let's revise the popular phrase "in, but not of." *DesiringGod Blog.* August 29. http://www.desiringgod.org/blog/posts/let-s-revise-the-popular-phrase-in-but-not-of.

McCurry, Don, ed. 1979. *The gospel and Islam: A 1978 compendium.* Monrovia, CA: MARC.

McDermott, Gerald, and Harold Netland. 2014. *A trinitarian theology of religions: An evangelical proposal.* Oxford university press.

McGavran, Donald. 1975. "The biblical base." In *Christopaganism or Indigenous Christianity?* ed. Tetsunao Yamamori and Charles R. Taber, 35–56. Pasadena, CA: William Carey Library.

McKeon, D. W. 2014. A response to some of the insider-movement leaning articles in *Perspectives on the world Christian movement, 4th ed.* textbook. *St. Francis Magazine* 10, no. 3: 25–45.

Metzger, Bruce. 1971. *A textual commentary on the Greek New Testament.* London: United Bible Societies.

Meyer, Lester V. 1995. "Remnant." In vol.5 of *Anchor Bible Dictionary*, ed. David Noel Freedman et al., 669–71. New York: Doubleday.

Millar, J. G. 2000. "People of God." In *New dictionary of biblical theology: Exploring the unity and diversity of Scripture*, ed. T. Desmond Alexander, Brian S. Rosner, D. A. Carson, Graeme Goldsworthy, 684–87. Leicester, England: InterVarsity.

Minear, Paul. 2004. *Images of the church in the New Testament.* Louisville, KY: Westminster John Knox.

Moltmann, Jurgen. 1993. *The church in the power of the Spirit.* Fortress Press.

Moreau, Scott. 2000. "Syncretism." In *Evangelical dictionary of world missions,* ed. Scott Moreau, et al., 924–25.Grand Rapids, MI: Baker.

———. 2010. "Evangelical models of contextualization." In *Local theology for the global church: Principles for an evangelical approach to contextualization,* ed. Matthew Cook, 165–93. Pasadena, CA: World Evangelical Alliance Theological Commission.

———. 2012. "Comprehensive contextualization." In *Discovering the mission of God: Best missional practices for the 21st century,* ed. Mike Barnett, 406–19. Downers Grove, IL: IVP Academic.

Morris, Leon. 1992. *The gospel according to Matthew.* The pillar New Testament commentary series. Grand Rapids, MI: Eerdmans.

Morton, Jeff. 2012. *Insider Movements: Biblically incredible or incredibly brilliant?* Eugene, OR: Wipf and Stock.

Naja, Ben. 2015. "Jesus movement: A case study from Eastern Africa." In *Understanding insider movements: disciples of Jesus within diverse religious communities,* ed. Harley Talman and John Jay Travis, Loc. 3397–3480. Pasadena, CA: William Carey Library. Kindle edition.

Newbigin, Leslie. 1954. *The household of God: Lectures on the nature of the church.* New York: Friendship.

———. 1988. "On being the church for the world." In *Leslie Newbigin: Missionary theologian: A reader*, compiled and introduced by Paul Wetson, 130–42. Grand Rapids, MI: Eerdmans. (Orig. pub. In G. Ecclestone, ed., *The parish church?Explorations in the relationship of the church and the world,* 25–42. Oxford: Mowbray.)

Nicuum, Curt. 2012. "Heaven can't wait: The church in Ephesians and Colossians." In *The New Testament Church: The challenge of developing ecclesiologies,* ed. John Harrison and James Dvorak, 130–47. Eugene, OR: Wipf and Stock.

Noll, Mark. 1974. "Martin Luther and the concept of a 'true' church." *The Evangelical Quarterly* (Oct-Dec): 79–85.

O'Brien, Peter. 1987. "The church as a heavenly and eschatological reality." In *The church in the Bible and the world: An international study,* ed. D. A. Carson, 88– 119.

Olbrict, Thomas H. 2012. "The church in the gospel and epistles of John." In *The New Testament Church: The challenge of developing ecclesiologies,* ed. John Harrison and James Dvorak, 61–84. Eugene, OR: Wipf and Stock.

Ott, Craig, and Gene Wilson. 2011. *Global church planting: Biblical principles and best practices for multiplication.* Grand Rapids, MI: Baker Academic. Kindle edition.

Padilla, Rene. 1979. "Why indigenous church principles?" In *Readings in dynamic indigeneity*, ed. Charles H. Kraft and Tom N. Wisley, 286–312. Pasadena: William Carey Library.

Parshall, Phil. 1974. "Obstacles encountered in the evangelization of Muslims." MA thesis, Trinity Evangelical Divinity School.

———. 1975. *The fortress and the fire.* Bombay: Gospel Literature Service.

———. 1979. "Evangelizing Muslims: Are there ways?" *Christianity Today* 23, no. 7: 28–31.

———. 1980a. "A contextualized approach to Muslim evangelization." DMiss diss., Fuller Theological Seminary.

———. 1980b. *New paths in Muslim evangelism: Evangelical approaches to contextualization.* Grand Rapids, MI: Baker Book House.

———. 1985. *Beyond the mosque.* Grand Rapids, MI: Baker.

———. 1998. "Danger! New directions in contextualization." *Evangelical Mission Quarterly* 34, no. 4: 404–10.

———, ed. 2000a. *The last great frontier: Essays on Muslim evangelism.* Quezon City, Philippines: Open Doors with Brother Andrew.

———. 2000b. Letter to the editor. *Evangelical Missions Quarterly* 36, no. 4: 414–19.

———. 2003. *Muslim evangelism: Contemporary approaches to contextualization.* Rev. ed. of *New paths in Muslim evangelism*. Waynesboro, GA: Gabriel Publishing.

———. 2013. "How much muslim context is too much for the gospel?" *Christianity Today* 57, no. 1 (January/February): 31.

Parsons, Greg. 2006. "What is the church?" *Mission Frontiers* (January-February). http://www.missionfrontiers.org/issue/article/what-is-the-church.

Patzia, Arthur G. 2001. *The emergence of the church: Context, growth, leadership, & worship.* Downers Grove, IL: IVP.

———. 2009. *Discovering church planting: An introduction to the whats, whys, and hows of global church planting.* Downers Grove, IL: IVP.

PCA Ad Interim Study Committee on Insider Movements. 2014. *A call to faithful witness, part two: Theology, gospel missions, and insider movements: A partial report (part two of two parts) of the ad interim study committee on insider movements to the forty-second general assembly of the Presbyterian Church of America, March 19, 2014.* http://www.pcahistory.org/pca/studies/scim02_2014.pdf.

Peters, Olutola K. 2012. "The church in the apocalypse of John." In *The New Testament Church: The challenge of developing ecclesiologies*, ed. John Harrison and James Dvorak, 243–68. Eugene, OR: Wipf and Stock.

Peterson, David G. 2009. *The acts of the apostles.* The Pillar New Testament Commentary series. Grand Rapids, MI: Eerdmans.

Pinault. 2016. "Imami (Twelver). Shi'a." *Encyclopedia of Islam and the Modern World.* Edited by Richard C. Martin. Pages 624–28. Macmillan Reference USA.

Piper, John. 2006. "Minimizing the Bible? Seeker-driven pastors and radical contextualization in missions." *Mission Frontiers* (January-February). http://www.missionfrontiers.org/issue/article/minimizing-the-bible. Reprinted from www.desiringgod.org.

Prenger, Jan Hendrick. 2017. *Muslim insider Christ followers: Their theological and missional frames.* Pasadena, CA: William Carey Library.

Priest, Robert. 2013. "Researching contextualization in churches influenced by missionaries." In *Communities of faith in Africa and the African diaspora: In honor of Tite Tienou, with additional essays on world Christianity*, ed. Casely B. Essamuah and David K. Ngaruiya, 299–318. Eugene, OR: Pickwick.

Rapinchuk, Mark. 2012. "Ecclesiology in the gospel of Mark." In *The New Testament Church: The challenge of developing ecclesiologies*, ed. John Harrison and James Dvorak, 26–40. Eugene, OR: Wipf and Stock.

Reinhardt, Wolfgang. 1995. Das wachstum des gottesvolkes: Biblische theologie des gemeindewachstums. Gottingen: Vandenhoeck and Ruprecht.

Riggs, Henry H. 1941. "Shall we try for unbeaten paths in working for Moslems?" *The Moslem World* 31: 116–26.

Romaine, Jim. 1999. Letter to the editor. *Evangelical Missions Quarterly* 35, no. 4: 397–98.

Sanchez, Daniel R. 1998. "Contextualization and the missionary endeavor." *Missiology: Introduction*. 318–33.

Sanders, Fred. 2010. *The deep things of God: How the trinity changes everything*. Wheaton, IL: Crossway.

Schaff, Philip. 1919. The creeds of Christendom, with a history and critical notes. Rev. and enl. 6th ed. Vol. 1: The history of creeds. http://www.ccel.org/ccel/schaff/creeds1.i.html.

Schineller, Peter. 1996. "Inculturation: Difficult/delicate task." *International Bulletin of Missionary Research* 20, no.3: 109–12.

Schlorff, Sam. 1999. Letter to the editor. *Evangelical Missions Quarterly* 35, no. 4: 394–402.

Schreiter, Robert J. 1985. *Constructing local theologies*. New York: Orbis.

Shenk, David. 1989. "Conversations along the way." In *Muslims & Christians along the Emmaus road*, ed. J. Dudley Woodberry, 1–17.

Shenk, David. 2014. Christian. muslim. friend. Twelve paths to real relationship. Harrison, VA: Herald.

Shorter, Aylward. 1999. *Toward a theology of inculturation*. Eugene, OR: Wipf and Stock.

Slaves of the Immaculate Heart of Mary. 2005. *Catholicism.org: An online journal edited by the slaves of the immaculate heart of Mary, St. Benedict Center, New Hampshire*. The popes on extra ecclesiam nulla sallus. http://catholicism.org/eens-popes.html.

Smith, Steve. 2012. The bare essentials of helping groups to become churches: Four helps in church planting movements. *Mission Frontiers* (Sept-Oct): 22-26.

Span, John and Anne. 2009. "Report on the common ground consultants meeting, Snelville (Georgia)." *St. Francis Magazine* 5, no. 4: 52–73.

Stegemann, Ekkehard W., and Wolfgang Stegemann. 1999. *The Jesus movement: A social history of its first century*. Translated by O. C. Dean, Jr. Minneapolis: Fortress. (Orig. pub. 1995, Verlag W. Kohlhammer, Stuttgart, Germany.)

Stetzer, Ed, and David Putman. 2006. *Breaking the missional code: Your church can become a missionary in your community*. Nashville: Broadman and Holman.

Stott, John. 1978. "Cornerstone: Christians and Muslims." *Christianity Today* 23, no. 5: 34–35.

Street, Jeff. 1999. Letter to the editor. *Evangelical Missions Quarterly* 35, no. 4: 399.

Talman, Harley. 2004a. Guest editor's page. *International Journal of Frontier Missiology* 21, no. 1: 5–2004b. Comprehensive contextualization. *International Journal of Frontier Missiology* 21, no. 1: 6–12.

———. 2014. "Is Muhammad also among the prophets?" *International Journal of Frontier Missiology* 31, no. 4: 169–90.

———. 2015a. "Acts 15: An inside look." In *Understanding Insider Movements: Disciples of Jesus within Diverse Religious Communities*, ed. Harley Talman and John Jay Travis, Loc. 6012-6300. Pasadena, CA: William Carey Library. Kindle edition.

———. 2015b. "Muslim followers of Jesus and the Muslim confession of faith." In *Understanding Insider Movements: Disciples of Jesus within Diverse Religious Communities*, ed. Harley Talman and John Jay Travis, Loc. 11435–11762. Pasadena, CA: William Carey Library. Kindle edition.

———. 2015c. "The old testament and insider movements." In *Understanding insider movements: disciples of Jesus within diverse religious communities*, ed. Harley Talman and John Jay Travis, Loc. 4447–4831. Pasadena, CA: William Carey Library. Kindle edition.

Talman, Harley, and John Jay Travis, eds. 2015. *Understanding insider movements: disciples of Jesus within diverse religious communities.* Pasadena, CA: William Carey Library. Kindle edition.

Tanchanpongs, Natee. 2010. "Developing a palate for authentic theology." In *Local theology for the global church: Principles for an evangelical approach to contextualization*, ed. Matthew Cook et al., 109–23. Pasadena: William Carey Library.

Taylor, Anthony. 2015. "The kingdom of God: A biblical paradigm for mission." In *Understanding Insider Movements: Disciples of Jesus within Diverse Religious Communities*, ed. Harley Talman and John Jay Travis, Loc. 4267–4431. Pasadena, CA: William Carey Library. Kindle edition.

Teeter, David. 1990. "Dynamic equivalent conversion for tentative Muslim believers." *Missiology: An International Review* 18, no. 3: 305–13.

Terry, John Mark. 2000. "Indigenous churches." In *Evangelical dictionary of world missions*, ed. Scott Moreau et al., 483–85. Grand Rapids, MI: Baker.

Tennent, Timothy C. 2005. "The challenge of churchless Christianity: An evangelical assessment." *International Bulletin of Missionary Research* 29, no. 4: 171–77.

———. 2006. "Followers of Jesus (Isa) in Islamic mosques: A closer examination of C-5 'high-spectrum' contextualization." *International Journal for Frontier Missiology* 23, no. 3: 101–15.

———. 2007. "Ecclesiology: Followers of Jesus in Islamic mosques." In *Theology in the context of world Christianity: How the global church is influencing how we think about and discuss theology*, 193–220. Zondervan: Grand Rapids.

———. 2013. The hidden history of insider movements. *Christianity Today* 57, no. 1 (January/February): 28.

Thielman, Frank. 2005. *Theology of the New Testament: A canonical and synthetic approach.* Grand Rapids, MI: Zondervan.

Tidball, Derek, J. 2000. "Church." In *New dictionary of biblical theology: Exploring the unity and diversity of Scripture*, ed. T. Desmond Alexander, Brian Rosner, D. A. Carson, Graeme Goldsworthy, 407–11. Downers Grove, IL: InterVarsity.

Tippet, Alan, R. 1975. "Christopaganism or Indigenous Christianity." In *Christopaganism or indigenous Cshristianity?*, ed. Tetsunao Yamamori and Charles R. Taber, 13–34. South Pasadena, CA: William Carey Library.

———. 1979. "Indigenous principles in mission today." In *Readings in dynamic indigeneity*, ed. Charles H. Kraft and Tom N. Wisley, 31–51. Pasadena: William Carey Library.

Travis, Anna. 2015. "In the world but not of it: Insider Movements and freedom from the demonic." In *Understanding insider movements: disciples of Jesus within diverse religious communities*, ed. Harley Talman and John Jay Travis, Loc. 11857–12192. Pasadena, CA: William Carey Library. Kindle edition.

Travis, John. 1998a. "The C1 to C6 spectrum: A practical tool for defining six types of 'Christ-centered communities' ('C') found in the Muslim context." *Evangelical Missions Quarterly* 34, no. 4: 407–8.

———. 1998b. "Must all Muslims leave 'Islam' to follow Jesus?" *Evangelical Missions Quarterly* 34, no. 4: 411–15.

———. 2006. Letters to the editor. *Mission Frontiers* (September-October): 7. http://www.missionfrontiers.org/issue/article/letters-to-the-editor.

———. 2012. "Reflections on Jesus movements among Muslims with special reference to movements within Asian Muslim communities." In *Toward respectful understanding & witness among Muslims: Essays in honor of J. Dudley Woodberry*, ed. Evelyne A. Reisacher et al., 233–44. Pasadena, CA: William Carey Library.

———. 2013. "Why evangelicals should be thankful for muslim insiders." *Christianity Today* 57, no. 1 (January/February): 30.

———. *Understanding insider movements: disciples of Jesus within diverse religious communities*, ed. Harley Talman and John Jay Travis, Loc. 798–871. Pasadena, CA: William Carey Library. Kindle edition.

———. 2015b. "The C1-C6 spectrum after fifteen years." In *Understanding insider movements: disciples of Jesus within diverse religious communities*, ed. Harley Talman and John Jay Travis, Loc. 11205–11349. Pasadena, CA: William Carey Library. Kindle edition.

Travis, John and Anna. 2005a. "Appropriate approaches in Muslim contexts." In *Appropriate Christianity*, ed. Charles Kraft, 397–414. Pasadena: William Carey Library.

———. *Frontiers* (January-February). http://www.missionfrontiers.org/issue/article/maximizing-the-bible.

———. 2007. "Responses to Gary Corwin" (in "A humble appeal to C5/insider movement Muslim ministry advocates to consider ten questions"). *International Journal for Frontier Missiology* 4, no. 1 (Spring): 5–21.

———. 2015. "Roles of 'alongsiders' in insider movements: Contemporary examples and biblical reflections." In *Understanding insider movements: disciples of Jesus within diverse religious communities*, ed. Harley Talman and John Jay Travis, Loc. 10513–10792. Pasadena, CA: William Carey Library. Kindle edition. (Orig. pub. 2013. *International Journal of Frontier Missiology* 30, no. 4: 161–69.

Travis, John and Anna, with contributions by Phil Parshall. 2008. "Factors affecting the identity that Jesus-followers choose." In *From seed to fruit: Global trends, fruitful practices, and emerging issues among Muslims*, ed. J. Dudley Woodberry, 193–205.

Travis, John, and Andrew Workman. 2000. "Messianic Muslim followers of Jesus." *International Journal of Frontier Missiology* 17, no. 1 (Spring): 53–59.

Travis, John, and Dudley Woodberry. 2015. "When God's kingdom grows like yeast: Frequently-asked questions about Jesus movements within Muslim communities." In *Understanding insider movements: disciples of Jesus within diverse religious communities*, ed. Harley Talman and John Jay Travis, Loc. 1353-1560. Pasadena, CA: William Carey Library. Kindle edition. (Orig. pub. 2010. *Mission Frontiers* 32 (July-August): 24–30. http://www.missionfrontiers.org/issue/article/when-gods-kingdom-grows-like-yeast.)

Travis, John, et al. 2006. "Four responses to Timothy Tennent's 'Followers of Jesus (Isa) in Islamic mosques: A closer look at c-5 "high spectrum" contextualization.'" *International Journal for Frontier Missiology* 23, no. 3: 124–26.

Uddin, Rafique. 1989. "Contextualized worship and witness." In *Muslims and Christians on the Emmaus Road*, ed. J. Dudley Woodberry, 269–72. Monrovia: MARC.

Van Engen, Charles. 1991. *God's missionary people: Rethinking the purpose of the local church*. Grand Rapids, MI: Baker.

Van Gelder, Craig. 2000. *The essence of the church: A community created by the Spirit*. Grand Rapids, MI: Baker.

Vanhoozer, Kevin. 2004. "Evangelicalism and the church: The company of the gospel." In *The futures of evangelicalism: Issues and prospects*, ed. Craig Bartholomew, Robin Parry, and Andrew West, 40–99. Grand Rapids, MI: Kregel.

———. 2013. "Response to Michael Bird." In *Five views on biblical inerrancy*, ed. J. Merrick and Stephen M. Garrett. Grand Rapids, MI: Zondervan. Kindle edition.

Volf, Miroslav. 1998. *After our likeness: The church as the image of the Trinity*. Eerdmans: Grand Rapids. MI.

Walls, Andrew. 1982. "The gospel as the prisoner and liberator of culture." *Missionalia* 10, no. 2: 93–105.

———. 2015. "The gospel as prisoner and liberator of culture." In *Understanding insider movements: disciples of Jesus within diverse religious communities,* ed. Harley Talman and John Jay Travis, Loc. 7095–7371. Pasadena, CA: William Carey Library. Kindle edition.

Walton, John. 2000. *The IVP Bible background commentary: Old testament.* Edited by John H. Walton, Victor H. Matthews, and Mark W. Chavalas. Downers Grove, IL: IVP.

Waterman, L. D. 2007. "Do the roots affect the fruits?" *International Journal of Frontier Missiology* 24, no. 2: 57–63. http://www.ijfm.org/PDFs_IJFM/24_2_PDFs/24_2_Waterman.pdf.

———. 2011. What is church? From surveying Scripture to applying in culture. *Evangelical Missions Quarterly* 47, no. 4: 460–67.

Watson, David, and Paul Watson. 2014. *Contagious disciple making: Leading others on a journey of discovery.* Nashville, TN: Thomas Nelson.

Webster, John. 2005. "The visible attests the invisible." In *The community of the Word: Toward an evangelical ecclesiology,* ed. Mark Husbands and Daniel Treier, 96–113. Downers Grove: IVP.

Wells, Jo Bailey. 2000. "God's holy people: A theme in biblical theology." *Journal for the Study of the Old Testament Supplement Series* 305. Sheffield, England: Sheffield Academic.

Wenham, Gordon. 1987. *Genesis 1-15.* Word biblical commentary. Waco, TX: Word.

Wilder, John W. 1977. Some reflections on possibilities for people movements among Muslims. *Missiology* 5: 301–20.

William, J. S. 2011. "Inside/outside: Getting to the center of the Muslim contextualization debates." *St. Francis Magazine* 7, no. 3: 58–95.

Williams, Mark. 2007. "What legacy do we leave behind to believers in contextualized communities?" *Journal of Asian Mission* 5, no. 1: 75–91.

Wilson, J. Christy. 1941. Public confession and the church. *The Moslem World* 31: 127–39.

Winter, Ralph. 2005. Editorial comment. *Mission Frontiers* 27, no. 5: 4.

Witherington, Ben, III. 1998. *The acts of the apostles: A socio-rhetorical commentary.* Grand Rapids, MI: Eerdmans.

Woodberry, Dudley. 1989. Contextualization among Muslims: Reusing common pillars. In *The Word among us: Contextualizing theology for mission today,* ed. Dean S. Gilliland, 282–312. Dallas: Word.

———. 2007. "To the Muslim I became a Muslim?" *International Journal of Frontier Missiology* 24, no. 1: 23–28.

———, ed. 2008. *From seed to fruit: Global trends, fruitful practices, and emerging issues among Muslims.* William Carey Library Publishers.

———. 2015a. "Contextualization among Muslims: Reusing common pillars." In *Understanding insider movements: disciples of Jesus within diverse religious communities,* ed. Harley Talman and John Jay Travis, Loc. 9321–10087. Pasadena, CA: William Carey Library. Kindle edition. (Orig. pub. in 1989, in *The Word among us: Contextualizing theology for mission today*, Dallas: Word. Also pub.1996. *IJFM* 13, no. 4 (Oct-Dec): 171–86. http://www.ijfm.org/PDFs_IJFM/13_4_PDFs/03_Woodberry.pdf.)

———. 2015b. "The incarnational model of Jesus, Paul, and the Jerusalem council." In *Understanding insider movements: disciples of Jesus within diverse religious communities,* ed. Harley Talman and John Jay Travis, Loc. 5836–6008. Pasadena, CA: William Carey Library. Kindle edition.

Wright, Christopher J. H. 2006. *The mission of God: Unlocking the Bible's grand narrative.* Downers Grove, IL: IVP Academic.

———. *The mission of God's people: A biblical theology of the church's mission.* Biblical theology for life. Gen. ed. Jonathan Lunde. Grand Rapids, MI: Zondervan.

Zwemer, Samuel. 1941. "The dynamic of evangelism." *The Moslem World,* vol. 31: 109–15.

Subject Index

A

Abraham 4–10, 13, 21, 25–26, 76–77, 87, 117, 136, 169, 177

apostles 12, 18–19, 22–24, 36, 40, 49, 57, 59–60, 66, 80–81, 95, 102, 128, 145, 183

apostolicity 57, 66, 150–152, 155, 166

ascension 17, 26, 32

Augustine 48–50, 149

B

baptism xvii, 10, 34–35, 41, 55, 58–62, 68, 70, 98, 101, 103–105, 109, 112–113, 122, 141–142, 153–154, 156, 165–166, 179, 181–182

Bible study 29, 33, 44, 60, 103, 106, 108, 122, 140, 144, 150, 165, 168

biblical ix, xii, xvi, xvii, xix, xxi, xxii, xxiii, 1, 4–5, 14, 19, 21, 23–27, 29–34, 36–37, 39, 42–51, 53–65, 68–69, 71–72, 74–76, 78–79, 82–88, 91–100, 102–106, 108, 110, 112, 115–118, 121–123, 125–132, 135–149, 152–156, 158–160, 162–166, 168–183

  elder 42–45, 69, 141–142, 154, 156

  narrative 5, 26, 30, 69, 87, 93, 126, 131, 136–137, 176–178, 180

  patterns 34, 42, 45, 64, 69, 88, 142, 156, 162

  story 5, 19, 24–25, 27, 93, 118

  theme 5, 32, 83, 97, 121, 126, 129, 135–139, 169

  theology 5, 51, 87, 97, 126, 129, 136–137, 165

Bonhoeffer, Dietrich 49–50

Buddhist xvi, 101, 138

C

C1–C6 spectrum xviii, xxi, 98, 106, 116

catholicity 56–57, 66, 75, 112, 150–151, 153, 155, 166, 180

church xi–xii, xv–xxiii, 1, 3–11, 13–27, 29–77, 79–89, 91–123, 125–132, 134–156, 158–183

  apostolic 26, 54, 66, 169

  biblical ix, xxiii, 26, 33, 36–37, 45, 48–51, 54, 58, 60, 62–63, 65, 68, 71, 88, 91, 98, 100, 104, 106, 112, 115, 117, 122–123, 125–126, 135, 139–140, 142–143, 154–156, 158, 162, 166, 168–170, 173, 175–183

  embyronic 176

  global 22, 46, 56, 86, 108, 145, 148, 182–183

  house 29, 44, 98, 125

  indigenous 73, 83, 86, 115

  insider 30, 71, 89, 93–95, 99, 101, 106, 108, 111, 113–114, 116, 119–122, 126–127, 135–137, 140, 147–148, 150–151, 153, 155, 159, 165–166

  invisible 48–50, 53–55, 58, 69, 93, 108–111, 122, 126, 147, 149–150

  local 19–20, 33–42, 44–45, 47–48, 51–52, 54, 57, 61, 65, 69, 86–87, 100, 102–105, 110–111, 115, 122, 140–144, 146–148, 154, 156, 165, 170–171, 178–180, 182

  New Testament 7, 38, 42, 51, 79–82, 105, 110, 141, 144, 153, 165, 179

  universal 33, 35, 45–47, 51–53, 57, 61, 69, 93, 106–108, 111–112, 122, 126, 144–148, 151, 153, 156, 163, 165, 170–171, 180

  visible 48–49, 51–54, 57, 68–70, 108–111, 148–149

Subject Index

church planting xvi, xx–xxi, xxiii, 22, 30, 34, 74, 94, 98, 102, 115, 128, 130, 137, 141, 150, 162, 169–170, 173–174, 176, 183

classical attributes 54–55, 63, 66, 70, 111–113, 150, 152, 154, 166, 180

communion 35, 48–50, 58–62, 64, 68, 98, 103–104, 109, 112–113, 122, 141–143, 153–154, 156, 165–166, 181–182

community xi–xii, xv–xxiii, 3–5, 7, 9–23, 26, 29, 31–42, 44–54, 56–59, 61–62, 64–70, 73, 77, 79–82, 84–87, 93–123, 125–128, 130–145, 147–163, 165–166, 168–174, 177–182

    Christ–centered xviii, xxi, 97–98, 100, 140, 144, 165

    Christian 3, 23, 45, 56, 79–80, 82, 96, 107, 111, 114, 125, 140, 148–149, 151, 155, 166, 173

    covenant 93, 126–127

    Kingdom 5, 10, 26, 67–70, 138, 144, 150, 182

    local 18–19, 33–34, 69, 140, 142, 165, 179

    membership 31, 49, 51, 53, 69–70, 87, 96–97, 99–100, 102, 109–110, 114–115, 120, 138, 147–148, 155

contemporary insiders 95, 111, 127, 130, 133, 135, 154

contextualization xi, xiii, xviii, xix, xxi–xxii, 56, 69, 72–76, 79, 83–86, 88, 116–117, 126, 162, 172–173

covenant 5–10, 17–18, 24, 26, 31–32, 61, 70, 76–77, 82, 93, 126–127, 130–131

crucifixion 17

cultural

    continuity 77, 162–163, 166

    expression 48, 97, 100, 137, 180–181

form xviii, 32, 41, 56, 60, 75, 79, 81–82, 86, 100, 113, 116, 120, 122, 140, 149, 152–153, 157, 180

    identity 46–47, 87, 135–136, 139–140, 158, 162

    structure 73, 75, 79, 84, 121, 160

D

death 8, 10, 14, 26, 32, 39, 58, 61, 70, 120, 128

disciples xii, xv–xxiii, 11–14, 16–19, 26, 34–35, 41, 45, 50–51, 53, 65–66, 68, 71, 81, 91, 99, 105, 110, 125, 128, 139–140, 156, 165, 168, 170, 172–174, 176, 178, 183

discipleship xii, xvi, xxi, 11, 17–18, 32, 47, 50–51, 57, 64–65, 100, 103, 113, 166, 169, 171, 173, 175, 183

E

ecclesiology xii, xxi–xxiii, 19, 34, 54, 58, 63, 75, 85, 92, 94–95, 99, 103–104, 106, 108–111, 114, 134, 141, 143–146, 157, 169, 171–172

edification 33, 39, 41–42, 44, 47, 68–69, 109, 156, 179

ekklēsia xxii–xxiii, 5, 10–11, 13–14, 17–20, 26, 30–31, 33–34, 36–38, 41–42, 54, 69, 72, 80, 82, 91–105, 107–113, 115, 117, 119, 121, 123, 125–129, 131, 133, 135, 137, 139–143, 145, 147, 149, 151–155, 157, 159, 161, 163, 165, 169–170, 176

elder 17, 33–34, 42–45, 69, 104–106, 134, 141–142, 154, 156, 165, 180

evangelical xii, xiii, xviii, xix, xx, xxii, xxiii, 30, 42, 60, 64, 73–74, 83, 107, 114, 146, 168

F

family xv, xvi, xxi, 3, 9, 11–13, 21–23, 25–26, 29, 32–33, 36, 38, 41, 45, 47–48, 52, 57, 67–70, 77, 79–82, 87, 96, 98, 100–106, 108–109, 111, 114, 116–117, 122, 125, 129–130, 138–139, 141, 145–147, 150, 155, 158–160, 163, 165, 168–170, 172, 177, 179–180, 182–183

family network 96, 101, 103–105, 155

fellowship xvi, xviii, 7, 14, 16–19, 33, 35, 37, 39, 41–42, 44–45, 47–52, 55, 65–66, 68–70, 80, 95–98, 100–109, 111–113, 115–116, 122, 140, 142–149, 152, 155–156, 158, 163, 165–166, 170–171, 176–183

G

gathering 8, 19–20, 24, 31, 34, 37–42, 45–47, 50–51, 53, 57, 66, 69, 79–80, 82, 95, 103–104, 108, 110–111, 141–143, 147, 154, 156, 165, 169–170, 173, 176, 179, 181

Gentile 8, 10, 12–13, 15, 17–19, 21–22, 52, 81–82, 94–96, 106–107, 130, 132–135, 144–145, 165

global xxi–xxii, 22, 45–48, 52–53, 56, 68–69, 86–87, 106, 108, 145–148, 151, 156, 158, 178, 180, 182–183

gospel xi–xii, xv–xxiii, 18–19, 21, 29, 32, 36, 45, 52, 57, 59–60, 68, 71–75, 82, 84–86, 101, 109, 111, 114, 118–119, 131, 145, 150, 159–162, 166, 170, 172–173, 180

Greco–Roman 76, 79–82, 93, 132–134

H

Higgins, Kevin xiii, 94–102, 104–108, 110, 112–120, 129, 132, 141–142, 144, 147–148, 155, 161

Hindu xvi, 101, 109, 114, 138

Hoefer, Herbert 109–110, 114–115, 117, 155, 161

holiness 8, 22, 55–56, 58, 67, 84, 135, 150–151, 155, 160, 166, 180

holy nation 8, 23, 26, 53, 66, 70, 77, 160–161, 163, 165, 177, 180

holy people 56, 58, 66, 69, 135

Holy Spirit xxi, 22, 26, 32, 35, 43, 46, 49–51, 55, 84, 99–100, 104–106, 114, 120, 127, 139, 151, 153, 162, 177

holy temple 55–56, 62, 70, 83, 158, 161

household 12, 22–23, 26, 33, 36, 42, 79, 81, 96, 104, 114, 117, 129–130, 141, 144, 150, 155, 158, 165–166

household conversion 96, 129

I

identity xii, xv, xvi, xvii, xviii, xix, xx, xxi, xxii, 3–9, 13, 18–19, 21, 23–25, 29–34, 36, 38, 40–41, 45–48, 51, 53, 55–63, 65–71, 76–77, 79–83, 85, 87, 92–93, 95–100, 102, 111, 113, 115, 117, 121–122, 126, 129–131, 133–140, 143–148, 150–158, 161–163, 165–166, 168–169, 172–173, 176–182

   cultural 87, 135–136, 139–140, 162

   dual 66, 95, 138, 148

   ecclesial 31, 98–99, 138, 140, 148, 153

   socioreligious 33, 98, 138–140, 144

   spiritual 51, 53, 55, 57, 61, 65, 97, 99, 138

   theological 33, 76, 79, 138–139, 143, 165

idol temple 133

image 4–5, 8, 11–12, 20–26, 33, 36, 45, 49, 69, 119, 135, 148, 159–160, 169, 176–178, 180

inculturation 73–74, 83–84

indigenous ii, 59, 73, 83, 86–87, 115

insider xi–xii, xv–xxiii, 4–5, 26–27, 30–31, 33–34, 54, 64–65, 67–69, 71–72, 88–89, 91–117, 119–123, 125–131, 133, 135–173, 177

Subject Index

advocate xvi, xix, xxi, 72, 92–97, 100–108, 110–116, 119, 121, 136, 141–142, 144–147, 153–157, 163, 169–170

believer 106, 116, 144, 146–147, 151, 157

community 100, 104, 108, 115, 149–150, 172

fellowship 96, 101, 103, 105–106, 112, 142–144, 147, 152, 166, 170

model 100, 102–105, 108, 121, 135, 137, 141, 147, 157

movement xi–xii, xv–xvii, xix–xxiii, 65, 72, 92–93, 96, 98–99, 101–102, 104–105, 108, 110–112, 116, 119, 122, 127, 129–130, 135, 143, 163, 167–169, 171–173

paradigm xvi, xvii, xix, xx, xxi, xxii, xxiii, 4–5, 26–27, 30, 54, 64–65, 67–69, 88, 91–98, 100–103, 106, 108, 110–117, 119, 121–122, 126–130, 133, 135–141, 144–164, 166, 168–172

Islamic ritual prayer 102, 153, 168

J

Jerusalem 4, 17–18, 24–26, 33, 36, 38, 41, 45–46, 51–53, 57, 66–68, 80, 95–96, 106, 130–135, 177

   church 33, 36, 41, 95, 106, 131–132

   council 18, 95–96, 133–135

Jesus Christ xi, xii, xv, xvi, xviii, xix, xx, xxi, xxiii, 5–6, 9–14, 16–26, 29, 32–33, 35–42, 44–55, 57–70, 72–73, 75, 80–87, 92–116, 118–122, 125, 128–132, 134, 136–151, 153–163, 165–166, 168–170, 172–183

Jew 9, 12, 15, 19, 21–22, 32, 52, 81–82, 94–95, 107, 127, 132, 134, 136, 145

K

Kingdom xii, xvii, 5, 7–8, 10–12, 14–17, 24–26, 32, 44, 46, 53, 58, 66–70, 75, 94, 97–99, 102, 106, 115, 117–122, 127–129, 138, 144, 150, 157, 159, 161–163, 165–166, 169, 177, 179, 182–183

L

laying on of hands 41

leadership 33, 42, 44, 95, 105, 108, 110, 131, 142

Lewis, Rebecca 98, 102–103, 116–117, 157

local xii, 14, 17–20, 22–23, 30–31, 33–42, 44–48, 51–54, 57, 61–62, 65, 67–69, 74, 82, 85–88, 93, 97, 100–106, 108, 110–112, 115, 119, 122, 126, 140–144, 146–148, 150–151, 153–154, 156, 158, 162–163, 165, 169–171, 178–180, 182

   church 20, 33–42, 44–45, 47–48, 51–52, 54, 57, 61, 65, 69, 86–87, 100, 102–105, 110–111, 115, 122, 140–144, 146–148, 154, 156, 165, 170–171, 178–180

   congregation 18, 20, 22–23, 35, 46–48, 148

   ekklēsia 100, 102–104, 110, 112, 140–141, 143

Lord's Supper 18, 22, 41, 60–62, 70, 104, 153–154, 181–182

Luther, Martin 49, 58, 62

M

missional xx, 8, 65–67, 69–70, 75, 79, 81, 151, 159, 163, 166, 182

mosque xv, 3, 91–92, 95, 102–103, 110, 122

movements xi, xii, xv, xvi, xvii, xix, xx, xxi, xxii, xxiii, 18–19, 34, 36, 42, 65, 67, 72, 80–81, 92–96, 98–99, 101–105, 108, 110–113, 115–116, 118–119, 122, 127, 129–130, 133, 135, 140, 143, 145–147, 154, 163, 165, 167–169, 171–173

Muhammad xv, xviii, 92, 102, 112, 136, 151, 161, 167–168

multicultural 69, 84, 86, 156, 163, 180

Muslim xv–xviii, xx, xxii, 3–4, 11, 31, 33, 35, 38, 42, 45, 61, 63, 65, 71, 75, 81, 88, 91–98, 100–103, 105–108, 110–111, 115–116, 119–120, 122–123, 125–126, 129–130, 133, 135–140, 144–145, 147–148, 150–152, 159–160, 162–163, 166, 168–174, 177, 180, 182–183

  context xvi, xvii, 4, 11, 35, 61, 63, 65, 107, 130, 137, 159, 169, 171, 173–174, 182

  culture xviii, 75, 81, 88, 126, 135, 137–138, 159, 162–163, 168

  family 98, 100, 103, 108, 145, 147, 159, 163, 172, 183

  follower xviii, 92, 95, 106–107, 110, 122

  identity xv, xvi, 93, 102, 111, 122, 129, 136–137, 151

  ritual 92, 102, 166

  world xv, xviii, 115, 135, 172, 182–183

Muslim–background believer 115, 138, 173, 177–178, 181

N

narrative 3–5, 7, 20, 25–26, 30, 46, 69, 87, 93, 97, 118, 126, 131, 136–137, 151–152, 165, 169, 171, 176–178, 180

Newbigin, Lesslie 16, 31, 49, 65–66, 157

new humanity 21–23, 26, 44, 46, 48, 80, 136, 145–146, 165

New Testament xii, 5, 7, 12, 19–20, 23–24, 31–44, 47, 51–52, 70, 76–77, 79–82, 93–94, 96–98, 102, 105, 107, 110, 127, 132–133, 139, 141–144, 147–148, 153, 165, 170–171, 173, 176, 178–179, 181

O

oikos 22, 79–82, 96, 101, 104, 114, 129, 141, 155, 165–166, 176

Old Testament 5, 8–10, 14–15, 22–23, 25, 37, 40, 56, 76–79, 82, 93–94, 126–127, 139

ordinances (sacraments) 54, 58–60, 64, 70, 104–106, 113, 152–155

P

partnership 52, 69, 146–147, 151

Paul (Apostle) 9, 18, 20–23, 33, 35, 40, 43, 49, 52, 56, 80, 82, 106, 121, 132–133, 142, 145, 183

Pentecost 17, 19, 25–26, 32–33, 35, 130

people of God xxii, 4–10, 12, 16–18, 20–21, 23–27, 30–32, 36–37, 53–54, 56, 65–66, 68–69, 76–77, 87–88, 93, 127, 134, 136–137, 139–140, 143, 149, 162–163, 165, 169, 176–178, 180–182

persecution 24, 39, 51–52, 125, 130, 175–177

Peter (Apostle) 13, 20, 23–24, 66, 145

pilgrim principle 86, 162–163, 166

prayer xv, xviii, 3, 29–30, 33, 41, 44, 92, 95, 102–104, 106, 113, 115, 122, 132, 140, 143–144, 151, 153–154, 161, 165, 168, 179

Protestant mark 54, 58–59, 62–63, 70, 111–113, 152, 154–155, 181

Q

Qur'an xv, 71, 92, 102, 112, 136, 151–153, 161, 166, 168

R

religious ritual 127

resurrection 10, 17, 26, 32, 61, 70, 120, 128

Roman Catholic 55–56, 73–74, 104, 143

S

salvation 6, 8–10, 15, 21, 30, 34–36, 55, 58, 61, 63–65, 68, 70, 93, 109, 113–116, 120, 122, 126, 134, 140, 155, 157–158, 162, 166, 169, 178

security 111, 145–147

social

    network 98, 100–102, 110–111, 116, 130, 144, 147, 150, 163, 165

    structure 79–80, 117, 122, 129, 159–160, 173

spiritual 12, 21–22, 32, 35, 40–45, 49–53, 55, 57, 61–62, 64–65, 67–69, 75, 96–97, 99–100, 106–109, 111, 114–116, 120–122, 129, 138, 140, 147–150, 152, 154–156, 158, 162, 165–166, 172–175, 179–181

    formation 68, 115–116, 122, 155–156, 158, 166

    maturity 155, 172–173

    nature 49, 52, 111, 122, 140

    reality 57, 69, 106–108, 111, 122, 147–150, 165, 181

syncretism xii, xviii, 72, 76, 78–79, 82–85, 88, 116, 162–163

T

Talman, Harley xix, xx, 77, 93, 95, 101–104, 106–107, 134, 141

teaching 4–5, 12, 14–16, 19–24, 26–27, 34, 39–42, 44, 59–60, 62, 70, 86, 98, 104, 112–113, 122, 127–130, 135, 142, 147, 151, 153, 155–156, 159, 163, 172, 176, 181

Travis, Anna 119–121, 161

Travis, John Jay xvi, xviii, xix, xx, 72, 94–98, 101–106, 110, 112, 114, 116, 141, 144–145, 147, 153, 155–156, 163

Trinity xii, xiii, 32

triune God 17, 32–33, 35, 37, 46, 66, 68–69, 178

U

underground 85, 110, 147

unity xx, xxii, 19, 22, 35, 45, 48, 52–53, 55–58, 81, 96, 108, 112–113, 144–145, 148–150, 155–156, 159, 166, 182

unleavened bread xvii, 22–23, 26, 169

V

Van Engen, Charles 57–58, 66–67, 150

visible expression 52, 107, 122, 148–149

W

Woodberry, J. Dudley xviii, 93–94, 96–97, 102–103, 105–106, 108, 110, 112, 119–120, 141, 144, 146, 153

Word of God xii, xv, xxii, 4, 10, 29, 33, 35, 44, 58–60, 74, 84, 91, 102–103, 106, 108–109, 115, 120, 122, 140, 144, 150–151, 156, 162, 165, 168, 170, 181

worship xv, 3, 8, 10, 18, 29–30, 37, 39–42, 44, 47, 49, 60, 62, 67–68, 70, 74, 77–78, 85, 92–95, 102–104, 107, 109, 116, 118, 127, 130–132, 134, 141, 152, 156, 171

Scripture Index

Genesis
12:1 77
12:1–3 5–6
12:2 64
12:7 6
12:8 77
14:18–20 93
15:1–21 6
17:7–8 6
20 93
45:7 9

Exodus
1–18 7
2:24 6
4:22 7
6:2–3 6
6:2–5 6
6:6–7 6
7:16 6
18 93
19:4–6 7, 139
19:5 7
19:5–6 135
19:6 7–8, 23, 66
20:3–6 78
20–24 7
23:20–26 161
25:31–40 24
27:1–8 77
33:16 8
34:10–16 77

Leviticus
1–6 77
11:44–45 56
18:3–4 8
19:2 56
20:24–26 8, 139
22:31–33 8
26:12 22, 32

Deuteronomy
4:10 14
6:5 78
7:1–6 77
7:6 7, 56
7:6–9 7
9:10 8, 14
14:2 56
18:16 14
23:1–9 14
32:10 7

Joshua
24:2–3 77

Judges
2:13 78

Ruth
4:11 14

1 Samuel
5:2 77
7:4 78
8:7 15

2 Samuel
12:1–15 160

1 Kings
6 77
10:1–13 93
11:8 77
12:25–33 78
19:14–18 53
19:18 9

2 Kings
5 93
17:7–23 78
17:17 78
21:13–15 9

2 Chronicles
33:15 77

Ezra
9:8 9
9:13–14 9
9:13–15 9

Esther
9:27 17

Psalm
13:19 15
118:22 14, 23
145:11–13 15
28:5 14

Proverbs
18:17 xvi

Isaiah

1:25–26 9
2:1–5 10, 46
2:2–4 8
4:2–4 9
5:17 22
9:6–7 15
10:20 9
10:22 9
11:10–16 10
14:1 17
17:4–6 9
25:6–8 8
28:5–6 10
43:20–21 23
52:11 22
66:18–19 10, 46
66:20–21 8

Jeremiah

1:10 14
2:1–3 6, 25
3:1–20 6
3:17 8
5:10 9
5:18 9
8:3 9
23:3 10
24:6 14
31:4 14
31:7–9 10
31:31–34 9
33:7 14
50:20 9

Ezekiel

37:24–28 15

Daniel

2:44–45 15
7 13
7:13–14 15
7:26–27 15
7:27 15

Hosea

1:2–3 6
1:9 8
1:10–11 8
1–3 25
2:1–13 6
2:14–23 6
2:23 8
3:1–5 6
3:16–22 8

Joel

2:29 46

Amos

2:6–8 78
9:11 14
9:11–12 18

Obadiah

17 9

Micah

2:12 9
2:12–13 10
3:1–4 160
5:2–5 15
7:18 9
7:18–20 9

Zephaniah

2:7–9 10
3:1–13 9
4:2–10 24
8:20–23 10, 46

Matthew

3:2–10 10
4:17 10–11
4:18–22 11, 129
4:19 11
5:14 11
5:22–24 11
5–7 60
7:3–5 11
7:14 12
7:21 15
7:21–23 59
8:11–12 15
8:21–22 12, 81, 129
8:22 11
9:15 6
10:8 16
10:17–18 159
11:28–29 11
12:1–8 81
12:28 15
12:49–50 12, 129
13:1–35 60
13:24 11
13:24–30 53, 121
13:33 xvii
13:36–43 60
13:37–43 121
13:43 15

14:4 160	3:30–32 15	**John**
15:1–20 81	3:31–35 12, 129	1:12 17
15:13 11	4:26 15	3:3 16
16:13–20 13, 60	8:31–35 15	3:16 32, 118
16:18 10, 13–14, 19, 45, 115	10:14–15 15	5:10 8
16:18–19 57	10:29–30 47	8:31 32
16:19 12	10:32–45 15	10:12 17
18 13	12:9 12	10:16 17
18:15 11	13:13 51	11:52 17
18:15–20 13, 62	**Luke**	14:15–17 32
18:17 10, 14	1:17 10	14–16 60
18:20 14, 34	3:4–6 13	15:1–6 22
18:21 11	4:17–21 13	15:5–6 17, 51
18:35 11	4:43 10	16:13 120
19:25 12, 129	4:43–44 60	17 17, 66
20:16 12	5:27–28 11	17:15 121
21:43 12	6:29–32 81	17:16–18 66
21:43–44 15	7:26–28 10	17:22 55
22:14 12	7:28 15	**Acts**
23:8 11	9:59–62 12, 81, 129	1:8 18, 32, 39, 45
23:8–9 11	10:9–11 15	1:15 17
24–25 60	10:17 16	2:1 17
25:1–13 15	11:20 15	2:1–4 32
25:40 11	12:32 11	2:1–10 18
26:26–29 60	12:51–53 12, 81, 129, 159	2:14–36 19, 131
28:10 11	13:24–30 15	2:16–21 13
28:19 60, 172	13:29 15	2:17–28 131
28:19–20 17, 45	14:25–27 12, 81, 129	2:29–36 131
Mark	17:20–21 15	2:38 35, 60
1:14–15 11	18:28–30 129	2:38–39 32
1:15 10	19:11–27 15	2:41 35, 60
1:16–20 11	21:16–17 12	2:42 41, 59, 64
2:19–20 6		2:42–47 18, 34, 36, 37, 14

Scripture Index

2:45   41
2:46   18–19, 38, 60, 141
2:47   17, 35, 40, 51
3:1   18–19
3:1–26   131
3:11–26   131
3:18–26   19
4:19–20   59
4:23–31   40
4:31   59
4:32–37   18, 36
5:14   17
5:34–37   41
6:1–7   15
6:7   17
7:2–4   77
7:2–53   131
8:1   37
8:14–17   18
8:48   18
9:2   95
9:13   55
9:29   60
9:31   17, 18, 45
10   81
10:44–48   127
10:44–49   18
10:47–48   61
11:19–26   18
11:22   18
11:22–25   52
11:24   17
12:1   37
12:12   51, 141

12:25   52
12:41   17
13:1   18, 37
13:1–3   52
13:3   40
13:14   43
13:14–15   18–19
13:15–47   60
13:16–41   131
14:1   43
14:8   43
14:21   43
14:21–23   179
14:23   17–18, 33, 43–44
14:24–28   52
15   18, 52, 95
15:10–11   18
15:14–17   134
15:15–18   13
15:17   18
15:19   18, 132
15:20   134
15:20–21   132, 134
15:36   179
15:41   33
15:45   18
16:5   17, 18
16:7   160
17:6   159
17:6–7   134
17:7   160
17:16–34   131
17:22–31   60
17:24–25   131

17:28   131
17:28–29   31
18:22   18
19:9   95
19:9–10   60
19:18–29   132
19:23–31   134
19:32   14
19:32–40   18
19:39, 41   37
19:41   37
20:1–6   179
20:7   38, 141
20:7–12   60
20:17   18
20:27   172
20:28   42, 43
21:17–20   147
23:1   80
24:5   130
24:14   130
28:22   130

Romans

1:7   21
1:18–20   160
4   21
4:12   21
5:12–21   22, 136
6:1–11   32
6:3–4   60
7:4   22
8:12–17   22
8:17   32
9:4–5   131

10:14–17 59	3:6 43	10:20 133
10:21–11:2 131	3:8 33	10:23–30 132–133
10:24–27 21	3:9 22	10:27–30 134
11:4–5 9	3:10–11 14	10:32 20, 37
11:17–24 22	3:10–14 21–22	11:16 20
12 148	3:16 22, 32, 33, 161	11:17 141
12:1–2 40	3:16–17 22, 55–56	11:17–22 60
12:3–8 41	4:17 20	11:17–34 41
12:3–13 37	5 56	11:18 20, 37
12:4–6 22	5:1–13 62	11:20 17
12:5 23, 46	5:4 37	11:22 20, 37
12:10 22	5:6–7 22	11:23–26 60
12:16 55	5:6–8 xvii	11:27 61
14:1–15:9 134	5:9 121	11:27–32 156
14:13–15:3 145	5:9–10 134	12 148
14:19 22	5:10 121	12:12–13 22, 32, 35, 51, 55
15:7 48	6:4 20, 37	12:12–27 22
15:16 183	6:11 55	12:12–30 148
15:20 21	6:15–20 56	12:12–31 36
15:25–29 52	7:17 20	12:13 21, 23, 35, 46–47, 60–61
15:27 52	7:20–24 79	12:14–30 47
16:1 20, 38	8:7–13 133, 145	12:27 23, 32–33, 35, 46, 158
16:1–2 52	8:10 132–133	12:27–28 46
16:1–16 147	8:11–12 47	12:28 20, 37
16:3–5 20	8:13 22	12–14 41
16:5 141	8–10 133	14:4 20
16:16 20	9:19–20 17	14:4–5 41
16:23 20	10 134	14:5 20, 22
1 Corinthians	10:1–22 133	14:12 20, 22, 41
1:2 20–21, 33, 38, 55–56	10:14–17 22	14:19 20, 37, 41
1:10 55	10:14–22 56, 82, 132–134, 161	14:23 17, 20
1:11–13 55	10:16–17 61	14:23 38
1:12–13 55	10:17 153	
1:13 55	10:19–22 132	

Scripture Index

14:24 40
14:26 22, 37, 41, 141
14:28 20, 37
14:33 20
14:34 20, 37
14:35 20, 37
15:3 57
15:9 20
15:20–23 22
15:21–23 136
15:45–49 136
16:1 20, 52
16:2 38
16:19 20, 52, 141

2 Corinthians
1:1 20
2:5–11 62
4:4 160
5:17 22
6:14 82
6:14–7:1 83, 135
6:14–18 151, 161
6:16 32
6:16–18 22, 55
8:1 20
8:1–9:15 52
8:15 147
8:16–24 52
8:18 20
8:19 20
8:23 20
8:24 20
10:8 21
11:1 6

11:8 20
11:28 20
12:13 20
12:19 21
13:10 21
13:14 41

Galatians
1:2 20
1:6 82
1:6–9 59
1:8 57
1:13 20
1:22 20
2:1–10 52
2:11–14 81, 145
2:11–16 135
2:18 21
2:20 32
3:6–29 21
3:27–29 21, 48
3:28 81
3:28–28 136
3:28–29 145
3:29 6
4:4–7 22, 31
4:26 46, 80
5:2–6 82
5:9 22
5:13 158
6:10 22, 129

Ephesians
1:1 21, 55
1:6 40
1:12 40

1:13–14 59
1:14 32, 40
1:20–23 46
1:22 20, 23, 45
1:22–23 46
2:6 24, 32
2:6–7 46
2:8–9 32
2:10 22
2:11–22 136, 145
2:12 21
2:13–14 55
2:13–22 46, 48
2:14–16 51
2:14–18 21
2:15–16 22
2:16 22
2:19 22, 47, 129
2:19–22 158
2:20 19, 21, 57
2:20 58
2:20–22 14
2:21–22 22, 32, 161
3:5 57
3:5–6 21
3:10 20, 24, 45
3:10–11 21
3:15 45
3:17 22
3:21 20, 45
3:28–29 81
4 148
4:1–6 145, 148, 156
4:3 55

4:4   22
4:4–5   51
4:4–6   35, 36, 55, 156
4:5   153
4:6   45
4:7–16   41
4:11   43
4:11–16   22, 40, 59, 13, 156
4:12   21
4:13   172
4:15–16   47
4:16   22–23
4:25   157
4:25–5:1   37
5:7   135
5:18–20   37, 156
5:19–20   40
5:22–33   23
5:22–6:9   81
5:23   46
5:23–32   20, 45
5:25–27   67
5:25–32   6
5:27   53, 56, 67
6:21–22   52

Philippians

1:3–11   52
1:5   41
1:5–7   41
1:9–11   179
1:27   80
2:1   41
2:16   183
2:25–30   52
3:6   20
3:20   80

4:14–16   41
4:14–20   52
4:15   20

Colossians

1:2   21
1:4–5   59
1:6   45
1:10   59
1:13–14   157
1:13–20   67
1:18   20, 23, 45–46
1:23   51
1:24   20, 45
1:28   172
1:28–29   183
2:1–7   82
2:7   22
2:8–11   82
2:11–13   32
2:16–29   82
3:1   46
3:1–3   32
3:1–4   24, 46
3:3   46
3:3–4   53
3:5–25   46
3:8   37
3:11   81
3:12–17   37
3:16   37, 40, 59
3:17   40
3:18–4:1   81
4:7–8   52
4:15   20
4:16   20, 37

1 Thessalonians

1:1   20, 38
1:2   179
1:6–9   52
1:9   132
2:14   20
5:12–13   44
5:27   37

2 Thessalonians

1:1   20, 38
1:4   20

1 Timothy

3:1–7   43
3:2   43
3:5   38
3:6   43
3:11   43
3:14   156
3:15   20, 33, 40, 129
5:16   20
5:22   43

2 Timothy

1:12–13   57
1:14   57
2:19   51

Titus

1:5   43–44, 143
1:5–7   42
1:5–9   43
3:7   158

Philemon

2   20
16–17   81

Hebrews

3:12   51
4:14–5:10   24
7:1–10   93
7:26–28   24
8:6   24
9:11–13   24
9:13–14   55
9:24   24
10:19–25   40
10:21   129
10:22   24
10:24–25   37, 51
10:25   24, 156, 158
10:25–26   141
11:10   80
12:18–21   24
12:18–24   8, 24
12:22   24
12:22–23   80
12:22–24   46
12:25–29   24
13:14   80
13:15   40
13:17   42–44

James

1:22–25   59
1:27   160
2:14–17   41

1 Peter

1:1   23, 66, 83
1:2   55
1:3   32
1:14–15   55
1:15   23
1:16   82
1:17   23, 66
1:22   23
2:4   40
2:4–5   156
2:4–8   14, 23
2:9   7–8, 23, 40, 66
2:9–10   45, 139
2:9–12   66, 135
2:11   23
2:11–12   23, 66, 83
2:13–17   159
2:17   23
2:21   23
2:25   23
3:8   23
3:9   23
4:3–4   134
4:8–11   41
4:17   129
5:1–5   42–43
5:2–4   23
5:9   23
5:10   23

1 John

1:3   41
2:15   160
2:18–24   160
2:19   51
3:2–3   56
3:16–17   41
4:1–6   59
5:18, 19   121

3 John

10   48

Jude

3   40, 65, 156
24   67

Revelation

1:6   7–8
5:9–10   25, 64
7:9–10   25
7:9–17   46, 57, 66
7:10   55
7:14   67
19:7–8   6, 56
21   67
21:1–4   6
21:2   80
21:2–4   53
21:3   25
21:5   119
21:9–10   25
21:14   14
21–22   66
22:1–5   25
22:17   25
22:20   25

www.ingramcontent.com/pod-product-compliance
Lightning Source LLC
Chambersburg PA
CBHW071340080526
44587CB00017B/2902